AN UNSHAKEABLE KINGDOM

The letter to the Hebrews for today

David Gooding

WILLIAM B. EERDMANS PUBLISHING COMPANY
GRAND RAPIDS, MICHIGAN

Library of Congress Cataloging-in-Publication Data
Gooding, D. W. (David Willoughby)
    An unshakeable kingdom : the letter to the Hebrews for
today / David Gooding.
       p.   cm.
    ISBN 0-8028-0471-3
    1. Bible.   N.T.   Hebrews — Criticism, interpretation, etc.
I. Title.
BS2775.2.G66   1989
227'.8707—dc20
                                     89-12085
                                      CIP

CONTENTS

To

JACK and ADA HARTBURN

in renewed gratitude

PREFACE

It has been a constant source of encouragement to me to find that from its earliest days the first edition of this book has proved helpful to an ever increasing circle of readers. To date it has been translated into half a dozen or so languages, and further translations are in progress.

In the course of the years I have naturally continued to think about the message of Hebrews against the background of developing contemporary issues. And since the relevance of Hebrews to contemporary life is something which many people do not immediately see for themselves, I am delighted at the opportunity this second enlarged edition gives me to explain that relevance to a new generation of readers.

The book's basic aims remain still what they always were. No attempt has been made to turn it into a formal commentary with a commentary's necessary rigour and exhaustive attention to detail. It continues to be, as its title indicates, a series of general introductory studies.

But such studies have their advantages. They have allowed me to concentrate on the broad themes of the epistle and particularly on matters which pastoral experience shows many people find difficult or even disturbing, without having to make matters even more difficult by exhaustive discussion of all the minor issues.

At the same time they have allowed me to go outside the limits of the epistle itself and to explore more extensively than the strict proportions of a formal commentary might allow, rich fields of Old Testament history, prophecy, ritual and poetry from which the epistle has drawn so many of its insights.

I have kept the informal conversational style of the original lectures on which the first edition was based. It may not be elegant; but it has been, so I am told, one of the secrets of the book's wide acceptance. It also serves the book's other major aim which is to bring home to its readers, more directly and personally than would be fitting in a formal commentary, the far-reaching practical and personal implications that the epistle carries for every one of us.

I am grateful to those who in various ways have contributed either to the contents or to the production of the book: Mr Stewart Hamilton, Dr John Lennox, Dr Roderic Matthews, Mr Michael Middleton and Dr Arthur Williamson. Mrs Barbara Hamilton deserves special mention for the artistry and efficiency of her typing. Members of the Inter-Varsity Press editorial team have laboured meticulously to turn my language into English fit to be read. My readers should know this so they can share my gratitude.

The first edition was dedicated to Jack and Ada Hartburn. Happily they are with us still, and I gladly rededicate the book to them.

David Gooding

1

THE HEBREWS

The letter to the Hebrews is ablaze with the glory of our Lord Jesus Christ; the glory of his deity, his manhood, his priesthood and sacrifice, his triumphant life of faith, his resurrection and ascension, and the certainty of his coming again. At the same time it contains dark and sombre warnings, which are longer and more solemn than any we find in the other letters of the New Testament. Because of these warnings many Christians have found Hebrews a difficult letter to understand – some have even found it frightening.

How then shall we proceed? In the first of these studies we shall examine the letter generally to discover to whom it was written, and for what reasons, and in what circumstances. As we first of all understand what bearing Hebrews had on the circumstances and lives of the people to whom it was originally written, we shall appreciate more fully and more accurately its bearing on our own situation.

The readers

The title that we find in the manuscripts, 'To the Hebrews', is obviously an appropriate title. The letter contains many things that would appeal to Hebrews even more than to us Gentiles. It is full of references to the Jewish priesthood, to the tabernacle, to its services and to its sacrifices. It has frequent references to Israel's history, and to the worthies of the Old Testament. Hebrews was obviously not written to former pagans who had now come to faith in Christ; it was written rather to Jews brought up in the Jewish faith, who had in addition professed faith in Jesus as the Jewish Messiah.

Where did they live? Many people have thought Jerusalem. Others think Caesarea or Rome or Antioch. We cannot know for certain. This much is obvious: they still had a tremendous regard for the temple at Jerusalem, its priesthood, sacrifices and rituals. This would have been natural if they lived in Jerusalem, and constantly visited the temple and took part in its services. But there is evidence enough from the ancient world that even Jews who lived in distant cities of the diaspora and who never visited the temple, or only rarely on some pilgrimage of a lifetime, could nevertheless feel great devotion to the temple and loyalty to the authority of the high priest (see p. 160). And it seems clear that the readers of this letter did so; for what would have been the point of talking at great length about the tabernacle, priesthood and sacrifices to Jews who no longer had any interest in, or attachment to, these things.

The date

As to the date of the letter we shall find hints here and there in the letter itself. For instance, in 13:7 we find an exhortation to 'remember your leaders, who spoke the word of God to you. Consider the outcome of their way of life and imitate their faith.' Apparently there had been time from the moment when the gospel was first preached for people to have been converted, for groups of Christians to have been formed, and for the senior Christians, who at the beginning had carried responsibility in these groups, to have died. On the other hand, at the end of chapter 8 we find more than a suggestion that the letter was written before AD 70: 'By calling this covenant "new",' says the writer, 'he has made the first one obsolete; and what is obsolete and ageing will soon disappear.'

He does not say that the old covenant and all connected with it *has* disappeared. He says that there is already a new covenant based on better promises than the old. The old covenant had the tabernacle and the priesthood and the sacrifices. The new covenant has another system of worship. And the very fact that there is a new covenant, says the writer, proves that the first one is old. Then he adds, 'what is obsolete and ageing will soon disappear'; it has not yet disappeared, but it soon will.

These facts, put together, tell us roughly just about when the letter was written: it was not yet AD 70, but it was getting very near to the time when, as you will remember, the Roman armies took Jerusalem, and fulfilled the prophecy of the Lord Jesus that not one stone of the temple would be left standing upon another (Lk. 21:6). It was that very short critical period when the old system was approaching its end. The new system was already there, but only in its infant days. Gradually it was gaining strength; and a time of crisis for both Judaism and Christianity was fast approaching.

The readers' spiritual state

We can come closer to the readers if we look again at 10:32–34. They had made a confession of faith in the Lord Jesus; and upon that confession they had been severely persecuted. Sometimes they were publicly exposed to insult and persecution; at other times they stood side by side with those who were so treated. They sympathized with those in prison and joyfully accepted the confiscation of their own property. Even at this distance in history we can still admire their courage and the firmness of their testimony to the Lord Jesus.

But the letter also reveals that things were not so well with them now as they had been. The writer indicates in 10:25 that some were giving up meeting together as Christians. Perhaps, if you had gone and asked them why they were not there, some of them might have turned round and said, 'Oh, we can still believe in Christ at home.' But, you know, it was a very suspicious symptom. Why were they now staying away? What did it imply about their faith? It is clear at any rate that the writer of this letter saw in this one symptom alone a very grave possibility. His letter is full of exhortations that they should hold fast the profession of their faith (see *e.g.*, 4:14) – not merely their keenness, not merely their form of godliness, but the profession *of their faith*. Obviously the writer feared that some of these people who had stood so boldly at the beginning might now abandon their profession of faith in Jesus as Messiah completely.

His fears, we gather, were reinforced by the memory of what had happened centuries before to their ancestors in the desert (see chs. 3 and 4). The Israelites had made a bold start, left Egypt and crossed the Red Sea crying triumphantly: 'I will sing to the Lord, for he is highly exalted. The horse and its rider he has hurled into the sea' (Ex. 15:1). But later on, when they got to the borders of Canaan, the great majority of them had refused point blank to go any further and enter the promised land. Haunted by this memory, our author warns his readers most seriously. He is afraid, he says, that some of them might be beginning to show the same pattern of behaviour as their ancestors (4:1).

Later, in his sixth chapter, he thinks it prudent to issue another similar warning. He describes in detail the serious consequences when people who have once been enlightened fall away. It is impossible, he says, to bring them again to repentance. And without repentance there can of course be no forgiveness, or salvation either.

Later still in his tenth chapter he reminds his readers that 'if we deliberately keep on sinning after we have received the knowledge of the truth, no sacrifice for sins is left' (10:26). Obviously there were symptoms in the behaviour of these early Hebrew converts that caused the writer grave concern.

Their history

In subsequent studies we shall attempt not only to understand what was said to them but also to apply it to ourselves, where and however it fits. We must, therefore (and I wish to emphasize this heavily), patiently try to understand what their situation really involved. Think again. Here were people brought up in the traditional Jewish faith. For centuries their nation's ideas of God had been bound up with the splendid temple at Jerusalem, with the chanting of the Levites and of the priests, with the wonderful ceremony and the delightful pageantry of those ancient services. There was incense to smell and music to listen to; the high priest in his spectacularly beautiful robes, the ordinary priests washing at the laver, worshippers confessing their sins, holy sacrifices being offered and an atmosphere of awe and devotion.

Our Hebrews, then, had been brought up in a religion honoured by the names of all their great ancestors, patriarchs, kings and prophets. Moses had worshipped in a tabernacle built according to plans given him by God himself. Solomon likewise had built his magnificent temple according to plans God had supplied to his father David (1 Ch. 28:19); and their present temple was basically an enlarged and enriched copy of these earlier sanctuaries. They, like most Jews, loved their temple with passionate fervour. Two hundred years earlier their ancestors in Palestine had endured bitter persecution when the Greek emperor, Antiochus Epiphanes, had turned their then existing temple into a pagan shrine complete with an idolatrous image of a Gentile deity. His banning of the worship of the one true God, and the law of God on which that worship was based had sent violent shock-waves throughout the whole diaspora. But the Jews in Palestine had refused to give in to Antiochus' blasphemies, and many of them had paid with their lives for their faith in the system of worship laid down by God in the Old Testament. Experiences like that had understandably driven devotion to the temple deep into the heart of the nation.

But then Jesus had come and claimed to be Israel's Messiah, to be the Son of God. The nation, as we know, had officially rejected that claim and had crucified him. But on the day of Pentecost the Holy Spirit had come, poured out by the exalted Jesus (Acts 2:33–35), mighty evidence that God had reversed the nation's decision and had made him both Lord and Christ. Together with a succession of outstanding miracles, performed in the name of Jesus, it had struck conviction into the hearts of some thousands of Jews. They had murdered the Messiah in ignorance (Acts 3:17); now they were glad to be allowed to repent; and in the very same city where their Messiah was crucified, they had been baptized in the name of Jesus, had been forgiven and had received the Holy Spirit.

A nation divided

Some of the older men and women among those to whom this letter was written may even have stood, as residents or visitors, in Jerusalem's streets when these mighty deeds were done. But for the most part that generation had passed on; the majority were younger and had had the gospel 'confirmed to them by those who had heard the Lord Jesus' (2:3). The nation's official leaders, of course, along with the majority of the nation everywhere, whichever one of the many Jewish sects they belonged to, still adhered to their decision that Jesus was not the Messiah. On the other hand right from the start there was a significant and constantly growing body of Jews including many priests (Acts 6:7), who asserted that Jesus was the Messiah, that he was the Son of God, that he was wrongly crucified. Now normally the non-Christian Jews would meet in their different synagogues, for in the Jewish nation there were different synagogues with different traditions and different views (see Acts 6:9). The Christian Jews would normally meet in homes (see Acts 2:46) or in their own synagogues (see Jas. 2:2; NIV's 'meeting' = Gk. *synagōgē*). But Christian as well as non-Christian would go up to the temple from time to time, and worship God there. In the Acts of the Apostles, you will remember, we find men like Peter and John in the early years of Christianity attending the temple. And much later we hear of Paul, on returning from one of his missionary journeys, visiting the temple. It was a natural centre both for Palestinian Jews and for Jews of the dispersion.

Of course the Christian Jews continued their witness to the Lord Jesus. The Old Testament, they pointed out, prophesied that the Messiah would suffer and then rise again from the dead. Jesus's death therefore, far from proving that he was not the Messiah, proved that he was. God, they proclaimed, had also appointed him Judge. The day was already set when God would judge the world with justice by this same Jesus (Acts 2:36; 10:42; 17:31). True, they realized that he must remain in heaven until the time came for God to restore everything as he had promised long ago through his holy prophets (Acts 3:21); but they did not think that that time was necessarily a long way off. Israel had only to repent and God would send the Messiah whom God had appointed for them (Acts 3:20); and then the Messiah would restore the kingdom to Israel, deliver them from the Romans and from all other Gentile imperialist oppressors, and make Israel the head of the nations.

Indeed, on the last occasion that the apostles had met the risen Lord before his ascension, they enquired if he was going to restore the kingdom to Israel there and then (Acts 1:6). Not there and then, he had replied. First they must spread their witness to him throughout all the nations. But by the time the letter to the Hebrews was being written, apostles such as Peter (not without some initial reluctance) and Paul, and crowds of Christian emigrants and expatriates, had obeyed the Lord and spread the gospel far and wide among the Gentiles. Not unreasonably, then, the Hebrew Christians expected the Lord to return soon. Adapting a phrase from an Old Testament prophet they encouraged one another in the hope that 'in just a very little while, "He who is coming will come and will not delay" ' (10:37). He would come, so they expected, and set up his kingdom in Jerusalem, in Palestine and throughout the whole world. And of course that would finally prove to their fellow-Jews that Jesus was the Messiah.

But the years went by and he did not come. The older Christians began to pass away. Still he did not come. As the new faith grew and spread, the attitude of official Judaism, far from softening or showing signs of conversion, or even of compromise, was in fact growing more intensely hostile. All round the Roman world, where new Christian groups were formed, the leaders of the local Jewish communities took every opportunity of turning the political authorities against the new 'sect'. Riots were not uncommon (see Acts 14:4–6, 19; 17:5–8, 13; 18:12–17).

And then there was another thing that troubled some of the Hebrew Christians. As a result of the preaching of apostles such as Peter and Paul, Gentiles all round the Roman Empire were coming to believe in Jesus as the Messiah. But the apostles were making no attempt to get them to practise Jewish rituals and ceremonies. Indeed, they discouraged some and altogether forbade others. Gentile believers were not required to be circumcised, did not observe the traditions of the scribes or the rabbinical rules, sent no tribute to the temple at Jerusalem. What did it all mean? What were things coming to?

Either-or?

When things had been going well and many of their fellow-Jews were getting converted, the Hebrew Christians had been strong and courageous. But now when their hopes for the conversion of Israel and the return of Christ seemed to be delayed and deferred, and persecution was rising and opposition hardening, it is understandable that some of them had doubts. What if their hopes were not true? What if they had made a ghastly mistake and Jesus was not the true Messiah after all?

On top of all that they were soon to face an unavoidable crisis. As the nation as a whole hardened in its unbelief, the apostles were beginning to withdraw the Christian Jews from their Jewish synagogues (see Acts 19:9) and to shake off the dust of their feet against their fellow-countrymen, explaining as they did so, 'We had to speak the word of God to you first. Since you reject it and do not consider yourselves worthy of eternal life, we now turn to the Gentiles.' It was becoming evident that Christianity could no longer be a part of Judaism. Soon they must part completely, Judaism must go its way, Christianity must take another road.

We can scarcely understand what it meant for people who had been brought up in Judaism, to whom it was dearer than life itself, to be forced to a decision either to keep with it or to leave it.

They would gladly have owned Jesus as Messiah if they could have had their temple and their high priest as well. But did it mean that it was an 'either-or'?

Either Jesus or the temple?

Was it in fact either his sacrifice or Israel's animal sacrifices, but not both?

Was it either Jewish politics and a Jewish homeland, with a capital, Jerusalem, on earth, or a coming outside of that gate, and outside of that camp completely (see 13:11–14) to a Jesus who was rejected and likely to stay rejected by the nation?

Was it an 'either-or'?

Yes, it was.

These people were soon to face the greatest crisis in all their spiritual experience. They deserve our deepest sympathy. Faced with problems like that some of them were wavering, some had stopped meeting with the believers; and I think we can now see what was going on in their minds. We can understand too what must have been going through the mind and heart of the person who wrote this letter. He cared for them and saw the grave crisis before them more clearly than they did. The all-important question was, which way would they go?

Go back?

What would be involved if they went back? Very carefully the Spirit of God spells it out in 10:29. Let us read his words and let us make sure, to begin with, that we notice exactly what he says.

Here is a literal translation of the verse: 'Of how much more severe a punishment shall he be considered worthy, who has trampled under foot the Son of God, and has considered the blood of the covenant by which he was sanctified common, and has insulted the Spirit of grace.'

Three things, therefore, would be involved if any of the Hebrews who had professed to accept Jesus as Messiah were to go back deliberately to the fold of Judaism and remain in it.

First, they would trample under foot the Son of God. Notice the verb 'trample under foot'. It describes a deliberate, and perhaps also a spiteful, action. Our Lord himself once spoke of some who fall over God's appointed foundation-stone (that is to say, himself); and the apostle Paul declares that many Jews have 'stumbled over the "stumbling-stone" ' (see Lk. 20:18 and Rom. 9:32). But 'trampling something underfoot and stamping on it' is a far more deliberate action than simply 'tripping over' or 'stumbling over' or 'falling over' something. The people envisaged in our verse have not simply been stumbled by the sheer size of the claims of Jesus: deliberately and with determination they have trampled him under foot. And notice exactly who it is that they are said to trample under foot: not Jesus, though of course it is he, but that is not the name which the Holy Spirit uses here – nor the Saviour, nor the Messiah, but the Son of God. They trample under foot the Son of God, says Scripture, that is, they deliberately and with determination deny the deity of the Lord Jesus.

Of course they do. From the very start this was the fundamental issue at stake between Judaism and Christianity: was Jesus, or was he not, the Son of God? The nation said, No, he was not. But the Hebrews to whom our letter was written had professed to believe that he was. Now, however, they were in danger of going back to their Judaism. What did it mean? They could not go back there unless once more they were prepared to say deliberately that Jesus was not the Son of God. Judaism would demand it of them. Originally, of course, in their pre-conversion ignorance they had joined with the nation in denying his deity. Since then, however, they had been enlightened by the Holy Spirit. They could no longer claim ignorance. To return to Judaism now would mean deliberately and wilfully and with their eyes open denying the deity of Jesus in spite of all the Holy Spirit's illumination.

The next step would follow logically. They would adopt the considered opinion that the blood of Jesus was an unholy, or, as the Greek has it, a common thing. Of course they would. It would be automatic and inevitable. If Jesus is the Son of God, his blood is of infinite value. If he is not the Son of God, then his blood has no more worth than anyone else's blood: it is common blood. Notice, moreover, that it is described here as the blood of the (new) covenant. The value of the covenant depends altogether on the blood that signs and seals it. If the blood is valuable, then the covenant is valid. But if the blood is common, the covenant is not worth the paper that it is written on. To go back to Judaism, then, involved first, that one denied the deity of Jesus; secondly, and logically, one said his blood was common and held that the new covenant was worthless.

And thirdly, to do this, says Scripture, was to insult the Spirit of grace. Notice again how he is described. It is the Holy Spirit, of course, but here he is referred to not as the Spirit of truth or the Spirit of holiness, but as the Spirit of grace. You see, the Jewish nation had crucified Jesus in their ignorance. How gracious it was of God not to wipe them out immediately, but after the resurrection and ascension to give them opportunity to repent. That was grace, indeed. But to that grace God added a super-abounding grace. The Spirit of God who came down from heaven on the day of Pentecost told the people of Jerusalem, 'Look, you murdered God's Son, but you did it in ignorance' (see Acts 3:17). 'Not only is God prepared to forgive you, but whereas formerly you tried to save yourselves by trying to keep God's law, now

God is prepared to save you freely and for nothing, by grace, without your works.' What a magnificent message of mercy and grace it was! Not only opportunity to repent but a salvation utterly by grace and altogether as a gift.

For anyone now to go back to Judaism meant turning round to God and saying, 'God I do not want grace. Mercy and forgiveness for crucifying Jesus? But we do not want forgiveness for that. We would do it again if it were necessary; we do not believe he is your Son.' To go back to Judaism was to turn to God and say, 'Salvation as a gift? Nonsense! We are prepared to work our way to heaven by keeping the law, observing its rituals and taking part in its sacrifices and ceremonies.' And to say that, was to offer terrible insult to the Spirit of grace.

Genuine believers?

Now as we have already noticed, some of the people to whom the letter was written had developed the habit of staying away from the meetings of the Christians. If that meant they were going back to Judaism, and if going back to Judaism meant denying the deity of Jesus, considering his blood common and insulting the Spirit of grace, how should we regard them? Were they true and genuine believers in the Lord Jesus Christ?

At first sight the answer might seem obvious: you can't deliberately and knowingly deny the deity of the Lord Jesus, deny the atoning value of his blood, and still be a genuine Christian, a true believer in the Lord Jesus.

But we mustn't be hasty in our judgment. The great apostle Peter himself at one stage, overcome by panic, denied the Lord Jesus and used all the oaths and curses he knew to convince the bystanders that he was not a Christian. But he was, of course. Outwardly he denied the Lord, but in his heart he remained a believer, as we know from our Lord's statements and from what subsequently happened (see Lk. 22:31–32). His faith did not fail, and he came back to the Lord. Could it not be that some of these Hebrews under pressure of persecution were temporarily behaving inconsistently as Peter did – outwardly going back to Judaism, though at heart still believers?

On the other hand, if Peter had carried on for the next ten or twenty years denying the Lord, avoiding the company of Christians, and taking his place fully in official Judaism, how could you have continued thinking he was a believer? After all, if someone himself consistently says he is not a believer, and demonstrates that he is not by deliberately denying all the fundamentals of the Christian faith, and shows no sign of remorse or of coming back to the Saviour, what's the use of our trying to say that he is a believer?'

But then if that is what some of these Hebrews were doing, or were in danger of doing, it raises another question. Were they ever true and genuine *believers* in the first place?

Many people feel they must have been, but that is not necessarily so at all. Consider a parallel case.

The apostle John in his first letter (2:18–19) refers to people who not only for some time professed to be believers and were members of a Christian church, but even, it appears, had played the role of teachers in it. Eventually, however, they abandoned the fundamental, apostolic doctrines, denied that Jesus was the Christ and left the church. John's comment is that in spite of earlier appearances, they never had been true believers at all. 'If they had belonged to us', he says, 'they would have remained with us'. Their departure from the church and from the apostles' fellowship revealed, according to John, that none of them had ever 'belonged to us', that is, been genuine believers.

Some argue, of course, that these Hebrews must have been believers at one time because the writer says explicitly (10:29) that they had been sanctified by the blood of the covenant even though now they were in danger of denying Christ. And you can't be sanctified, they assume, without being a genuine believer.

But again, this assumption is not necessarily correct. Scripture itself indicates that there are senses in which you can be sanctified without being a believer. 1 Corinthians 7:14 says that the *unbelieving* husband is sanctified by the wife. Notice how impossible it would be to substitute the word 'justified' for 'sanctified' in this statement, for no-one can be justified without faith. But obviously there are senses in which people can be sanctified without being genuine believers.

Let's look again at 10:29. It speaks of our Hebrews having

been sanctified by the blood of the covenant. It will help us understand this phrase if we remember that their ancestors in the desert had similarly been sanctified by the blood of the old covenant. Moses, we are told, took the blood of the calves and the goats and sprinkled both the book itself (*i.e.* the book containing the terms of the covenant) and the people, saying, 'This is the blood of the covenant which God has enjoined on you' (See Ex. 24:5–8 and Heb. 9:18–20). So they were sanctified by the blood of the covenant. But in spite of that most of them later refused to enter the promised land. And what did that show? It showed, says our writer, who recalls this incident in great detail, that they did not believe the gospel. They never had believed (see 4:2 and Nu. 14:11,22).

Similarly, then, these Hebrews had professed to believe in the Lord Jesus, and to accept the new covenant, and they had taken their stand with the Christians and had separated themselves from the murderers of the Messiah (see Acts 2:40). They had been sanctified by the blood of the new covenant. But as with their ancestors, so with them, that still leaves open the question whether they had ever genuinely believed the gospel. And it was precisely this that their behaviour was beginning to put in doubt.

We should observe how carefully the writer chooses his words when he recalls their initial experience of Christianity. At 6:4 he talks of 'those who have once been enlightened' – not 'saved', mark you, but 'enlightened'. At 10:32 again he says, 'Remember those earlier days after you had received the light' – not 'after you were saved', or 'after you believed', but 'after you received the light'. So once more at 10:26: 'If we deliberately keep on sinning after we have received the knowledge of the truth . . . not 'after we have believed the truth', or 'have received the love of the truth', but simply 'have received the knowledge of the truth'. And it is all too possible to know the truth without believing it.

Granted. Yet many people still feel that other phrases which the writer uses elsewhere imply quite clearly that his readers were, or at one time had been, true believers. He may not use the actual word "saved", but he uses other equivalent terms which imply the same thing.

Well, later on we shall investigate these terms in detail. But for the moment let us notice that the writer himself tells us explicitly how he assessed the spiritual history and state of the people to whom he was writing. We had better let him speak for himself. After describing the sad fate of those who, after being enlightened, go back to Judaism, he remarks, 'Even though we speak like this, dear friends, we are confident of better things in your case – things that accompany salvation' (6:9). That makes his position very clear. He is speaking *as if* they were not saved, although in actual fact in his heart of hearts he feels sure they are. He thinks indeed that he can see evidence in their lives that they are saved; things, as he puts it, that accompany salvation. But he is speaking as if there were no evidence that they had genuinely been saved. He will take no risks. A whole generation of their ancestors had professed to believe Moses and God, but in the end it became apparent that they had never believed the gospel. So he holds up their experience to warn his readers against – not ungodliness, or worldliness – no, against something more serious than that: unbelief. You see, if you have never believed the gospel, you are an unbeliever, whatever spiritual experience you may have subsequently had.

Therefore we shall find, as we read this letter, that the one great cardinal point that is stressed time and time again is the all-importance of faith. 'My righteous one will live by faith', declares 10:38, and chapter 11 follows with a whole forty verses on the utterly indispensable requirement of faith.

This then is the question this letter will confront us with: are we genuine believers? Do we really believe that Jesus is the Son of God? And are we behaving in everyday affairs and especially in religious contexts in a way that is straightforwardly consistent with our professed belief? 'Everyone who believes that Jesus is the Christ is born of God,' says Scripture (1 Jn. 5:1). And all who so believe will find tremendous encouragement in this letter to the Hebrews. It will remind them that God's word and God's oath give them a hope like an anchor for the soul, undrifting and firm. Every believer is secure (6:17–20). It will urge every believer to take courage and 'approach the throne of grace with confidence' to find 'mercy' for past mistakes and failures, and 'grace' for the future (4:16). Even if, like Peter, they have been inconsistent and have fallen and temporarily denied the Lord who redeemed them, they have a high priest who prays for them as he prayed for Peter that their faith shall not fail (Lk. 22:32). And because he ever lives, 'he is able to save completely all who come to God through him' (7:25). He will not lose one true believer. Indeed, everyone who rests only and altogether on the sacrifice of Christ is assured that 'by one sacrifice' for sin 'he has made perfect for ever those who are being made holy' (10:14).

So none of us need be uncertain, or insecure, or debilitated by doubts about the completeness of our salvation through Christ. This very letter abounds with assurances that every believer, however weak, shall certainly be saved. But its powerful and insistent question will be: Do you really believe? Not, 'Have you made a profession of being a Christian?', but 'Are you a genuine believer?'

And so we shall be led to ask ourselves: is our behaviour consistent with the gospel we profess to believe? Is our faith for salvation in Christ alone, or partly in him and partly in some ritual or sacrament? Is he our sole mediator with God, or are we compromising our faith in him by relying on other mediators as well? Are we intellectually loyal to Christ? Or do we, while professing faith in him for salvation, allow ourselves to hold theories that by implication deny his divine authority in other areas? Are we allowing our background and culture to pressure us into continuing practices that are inconsistent with the gospel we profess to believe? Do we really believe that Jesus is the Messiah-King and is coming again to reign? And are we taking up our cross and bearing his reproach, or compromising with the world that crucified him? Does our pursuit of holiness make it clear that we are genuine believers in the true grace of God? Or are we trying to mix faith in Christ with a permissive lifestyle that changes the grace of God into a licence for immorality?

If we are genuine believers, Christ will save us completely. But then, if we do really believe, others will be able to see evidence in our lives that we are believers, 'things that accompany salvation'.

Questions

1 What may we learn from the letter to the Hebrews about the religious background and the personal spiritual experience and circumstances of the people to whom it was originally written?

2 According to 10:29, what would be involved if a Jew who had professed faith in Jesus went back to Judaism? Would anything similar be involved if an atheist, who had professed conversion to Christ, went back to atheism?

3 How important is it that our behaviour should be consistent, and be seen to be consistent, with the gospel we profess to believe? Consider 6:9–12; 11:14–16 and 13:12–14.

4 What do you take the phrase 'things that accompany salvation' (6:9) to mean? List some of these things.

5 What passages would you choose from the letter to illustrate the completeness of our Christian salvation and the certainty and security of our Christian hope?

2

THE DEITY OF CHRIST ASSERTED
Hebrews 1:1–4

The writer of the letter to the Hebrews is nothing if not a superb spiritual tactician. He wastes no words on secondary matters. In his first chapter he comes straight to the fundamental issue between Judaism and Christianity: is Jesus, or is he not, the Son of God?

For his readers this was no merely academic question. They were not themselves learned theologians. They were, for the most part at any rate, ordinary people. So it doesn't take much imagination to visualize the difficult situations they would frequently have found themselves in when faced with their former religious leaders. The rabbis would want to know why they were abandoning the faith of their fathers, throwing overboard the religion that God himself had ordained in the Old Testament, and going over to the absurd and blasphemous Christian idea that the carpenter of Nazareth was God incarnate and equal with God.

'Look,' the rabbis would say, 'does not God's inspired Word, the sacred Torah, declare plainly enough, "Hear, O Israel: the Lord our God, the Lord is one" (Dt. 6:4)? Has it not been Israel's glory all down the centuries to witness to the fact that there is only one true God and to protest at the absurdity of the Gentiles who have deified mere men and worshipped a thousand and one false gods? And to think that you – you who as Jews have heard the oneness of God proclaimed ten thousand times in your home, in the synagogue, in the temple, ever since you were children – to think that you could be taken in by this fanatical sect who worship the man Jesus as if he were God!

'And who are you to say that our high priest and Sanhedrin

were wrong to have Jesus crucified? And what do you know about the Bible? Just because you have heard stories of the miracles Jesus is supposed to have done and have been impressed by his popular religious propaganda, you imagine he must have been more than human. But our high priest and rabbis knew what they were doing. They saw through his deceptions and had the courage to do what the Bible commands to be done with such deceivers – have him executed.

'So be sensible. Stop imagining you know better than your rabbis. Show some respect and gratitude to your father and mother for your upbringing. Come back to the faith of your fathers, and don't ruin your lives and break your parents' heart and disgrace your family by abandoning everything you were brought up to believe by running off with this fanatical sect.'

Faced with repeated barrages like that, it's no wonder if the Hebrew Christians began to have doubts. Could they be right and their learned rabbis and all the rest of the nation be wrong? After all, the Old Testament was very clear: there is only one God. And there was no denying that many of the Christian apostles had been no more than fishermen and tax-collectors and such like. How could they know better than the rabbis?

Jesus, the Son of God?

Concerned, therefore, for the spiritual and emotional storms which his friends were encountering, our unknown Christian author sits down to write to them. They have been staying away from the meetings of the church, but he won't mention that until near the end of his letter. He will not begin by chiding them; he has too large a heart, too understanding a spirit, for that. The people are deeply troubled and in grave danger. Their faith is wavering. The question that haunts them is not the kind of superficial difficulty that often troubles us. It concerns the most fundamental thing of all. Is Jesus, or is he not, the Son of God? Everything else depends on this. As the apostle John remarked to his Gentile converts: 'This is the victory that has overcome the world, even our faith. Who is it that overcomes the world? Only he who believes that Jesus is the Son of God' (1 Jn. 5:4–5).

28

We should note that. The secret of overcoming the world is a living and vigorous faith that Jesus is in fact the Son of God. It is well to believe that our sins have been forgiven; it is well to believe that we have eternal life. But if Jesus is not the Son of God, then our Christian gospel is a delusion; our sins have not in fact been forgiven; we have no eternal life; and if there's a God at all, we are guilty of idolatry and blasphemy all rolled into one in attributing divine honours to a mere man, Jesus. Then again, if Jesus is not the Son of God, we would be fools to sacrifice anything for his sake. To sacrifice for anyone's sake is costly; to sacrifice for the sake of an imposter would mean loss in this life, and disastrous, irretrievable loss in the next. On the other hand, if Jesus is the Son of God, not to sacrifice for his sake would be the height of folly. We must decide. Clearly then the sheet anchor that will keep us from dithering or drifting disastrously in face of the world's opposition is an unshakeable faith in the deity of the Lord Jesus.

With great understanding, therefore, the writer proceeds at once to deal with this fundamental question. His approach is twofold. First (1:1–4), he calmly and firmly reasserts the deity of the Lord Jesus; and then (1:5–14) he proves it.

There is wisdom in his tactics. It is so easy in the course of endless arguments for the basic facts of the case to get lost sight of. So the writer re-states them. And of all the relevant facts the most important and fundamental is this: Jesus, having been crucified and buried, rose again from the dead and ascended into heaven. It is this that marks him out as the Son of God: he 'was declared with power to be the Son of God', says Paul, 'by his resurrection from the dead' (Rom. 1:4). The deity of Christ is not an idea arrived at by difficult, intricate theological or philosophical speculation. It is a fact declared by the historical event of the resurrection and ascension. Watch how the writer builds this great event into the climax of his opening proclamation:

God has spoken by his Son,
1 whom he appointed heir of all things,
2 and through whom he made the universe,
3 who, being the radiance of God's glory,
4 and the exact representation of his being,

29

5 and sustaining all things by his powerful word,
6 when he had provided purification for sins

– six subordinate clauses in the Greek, all of them mighty statements in themselves, but leading to the triumphant climax:

He 'sat down at the right hand of the Majesty in heaven'.

Here then is the bedrock of the Christian faith. Let the swirl of religious debate rise and fall as it will; Christians stand on the unalterable fact of the resurrection and ascension of Christ, observed by numerous witnesses of unquestionable honesty and reliability and validated by the coming of the Holy Spirit in his name.

But if the great climax serves to validate the claims made in the six subordinate statements, those six statements themselves perform a powerful function. They present the Saviour. They describe in detail who it was that triumphantly rose from the dead and ascended to God's right hand. They explain the significance of his death, of his resurrection and ascension; in other words they proclaim the person and the work of Christ. These are wise tactics indeed, and all Christian teachers and preachers do well to copy them.

We should always remember that God is, so to speak, his own evidence. That is to say, since he is the Creator, he is the ultimate source of everything. There is no being in the universe who is altogether independent of God and is able on that account to give us an independent assessment of God's claims to be God! Neither is there anyone able to provide us with evidence that did not ultimately originate with God himself. God is self-evident; and true faith on our part is our response to God's self-revelation.

And so it is with the Son of God. He is his own evidence. If you wish to provoke faith in him, proclaim him himself. Preach his person; repeat his words and sermons; relate his deeds and miracles; tell out his virgin birth, his cross, his death, his resurrection; relay the interpretation that he himself gave of these great events. It is this that creates and draws out people's faith. Of course we can each do what John the Baptist did and give our own personal testimony to Christ and to what he has done for us. That is certainly valid and helpful; and the Lord will use it to lead other people to himself and to salvation. But at the ultimate level, as our Lord himself pointed out (Jn. 5:33–34), he does not 'accept human testimony', that is as though it were some independent source of validation for his claims. There is, and can be, no such independent evidence. The divine persons themselves must be, and are, the source of all the evidence that calls forth our faith in the Father, the Son and the Holy Spirit. The Samaritans spoke wisely – perhaps more wisely than they knew – when they said to their fellow-townswoman, 'We no longer believe just because of what you said; now we have heard for ourselves, and we know that this man really is the Saviour of the world' (Jn. 4:42).

But then there is a second part to the writer's tactics. There has to be. You see, the Jews would not accept, as Christians do, that he was inspired by the Holy Spirit, and that therefore his statements were authoritative. They would argue that the early Christians simply invented the idea of the deity of Jesus, and that this idea flagrantly contradicts the basic doctrine of the Old Testament, the oneness of God. The writer must show, therefore, that the Jews are quite mistaken. Their Old Testament itself, so he will argue (1:5–14), announced that the Messiah, when he came, would prove to be a divine person. To believe their own Scriptures, therefore, the Jews must believe in the deity of the Messiah. Once that has been established by quotations from the Old Testament, all he will then need to do is to demonstrate that Jesus is that Messiah whose coming the Old Testament foretold.

So now for the statement of the facts; and then in our next chapter we will examine the statements and promises of the Old Testament.

Still only one God

'In the past, God spoke to our forefathers through the prophets at many times and in various ways, but in these last days he has spoken to us by his Son' (1:1–2a).

We begin, then, with God; with the God of Abraham, of Isaac and of Jacob; the God who spoke to the patriarchs, to Moses, to Joshua, to the priests, prophets and kings of the Old Testament. Here Judaism and Christianity stand together, and it is worth underlining the fact. Christians do not believe in just any god, but in the God of the Jews. And what is more, they believe that the Old Testament is his inspired and authoritative Word.

But if the writer begins by affirming that it was God who spoke in the past to the fathers, will he not now claim as a Christian that as far as Christians are concerned it is Jesus who has spoken to us?

No! Not but what it would be true if he claimed it. But that's not the point he wants to make. What he stresses is this: it is the very same God who spoke in the past to our forefathers through the prophets that has spoken to us in Jesus. As a Christian Jew on behalf of all other Christian Jews he is making the point that though they follow Jesus, they still believe in exactly the same God as they did before! They have not gone off into the worship of some other god or gods. They affirm with all their hearts the age-old declaration of the faith: 'Hear, O Israel: the Lord our God, the Lord is one' (Dt. 6:4), and 'You shall have no other gods before me' (Ex. 20:3).

And incidentally it should not be overlooked what effect Jesus and his teaching have had on Gentiles. He has led multi-millions of Gentiles who originally worshipped all kinds of false gods to abandon their idolatry and to put their faith in the one true God, the God of Israel. There has never been any other Jew like him for this.

But while it is the same God who has spoken to us as spoke to Israel in the past, there are three great differences in his speaking.

First, in the *time* of his speaking: 'In the past God spoke . . . but in these last days . . .'

Secondly, in the *mode* of his speaking: 'God spoke at many times and in various ways . . . he has spoken to us by his Son.'

Thirdly, in the *status* of his spokesmen: 'God spoke . . . through the prophets . . . he has spoken to us by his Son.'

Who Jesus is

Take the first difference. The NIV's phrase 'in these last days' is literally 'in the end of these days'. That sounds odd to us, but it comes straight from the Septuagint, the ancient Greek translation of the Old Testament, which in turn is based on the original Hebrew. Ancient Jews divided human history into two major periods: world history up until the coming of the Messiah ('these days'), and then the age to come, the age of the Messiah. The transitional period between the two would be 'the end of these days'.[1] It is this terminology that the writer is using, and he is using it to make a tremendous claim. He is standing at the turning-point of the ages. In all the past centuries, he says, Israel has been waiting for the coming of the Messiah and for the dawning of the messianic age. Now at last the Messiah has come. We are standing in 'the end of these days', or as the apostle John would put it, 'Dear children, this is the last hour' (1 Jn. 2:18).

God did not wait of course until Messiah came before he spoke to human beings, nor did he eventually send the Messiah as an unannounced surprise. From the time when he spoke to Eve about the triumph of the offspring of the woman (Gn. 3:15) to the time when he spoke through Malachi about the rising of the sun of righteousness with healing in its wings (Mal. 4:2), promise after promise, prophecy after prophecy, repeated God's assurance that one day the Messiah and Saviour of the world would come.

And now he has come! 'We have found the Messiah,' says Andrew to his brother Simon. 'We have found the one Moses wrote about in the Law, and about whom the prophets also wrote,' says Philip to Nathanael (Jn. 1: 41, 45). The long centuries of waiting are over, says the writer to the Hebrews. The end of these days is here. The Messiah has come and all that God has ever promised, has been, or is being, or is about to be, fulfilled in him.

Even at this distance in time we sense the thrill in the voice of these early Christians. What a gospel is theirs! They have found the key to the meaning and purpose of life, of history, of the universe! The promises, prophecies and visions of the Old Testament have turned out to be true! In past times God's speaking was in the form of promise; but now, in the end of these days, he has spoken at an altogether higher level:

[1] See *e.g.*, Dn. 10:14, and for details, together with a very helpful exposition, F. F. Bruce, *The Epistle to the Hebrews* (Marshall, Morgan and Scott, 1965), p. 3.

in fulfilment, in reality, in the person of the Messiah, formerly promised, but now actually arrived.

Then take the second difference, the difference in the mode of God's speaking. 'In the past God spoke to our forefathers.' Christians assert this as firmly as the most orthodox Jew; and they believe on the authority of the Lord Jesus himself that the Old Testament is the inspired record of that speaking. But when you look at it closely, you will find, as the writer points out, that there was never one single occasion in the past when God said everything he had to say, or one single person to whom and through whom he communicated everything about himself that he intended to tell us.

What tremendous revelations he gave to the father and founder of the Hebrew race! The fundamental principle of man's relationship to God, justification by faith, is as valid for us today as it was when God first taught it to Abraham (Gn. 15:6). But there was a tremendous amount that God did *not* tell Abraham, and only revealed centuries later through Moses. Nor did God tell Moses everything; for there were prophets after Moses who did far more than simply repeat or expound what Moses had already said. Indeed, as our writer will eventually point out (*e.g.* 7:11–16; 8:7–13; 9:10), God revealed through those later prophets that some of the regulations he had laid down through Moses were never, in fact, intended to be more than provisional. Through some prophets God spoke a great deal, through others very little. There are sixty-six chapters in Isaiah, but only one in Obadiah!

In the past, then, God's revelation of himself was piecemeal and progressive. But in Christ it is full and final. In Abraham, for example, God showed how he was prepared to justify anyone that 'believed God'. But it remained a secret how God could possibly be just and righteous himself and yet declare sinners like Abraham – and us – to be right with God and accepted by him. In Christ and in his death as an atonement for sin, that long-kept secret is now fully revealed (Rom. 3:25–26). Through Moses' law, to cite one more example, God indicated the standard of behaviour he required from man. But Moses never showed us how fallen, sinful people such as we could possibly keep that law and meet its requirement. Christ has (Rom. 8:2–4). In Christ God says everything he has to say. Christ is God's last word to man. Beyond him

God has nothing more to say. Nothing more needs saying.

In the past then God's revelation was not only piecemeal: it came in different forms. God showed us something of his sympathetic heart in appointing priests in Israel; and something else about himself and his purposes by instituting kingship. He raised up judges to be the people's deliverers and saviours (Jdg. 2:18). He spoke through sacrifices, rituals and ceremonies. But the priests were at best weak and failing men. The kings were often disobedient to God and tyrannical towards the people. The saviours and deliverers were never totally free from the slavery of sin themselves; and the sacrifices, rituals and ceremonies were only symbols: they could not effect the inner spiritual cleansing which they outwardly symbolized.

But one and all these different modes of revelation pointed forward to Christ, and in him they all unite. What they said partially and indistinctly, he expresses to perfection. He is the perfect priest *and* the ideal king – because he was the unfailingly obedient subject *and* the sinless saviour *and* the adequate, effective sacrifice.

If we ask how all this can be true of Jesus, the answer is to be found in the third difference, the difference in status between God's spokesmen in the past and his final spokesman. In the past, says the writer, God spoke through the prophets: in the end of these days, he has spoken through his Son. Notice at once that we are being asked to consider two different categories of spokesman: the prophets on the one hand, and God's son on the other. He does not say 'God spoke through prophets', but 'through *the* prophets'. *The* prophets were a well-known group or category in Israel. They held high office indeed. They 'spoke from God as they were carried along by the Holy Spirit' (2 Pet. 1:21). Some were more exalted, some less. Some were more effective and famous than others. But whatever their degrees of greatness, they could all rightly be bracketed together in one group: 'the prophets'.

Jesus is not to be placed in that group; he belongs to a category all of his own. 'The prophets' were inspired men, spiritual giants, but at their highest only men. Jesus is more than man. His relationship with God is unique. Greek idiom permits the writer to express it with a brevity unmatchable in English. God spoke in the past in, or through, the prophets, he says; but at the end of these days he has spoken in, or through, Son. It sounds odd in English to use the word 'Son' like that without either the definite article (through *the* Son), the indefinite article (through *a* Son) or a possessive adjective (through *his* Son). But you cannot translate the Greek 'through *a* Son, for the writer does not mean that Jesus is one of many sons. No, what he is saying by his Greek idiom is that God has spoken to us through someone who is essentially Son of God, who is related to God as Son to Father, the Son having the very same nature as the Father. He is not only a spokesman for God; in his essential nature he *is* God. When you meet him, when you hear him, you meet God and you hear God.

As human beings we can use words to convey our meaning, to convey, if we wish, what we are and what we feel in our innermost personality. But often our words are inadequate, and we find ourselves complaining, 'I cannot express what I really feel.' Our words are inadequate to express ourselves, precisely because our words are not us, so to speak. We are persons, but our words are something very much less than persons. When God expresses himself, however, his expression, his word, is a person, who perfectly expresses what God is, because he is God himself. 'In the beginning was the Word,' says John, 'and the Word was with God, and the Word was God' (Jn. 1:1).

That is not to deny the Old Testament's declaration of the oneness of God. The New Testament asserts as unreservedly as the Old that 'there is one God' (1 Tim. 2:5). But as God has gone on speaking throughout the centuries, gradually revealing more of himself, it has become apparent that God's unity is not monolithic. We human beings, humble and lowly creatures though we are, are not monoliths either. Listen to us speaking about ourselves and you will find that we naturally think of ourselves as being a plurality within a unity. For instance, we find the pious, Old Testament Hebrew facing death of the body and saying to God, 'Into your hands I commit my spirit' (Ps. 31:5). We know exactly what he meant. But obviously, the fact that he distinguished between his body and his spirit does not imply that he believed he was two people, or on the other hand that his body was not a part of him. Nor do Christians imply that there are three Gods when they say that the one true God is infinitely more complex than we his humble creatures are, and that the Godhead is composed of the Father, the Son, and the Holy Spirit. Indeed, the Old Testament itself more than hints at this plurality within the unity of the Godhead. In its very first chapter God says, 'Let *us* make man in *our image, in our* likeness' (Gn. 1:26) – and obviously God was not talking to the angels; man is not made in the image of God-plus-the-angels!

The person of the Son

What then is meant by the term 'Son of God'? The writer proceeds to tell us. He makes no attempt to give us a definition, either theological or metaphysical. Wisely enough! Even if it could be done in merely human language and using finite thought-forms, the resultant definition would be altogether beyond the grasp of the vast majority of believers. (Compared with the Godhead, the atom is a simple, lowly thing. Has anyone fully understood and correctly visualized its structure yet?) What the writer chooses rather to do is to give us a description of the person of the Son of God and of his role first in creation and secondly in redemption.

a. The Son in relation to the creation of the universe

The Son is the one for whom the universe was made. He is, says the writer, the appointed 'heir of all things'.

The universe is not self-existent. It was made. And that inevitably raises the question, 'What was it made for?' Instinctively we reject the idea that there is no purpose or goal behind its existence. The study of the purpose and function of each individual part and mechanism within our bodies, or within the universe as a whole, is one of the most stimulating and gratifying intellectual exercises we can engage in. Our minds refuse to be satisfied with the idea that while each part of the universe has a purpose and a function in regard to the whole, the whole itself has no purpose or function.

We ourselves are not self-existent either, and we certainly

did not make ourselves. Sooner or later we each start asking, 'Why am I here? What is the purpose of life?' Most of us find that we ourselves are too small to be a satisfying goal and purpose for our own lives. We must seek a bigger and more satisfying purpose. But what? The family? Society? The nation? The race? The behaviour of the nations and of the human race so far, as history reveals it, seems to show the human race as a pretty unsatisfactory goal to live for.

'Ah, but the human race', you say, 'has made, and will continue to make, great progress; and I am satisfied if my individual life serves the noble purpose of the progress of the human race.'

Well said; but if the race is making progress – and it certainly is in some directions – that raises once again the same question: progress to what goal? And if there is no answer to that question, 'serving the progress of the race' would ultimately be pointless. What's the point of being a cog in the engine of a bus that serves the purpose of making the bus go, if the bus itself doesn't know where it is going, and there is in fact no place for it to go to and no reason for going anywhere anyway?

Where then shall we find a satisfactory and satisfying purpose and goal for our existence? The answer is: in the Son of God. It was for him and for his pleasure that the universe, and we within it, were made. He is the appointed heir of all things; of the material universe, of all its creatures, of its history and progress. Almighty and eternal Son of God, he alone is big enough and worthy enough to be the final goal of the life of the individual and of the human race and of the universe.

What is more, he is not only the goal of the universe; he is its Creator as well. He is the one by whom God created the universe. When the author of the Old Testament book of Proverbs talked of the wisdom by which God created the world, he spoke of wisdom in almost personal terms (Pr. 8:22ff.). His instinct was true; truer perhaps than he realized, for he was inspired by God. That wisdom was indeed a person, the Son of God. What a gospel this is! We human beings are not the mere products of impersonal, purposeless forces working through chance on blind, unfeeling matter. We are the creatures of a personal Creator, who has become incarnate in Jesus our Lord so that we might get to know him personally and serve him lovingly and intelligently.

b. The person of the Son of God

We have thought of the Son of God in relation to creation. But what is he in himself? He is the radiance of God's glory and the exact representation of his [essential] being (1:3). Notice the present tense. These are things that Christ has ever been, is and will always continue to be. He is the radiance of God's glory. None of us has ever seen God the Father at any time. Not even Moses. When Moses stood in the cleft of the rock and God made all his glory to pass by, Moses did not see the one whom we know as God the Father (Ex. 33:17ff.). He saw the one who subsequently became Jesus of Nazareth, but who ever was, and is through all eternity, the radiance of God's glory. He has displayed God's glory by creating the universe – showing that God is a God of colour and music and beauty and grandeur and might. Through Moses and his law he made God known as a God of moral order and purity, of righteousness and holiness. But in his own incarnation, death, resurrection and ascension, he has revealed the glory of the Father as only the Son could do. 'The Word became flesh and made his dwelling among us,' says the apostle John. 'We have seen his glory, the glory of the One and Only, who came from the Father, full of grace and truth' (Jn. 1:14).

Not only in his acts but in his own self he is the radiance of God's glory. Isaiah once looked up into heaven and saw the Lord high and lifted up and his train filled the temple. The seraphim were veiling their heads and feet as they cried, 'Holy, holy, holy is the Lord Almighty.' Isaiah saw, so he tells us, 'the King, the Lord Almighty' (Is. 6:1–5). John, the inspired gospel-writer, adds the information that the person whom Isaiah saw was the one whom we call Jesus (Jn. 12:41). He is that person of the Trinity who reveals the glory of the Godhead. He does not merely reflect it as a mirror might reflect the rays of the sun but has no light of itself. Rather, just as the sun's rays reveal to us what the sun is like because they possess the same nature as the sun, so Christ reveals God because in his essential being he *is* God.

He is, says Scripture, the exact representation of God's

essential being. Just as you might get a die and impress it on metal and from the marks made on the metal you could tell what the die was like, so if you look at Christ you will see what God is like. But our illustration breaks down, for the metal which received the die-marks need not be of the same metal as the die. But Christ, as we have seen, not only represents God's essential being exactly; he does so in virtue of the fact that he possesses the same essential being.

c. The Son of God and the maintenance of the universe

There is something else that Christ has ever done and ever will do. He upholds all things by the word of his power. He sustains the universe, which he himself made. He not only sustains it as though it were some dead weight that he has to hold up. He bears it in the sense that he is conveying it along, conveying it to its final goal and destiny.

The scientists talk about the possibility of nuclear fission or fusion, about the possibility of man's blowing up the world on which we live. You need not be worried, for it is Christ whose powerful word maintains and guards its existence. We are told that the universe is expanding, that stars already millions of light years away are constantly travelling farther away from the earth at tremendous speeds. Where is it all going to? Where will it end? The fact is that the Son of God is upholding it all and leading it to its destiny.

d. The Son of God and the redemption of the universe

There is more. He 'provided purification for sins', says Scripture. The Authorized (King James) version reads: 'when he had by himself purged our sins . . .'; but the thought is bigger than that. It is not a question of *our* sins only – bad and big as they are – but of the whole defiled and disjointed universe. He made it all, he sustains it all; and when sin spoiled everything he himself came to put it right. He is not a mere creature, tinkering with a universe which he did not himself make. The universe's Creator, he has also become its redeemer. He has done the work that makes possible the eventual reconciliation of all things to God 'whether things on earth or things in heaven, by making peace through his blood, shed on the cross' (Col. 1:20).

e. The glorification of the Son of God

'After he had provided purification for sins, he sat down at the right hand of the Majesty in heaven' (1:3).

There is an allusion here to Psalm 110:1 where through the prophet David, God issues his invitation to David's Lord: 'The Lord says to my Lord: "Sit at my right hand until I make your enemies a footstool for your feet." ' This verse became very popular with the early Christians, because Jesus called their attention to it and applied it to himself (see Lk. 20:41–44; 22:69–70). We shall meet it many times in this letter. But for the moment consider its implication. When the high priest's court heard Jesus claim, 'From now on, the Son of Man will be seated at the right hand of the mighty God,' they all exclaimed: 'Are you *then* the Son of God?'

'Yes,' he replied.

Their deduction was absolutely correct.

f. The Son of God and the angels

Finally the writer adds, 'So he became as much superior to the angels as the name he has inherited is superior to theirs' (1:4). It is of course natural that he should remind his fellow Jewish Christians that the Lord Jesus, the captain of their salvation, is better than what they have known in Judaism; and he warms to his theme as his letter proceeds. Christ is better than angels (1:4ff.); he is better than the sacrifices (10:3–10), and his covenant is better than the old covenant (8:6). They lost nothing by following Christ.

But there was a special reason for reminding his readers that Jesus is superior to angels. The Jewish law was put into effect through angels (see Acts 7:53; Gal. 3:19); hence their respect for that law. Were they not a privileged nation? What other nation could claim that God had spoken to them and delivered his law to their leader, Moses, through the agency of angels? And what a spectacle the giving of the law on Mount Sinai had been (Ex. 24:16–17)! By contrast, in their estimation Jesus was a nobody. As the Pharisees once remarked, 'We know that God has spoken to Moses, but as for this fellow, we don't even know where he comes from'

41

(Jn. 9:29). So they would constantly deride the Christian Jews for having abandoned the law given by the mediation of exalted angels in order to follow the teachings of an obscure carpenter.

Not so! says our writer. Jesus is doubly superior to angels. As Son of God he always had by divine inheritance a name superior to theirs. Now incarnate as Jesus, he sits enthroned in his exaltation far above them all.

Questions

1 What similarities in detail do you see between what Hebrews 1:1–4 says about our Lord and what other New Testament writers say about him (*e.g.* Col. 1:15–17; Jn. 1:1–4)?

2 What would you say to someone who accused you of believing in three Gods?

3 In what sense is Christ 'heir of all things'?

4 What is the meaning of the phrases 'the radiance of God's glory' and 'the exact representation of his being'?

5 How did the universe created by Christ come to need purification? Has Colossians 1:20 anything to teach us in this connection?

6 'Sat down at the right hand' (1:3) is an allusion to Psalm 110:1. Consider the lessons drawn from this verse (a) in the rest of this letter; (b) in the rest of the New Testament. Use a good concordance to find the places where it is quoted.

7 In what particulars is Hebrews 1:1–4 good news for modern man?

3

THE DEITY OF CHRIST PROVED
Hebrews 1:5–14

(This is a long and difficult but extremely important chapter. You may prefer to read Part One now, and come back to Parts Two, Three and Four later.)

Part One

In Hebrews 1:1–4 the writer asserts the deity of Christ. In 1:5–14 he sets out to prove it. Not of course to agnostics and atheists and people of other faiths who do not accept the Old Testament as the Word of God – or at least not in the first place to them, though what he has to say may well in the end provide even them with powerful evidence that Jesus is the Son of God. But in the first place he is writing to Christian Jews to strengthen their faith and to help them answer the criticisms of their fellow-Jews who denied the deity of the Lord Jesus and considered it blasphemous idolatry to worship Jesus as God. It would have been no good expecting the non-Christian Jews to accept the deity of Jesus on the authority of the Christian apostles. They did not accept that authority. But both the Christian and the non-Christian Jews accepted the Old Testament as the divinely inspired and authoritative Word of God; and it is to the Old Testament that the writer to the Hebrews appeals in order to prove his case.

Let us notice at once that the issue at stake is not victory in some wordy and utterly unpractical theological debate. It is nothing less than the very heart and credibility of the Old Testament's announced programme for the salvation of the world. The Old Testament has more to offer the world than the doctrine of monotheism, glorious and liberating and life-

43

giving though that doctrine is; and more to offer than its God-given, sane, wholesome code of morality, necessary for the moral health of the world though that is. The Old Testament presents a programme for the salvation of the world, for the putting down of evil, for the establishment of the kingdom of God on earth. The world certainly needs it.

Key and kingpin in this programme according to the Old Testament is the coming of the Messiah. Take two prophecies typical of many. 'A shoot will come up from the stump of Jesse; from his roots a Branch will bear fruit. The Spirit of the Lord will rest upon him . . . with righteousness he will judge the needy, with justice he will give decisions for the poor of the earth. He will strike the earth with the rod of his mouth; with the breath of his lips he will slay the wicked . . . The wolf will live with the lamb . . . the calf and the lion and the yearling together; and a little child will lead them . . . for the earth will be full of the knowledge of the Lord as the waters cover the sea. In that day the Root of Jesse will stand as a banner for the peoples; the nations will rally to him, and his place of rest will be glorious' (Is. 11:1–10). 'In the last days', says Isaiah elsewhere (2:1–4), ' . . . he (God) will judge between the nations and will settle disputes for many peoples. They will beat their swords into ploughshares and their spears into pruning hooks. Nation will not take up sword against nation, nor will they train for war any more.'

The hope of such a future haunts mankind. In our hearts we know it is the only sane way to live. But centuries of hope unfulfilled and of continuing wickedness and war have made people sceptical. There have been so many promises of utopia, based on political theories or religious faiths, that have proved illusory and have themselves sometimes contributed massively to the world's misery and suffering. Hope gets blunted. People naturally ask what credibility the Old Testament's programme has. Are its visions and promises anything more than wishful thinking or religious castles in the air? Who is this 'shoot from the stump of Jesse', this 'Branch from his roots', who is to rally the nations to himself and introduce universal peace based on perfect justice?

The description of him as a branch from the root of Jesse (Jesse was King David's father) indicates that he is to be a king from David's royal line. Is he then to be no more than that? If so, what conviction would that create in our hearts that here is the key to the salvation of the world? David himself gained many military victories; he enjoyed great popularity with his nation (though even that declined seriously at one point); and his religious poetry still comforts and inspires millions of people round the world (witness Ps. 23). But he was king of only a little pocket-handkerchief-size state. The great Gentile nations did not exactly come rallying to his banner. He was guilty, too, of acting like an oriental despot and committed adultery and murder. His commander-in-chief, Joab, was a ruthless, power-hungry, unprincipled schemer whom David never managed to control satisfactorily. David's merely human successors were none of them greater or better than he; many of them were a lot worse. How could we take the Old Testament seriously if its promised programme for the salvation of the world depended on a Saviour-Messiah-King who was nothing more than a merely human descendant of David, however brilliant – or of any other famous leader for that matter, Alexander, Caesar, Napoleon, or who you will?

But then what the Old Testament promises is a Saviour-Messiah-King who is far more than that. He is of course to be a son of David; and therefore many prophets in the Old Testament take the experiences of King David, and of his successors, as a kind of prototype or prefigurement of the Messiah. But the Old Testament itself makes it quite clear that Messiah will not only be David's son, he will be David's Lord (see Ps. 110:1 and Christ's comment on the verse in Lk. 20:41–44). Human certainly, as David was, but more than human. Nothing less than the Son of God, God incarnate (see Is. 9:6–7). It is this part of the Old Testament's programme (if it is true) that, miraculous though it is, gives the programme a realistic hope of being fulfilled.

Nor has the writer to the Hebrews any difficulty in showing that this is what the Old Testament says the Messiah will be. To cite for the moment three of his Old Testament quotations. He quotes Psalm 2:7 where God says to the Messiah, 'You are my son; today I have begotten you' (AV, RV, NIV footnote). He quotes Psalm 45:6–7 where God says to the Messiah (through the divinely inspired poet-prophet), 'Your throne, O God, will last for ever and ever . . . God,

45

your God, has set you above your companions.' And he quotes Psalm 110:1 where God invites David's Lord, that is the Messiah, to sit at his right hand until God makes his enemies into a footstool for him. This is language so exalted that it goes far beyond either David or any ordinary successor in his royal line. The inspired composers of these psalms were more than poets: they were prophets. Using King David or one of his successors as models to help people conceptualize God's promised Saviour-King, they then talked of that King in language that went far beyond anything that could be said, without gross exaggeration, of David. In its full and natural meaning it could only be meant to apply to the Messiah.

The meaning of the term 'Son of God'

Let us look, to start with, at a skeleton outline of the writer's Old Testament quotations. This is how he sets them out:

'For to which of the angels did God ever say,'

1 Psalm 2:7;
2 2 Samuel 7:14;
3 Psalm 97:7?

'In speaking of the angels he says, "He makes his angels winds, his servants flames of fire" [Ps. 104:4]. But to the Son he says,

4 Psalm 45:6–7;
5 Psalm 102:25–27.

'To which of the angels did God ever say,'

6 Psalm 110:1?

'Are not all angels [simply] ministering spirits sent to serve . . .?'

We notice at once that the first thing the writer aims to show is that the Messiah, Son of God, is infinitely superior to angels. You see, there are places in the Old Testament where angels are referred to as 'the sons of God' (see *e.g.*, Jb. 1:6, NIV footnote). Some people might have argued therefore that when the Old Testament refers to the Messiah as Son of God, it means no more than it does when it calls the angels sons of God. But such an argument is false, as the writer shows. Notice how he argues. Proof of the deity of the Messiah is not made to depend on his readers' ability to grasp fine distinctions in the possible meanings of the Hebrew word for 'son'. The writer takes a far more direct route. Granted that angels as a group are sometimes called 'sons of God' in Scripture; yet to which individual angel, he asks, did God ever at any time in Scripture say, 'You are my Son' (Ps. 2:7)? And when did God ever tell an angel that he had begotten him (Ps. 2:7)? And when did God ever address an individual angel through an inspired biblical poet or prophet as 'God', and declare that the angel's throne would last for ever (Ps. 45:6–7)? And to which angel did God ever say, 'Sit at my right hand until I make your enemies a footstool for your feet' (Ps. 110:1)?

These questions answer themselves. As Son of God the Messiah is unique and infinitely superior to angels. Things are said by God in the Old Testament both of him and to him that have never been, and could never be, said of any angel; and if not of any angel how much less of any mortal king like David or his ordinary successors.

A survey of the quotations

Now let us survey the quotations. They all state or imply the deity of the Messiah. But we shall find two very important things about them. First, they are not mere proof-texts wrenched out of their contexts and made to mean something quite foreign to what was originally intended. The very opposite is true. It will be by studying their contexts that we shall come to see how powerful their support is for the writer's case. Studying their contexts, of course, will involve us in hard work. But it will be worth it.

Secondly, the successive quotations do not simply repeat the deity of the Messiah. When read along with their contexts, they form a logical progression, and sketch for us the various stages in God's programme for the establishment of his kingdom on earth; and they also show how the deity of the Messiah is the key element in each of these stages.

Here is a bird's-eye view of the quotations:

First group: King Messiah's relationship to God

1 Psalm 2:7   *The declaration of the relationship* by the installation of Messiah on God's holy hill of Zion: fulfilled at the resurrection and ascension of Christ.

2 2 Samuel 7:14   *The perpetuation of the relationship* unbroken throughout all subsequent ages.

3 Psalm 97:7   *The universal acknowledgment of the relationship* at the coming of the Lord to judge the world and to set up his kingdom.[1]

Second group: The permanence of Messiah's reign: the quality of his rule: the permanence of Messiah himself and of his subjects

4 Psalm 45:6–7   *The permanence and quality of Messiah's reign,* based both on his deity and on the perfect justice of his rule. That justice itself is based on Messiah's previously demonstrated love of righteousness and hatred of wickedness; which in turn is why God has exalted him, has given him the name that is above every name, and will yet require everyone to acknowledge him as God at the coming cosmic celebration of the marriage of the King.

5 Psalm 102:25–27   *The permanence of Messiah himself and of his subjects.* What use to us the certainty of a coming kingdom of God on earth, if we ourselves never live to see it or enjoy it? What use to us or to any others of God's creatures, if eventually all God's creatures, we included, are doomed to perish along with the heavens and earth and the rest of the created universe? But in the Messiah

---

[1] See Additional Note 1 at the end of this chapter for the evidence that this third quotation is based on Ps. 97:7.

the Creator has become a man. Being the eternal Creator he will outlast his creation. But so he will as man. In relation with him all his true servants already enjoy eternal life and will likewise last eternally.

Final quotation: Messiah's present position while he waits for the establishment of his kingdom

6 Psalm 110:1 *Messiah's present position and status* are indicated by God's invitation: 'The Lord said to my [David's] Lord, "Sit at my right hand." ' This could never have been addressed to any angel. It refers to Messiah's ascension and his position in the place of honour on God's throne. The next words, 'until I make your enemies a foot-stool for your feet', show that it was never planned that his ascension should be immediately followed by the subjugation of all evil. The plan was that there should be an interval of waiting. But the invitation points to the coming reign of Christ when evil will be put down and the last enemy will be destroyed.

Brief, then, as this survey has been, it has shown us, first, that each of these Old Testament quotations declares in one way or another the deity of the Messiah; and, secondly, that the quotations studied in their original contexts take us from the resurrection and ascension of the Son of God through this present age to his second coming, the marriage of the King, and the establishment of his reign on earth; the nature and quality of that reign, and the eternal permanence not only of the Messiah himself but of all his true servants.

We shall get down to the detail in Parts Two, Three and Four. (For questions on Part 1 see p. 81.)

Part Two

At this point let us just remind ourselves that there are two things which the writer must show by his quotations. First, that the Messiah is the Son of God. This he will do easily enough. If in Psalm 2:7 God explicitly acclaims the Messiah as his Son, and if in Psalm 45:6–7 God, through the poet-prophet, addresses the Messiah as God – that is enough. The case is proved. The deity of the Messiah is established; and all that is said elsewhere in the Old Testament about the Messiah must be read and understood in the light of it.

Secondly, he has to show that Jesus is the Messiah spoken of in the Old Testament. Here he starts from the historical fact of the resurrection of Jesus. Not only does that resurrection itself declare Jesus to be the Son of God, but it shows us what God's full meaning and intention were when he made the statements, promises and predictions which are now to be quoted.

The first group of quotations

1. *The declaration of the relationship (Ps. 2:7)*

> Why do the nations conspire
> and the peoples plot in vain?
> The kings of the earth take their stand
> and the rulers gather together
> against the Lord
> and against his Anointed One
> 'Let us break their chains,' they say,
> 'and throw off their fetters.'
>
> The One enthroned in heaven laughs;
> the Lord scoffs at them.
> Then he rebukes them in his anger
> and terrifies them in his wrath, saying,
> 'I have installed my King
> on Zion, my holy hill.'
>
> I will proclaim the decree of the Lord:
> He said to me, '*You are my Son,*
> *today I have begotten you*
> Ask of me,

> and I will make the nations your inheritance,
> the ends of the earth your possession.
> You will rule them with an iron sceptre;
> you will dash them to pieces like pottery.'
>
> Therefore, you kings, be wise;
> be warned, you rulers of the earth.
> Serve the Lord with fear . . .
> Kiss the Son, lest he be angry
> and you be destroyed in your way . . .
> Blessed are all who take refuge in
> him (Ps. 2:1–12).

We have given the quotation in its context. It is concerned, as we now see, with the proclamation, or declaration, of the Lord's decree. The 'I' in 'I will proclaim the decree' is not of course the author of the psalm. It is the Messiah whom the psalmist in true dramatic and prophetic style has introduced as speaking in his own (*i.e.* the Messiah's own) voice. What we are concerned with here, therefore, is not the question: 'When did God say to Messiah, "You are my Son, today I have begotten you"?' but the question 'When and how was this decree of the Lord proclaimed by Messiah and demonstrated to the world at large?'

The earlier context in the psalm supplies the answer. It pictures first an international attack of kings and rulers against God and his Anointed One. It then describes God's response: 'The One enthroned in heaven laughs; the Lord scoffs at them. Then he rebukes them . . . saying, "I have installed my King on Zion, my holy hill." '

So the question now becomes: What event in all history matches the situation described here and gives it the fullest possible, and therefore the most convincing, fulfilment? Christians answer without hesitation: the crucifixion, death, burial, resurrection and ascension of Jesus.

It took the early Christians very little time to see how the situation depicted in Psalm 2 had been vividly fulfilled in the Jerusalem of their day. 'Sovereign Lord,' they prayed as they faced the opposition of their rulers, 'you made the heaven and the earth and the sea, and everything in them. You spoke by the Holy Spirit through the mouth of your servant, our father David:

> "Why do the nations rage
>   and the peoples plot in vain?
> The kings of the earth take their stand
>   and the rulers gather together
> against the Lord
>   and against his Anointed One."

'Indeed Herod and Pontius Pilate met together with the Gentiles and the people of Israel in this city to conspire against your holy servant Jesus, whom you anointed. They did what your power and will had decided beforehand should happen.' And they concluded their prayer with an appeal to God to vindicate the resurrection and ascension of Jesus by performing 'miraculous signs and wonders through the name of . . . Jesus' (Acts 4:24–30).

Paul later made the same point theologically. The gospel, he says, was 'promised [by God] beforehand through his prophets in the Holy Scriptures regarding his Son, who as to his human nature was a descendant of David, and who through the Spirit of holiness was declared with power to be the Son of God by his resurrection from the dead' (Rom. 1:2–4).

It is no accident, of course, that this first quotation from the Old Testament points to the crucifixion, death, resurrection and ascension of the Son of God Any realistic programme for putting down evil in the world and introducing an age of peace must be based on a thorough diagnosis and exposure of where the trouble lies. The crucifixion, by responsible rulers, of one whose claim to be the Son of God was subsequently vindicated by his resurrection, gives us that diagnosis as nothing else could. Pontius Pilate and Herod were not extraordinary villains like, say, Hitler. They were comparatively medium-to-small-sized military/political rulers, no more despotic, cruel, weak, ambitious, no less sincerely concerned for the good of those they ruled than the average politician or ruler today. The Jewish high priest and his colleagues were not fiends incarnate either, nor despicable charlatans. They were responsible religious leaders, caught up, and sometimes perhaps compromised, by the difficulties of solving complex religio-politico-social problems; but no less sincere, no more career-minded or power-blinded than the average religious leader is today.

Yet their united opposition to Jesus, their crucifixion of the Son of God, exposes what the real problem was for them and is still for every man and woman today. It is not simply a careless attitude to justice, not simply a somewhat selfish concentration on one's own interests to the neglect of other people's rights; or simply a rather less than vigorous determination to keep the moral code, or to say one's prayers regularly and to lead a life of purity. No, the problem is that in the heart of every person there is a basic rebellion against God, such that faced with God's own Son, and his claim to be our rightful Lord and King, we refuse to submit. This basic rebelliousness can often remain undetected beneath genuine political concern for others and sincere religious endeavour. But it is there nonetheless. It is direct encounter with the claims of the Son of God incarnate that removes the upper layers of political and religious respectability and exposes our basic, inherent rebellion against God. 'The mind of the flesh', says Scripture, is enmity against God; for it is not subject to the law of God, neither indeed can it be' (Rom. 8:7, RV).

The first step, therefore, in the salvation of the individual or of society, is the exposure of the real trouble. That, the cross of Christ does. The second step is the provision of an effective incentive to repentance. That, the resurrection of Jesus and his vindication as God's Son provide. Hear this stated in the language of this same Psalm 2:9–12: 'You [the risen and ascended Son of God] will rule them with an iron sceptre; you will dash them to pieces like pottery. Therefore, you kings, be wise; be warned, you rulers of the earth. . . . Kiss the Son, lest he be angry and you be destroyed in your way.' Hear it stated, if you prefer, in the language of the New Testament: 'God . . . now . . . commands all people everywhere to repent. For he has set a day when he will judge the world with justice by the man he has appointed. He has given proof of this to all men by raising him from the dead' (Acts 17:30–31). But hear also the comfort offered by the psalm to all who repent and believe: 'Blessed are all who take refuge in him' (Ps. 2:12).

2. The perpetuation of the relationship (2 Sa. 7:14)

The Lord declares to you [King David] that the Lord himself will establish a house for you: When your days are over . . . I will raise up your offspring to succeed you, who will come from your own body, and I will establish his kingdom. He is the one who will build a house for my Name, and I will establish the throne of his kingdom for ever. *I will be his father, and he shall be my son.* When he does wrong, I will punish him with the rod of men . . . But my love will never be taken away from him, as I took it away from Saul, whom I removed from before you. Your house and your kingdom shall endure for ever before me; your throne shall be established for ever (2 Sa. 7:11b–16).

The second quotation comes, as we see, from a long and elaborate promise made by God to David about the perpetuation of David's throne and royal line. Now obviously this promise referred in the first place to David's first successor, Solomon. He it was who built the temple for God's Name. If God had removed the kingship from him, as he did from Saul, and had given it to a different family altogether, David's royal dynasty would have been strangled at birth so to speak. We should not underestimate therefore the primary meaning of the passage: the special relationship of father and son and the discipline involved in it which God announced between himself and Solomon. But it is equally obvious that this elaborate promise cannot have been meant to apply only to Solomon. If it had, and God in his fatherly loyalty had maintained Solomon's throne, but then allowed the throne to be taken away from his successors, what would have become of the rest of God's promise to David: 'Your house and your kingdom shall endure for ever before me; your throne shall be established for ever'? It must therefore have been intended to apply to more of David's successors than Solomon.

But then again if God's promise was meant to apply only to David's merely human successors, we meet another problem. This time it is a colossal one. David's merely human successors have long since lost their kingdom! David's earthly throne has not been maintained! For ancient Judaism this was a very serious difficulty. Long before the writer to the Hebrews wrote his letter, the pre-Christian Jewish author of Psalm 89 was wrestling with the problem that the destruction of David's earthly throne and dynasty posed for his faith.

He quotes at length the promise, the oath and the covenant made by God with David and his seed guaranteeing to him an everlasting throne (verses 19–37). But then he frankly admits that by the time he was writing his psalm God had 'rejected . . . spurned . . . been ˎvery angry with your anointed one . . . renounced the covenant with your servant . . . defiled his crown in the dust' (verses 38–39). As he contemplates it, his sorrow, misery and perplexity drive him to ask, 'O Lord, where is your former great love, which in your faithfulness you swore to David?' (verse 49).

This is a serious problem not only for a Jew who believes that 2 Samuel 7 and its promise are God's inspired and unfailing word. It is a problem for Christians. We Christians too believe that the Old Testament is God's Word. Our very gospel is built on, and witnessed to, by the Old Testament (see Rom. 1:2; 3:21). How shall we hold up our heads to the godless despots, humanists, atheists, agnostics and general unbelievers of this world, if it has to be admitted that the Old Testament's announcement of a divine purpose and plan for the world, to be accomplished through the royal house of King David of Judah, all petered out and came to nothing?

But then, of course, it has not petered out. The answer to the problem is to be found in Jesus. In so far as God's covenant promise to David referred to David's merely human successors, it was set aside because their flagrant apostasies broke the covenant. But the covenant promise in its fullest sense has been gloriously maintained, and what is more, fulfilled in Jesus. He was born a physical descendant of David. That satisfied one part of the promise. Then his resurrection showed him to be the Son of God in the highest possible sense of the term. That has satisfied the other part of the promise. In other words, the solution to the problem is not to say that the original promise, 'I will be his father, and he shall be my son', was only a pious piece of wishful thinking and exaggeration on the part of the prophet Nathan; and that it was fulfilled (if at all) only at a very lowly and temporary level. The solution is that the promise was indeed the word of God. It meant what is said. But it also meant far more than it appeared to say, as we can now see since the resurrection of the Lord Jesus. God had always intended to fulfil his promise not only at its primary level in connection with Solomon, but also at an infinitely higher level. Behind the lesser relationship of father and son, God always had in mind the greater relationship of Father and Son. That's God! To recognize the fulfilment of his promises, you must base your expectations not on a minimal but on a maximal interpretation of their terms.

It was of course the resurrection of Jesus that opened the eyes of the early Christians to see the full meaning of God's promises to David in 2 Samuel 7. Listen to Peter on the day of Pentecost: 'Brothers, I can tell you confidently that the patriarch David died and was buried . . . But he was a prophet and knew that God had promised him on oath that he would place one of his descendants on his throne. Seeing what was ahead, he spoke of the resurrection of the Christ . . . (he has been) exalted to the right hand of God . . . God has made this Jesus . . both Lord and Christ' (Acts 2:29–36).

But there is another piece of highly significant evidence bearing on the question of the fulfilment of the promise, 'I will be his father, and he shall be my son.' With the birth of Jesus Christ in the royal line of David there entered our world someone who had an unparalleled sense of God as his Father and of himself as God's Son. As a boy of twelve he astounded his hearers by referring to the temple as 'my Father's house' (Lk. 2:49). In the twenty-one chapters of the gospel of John's record of his life and teaching he refers to God as his Father over 100 times.

We are so used to thinking of God as Father that if we are not careful we shall fail to see how doubly unique Jesus was in this respect. First, no prophet, priest, poet or king in the Old Testament ever spoke of God as his personal Father in the way and to the extent that Jesus did. Verify this claim for yourself. Secondly, though Jesus taught his disciples that God was their Father, he consistently maintained that God was his Father and that he was God's Son in a unique sense. He taught his disciples, 'This, then, is how you should pray:

'Our Father . . ." ' (Mt. 6:9); but he never joined them in saying '*Our* Father'. Rather he expressed himself, as to Mary in the Garden: 'I am returning to my Father and your Father' (Jn. 20:17). Or as in Matthew 11:27: 'All things have been committed to me by my Father. No-one knows the Son except the Father, and no-one knows the Father except the Son and those to whom the Son chooses to reveal him.' It was language like this that astonished, and then infuriated, many of his contemporaries: 'he was even calling God his own Father, making himself equal with God' (Jn. 5:18).

The resurrection has vindicated his teaching about himself, and it becomes apparent that God's promise to David has been fulfilled magnificently. David's line will never peter out. God's promise to provide the world with a Saviour-King is secure. The Messiah is not a mere man or even an angel, both of whom might fall out of divine favour. He is the eternal Son of the eternal Father. The relationship is indestructible; and the future is in his hands.

3. The universal acknowledgment of the relationship (Ps. 97:7)

Say among the nations, The Lord reigns . . .
   he will judge the peoples with equity.
Then all the trees of the forest will sing for joy;
   they will sing before the Lord, for he comes,
   he comes to judge the earth.
He will judge the world in righteousness.
(Ps. 96:10, 12–13)

The Lord reigns, let the earth be glad;
   let the distant shores rejoice. . . .
   righteousness and justice are the foundation of his throne.
Fire goes before him
   and consumes his foes on every side . . .
The heavens proclaim his righteousness,
   and all the peoples see his glory.
All who worship images are put to shame . . .
(Ps. 97:1–3, 6, 7a)
   Let all God's angels worship him.
(verse 7c, my translation)

The Lord has made his salvation known
  and revealed his righteousness to the nations.
He has remembered his love
  and his faithfulness to the house of Israel;
all the ends of the earth have seen
  the salvation of our God. . . .
  shout for joy before the Lord, the King . . .
let them sing before the Lord,
  for he comes to judge the earth.
He will judge the world in righteousness
  and the peoples with equity.

(Ps. 98:2–3, 6, 9)

The Lord reigns . . .
Great is the Lord in Zion;
  he is exalted over all the nations.

(Ps. 99:1–2)

The first quotation, Psalm 2:7, pointed to the declaration of the Son's relationship with the Father at the resurrection and ascension. The second quotation, 2 Samuel 7:14, dealt with the perpetuation of that relationship throughout all the ages. Now the third quotation moves on to the universal acknowledgment of that relationship at the second coming of the Lord.

But first a few minor technicalities. This third quotation, 'Let all God's angels worship him', is based on the phrase in Psalm 97:7 which in Hebrew reads, 'Worship him, all you gods!' (see NIV). Following a long-established tradition in the Septuagint (that is, the pre-Christian, Jewish translation of the Old Testament into Greek) the writer to the Hebrews has understood the term 'gods' to refer to the angels. Very reasonably so; God does not require the worship of false gods. He has also borrowed the wording of a rendering of this verse which is found in another passage in the Septuagint.[2]

A major question, however, is raised by the writer's interpretation of the command, 'Let all God's angels worship him.' He takes the 'him' to refer to the Messiah; and he argues that the Messiah must be the Son of God, for this verse

[2] See Additional Note 1 at the end of this chapter for the evidence that this third quotation is based on Ps. 97:7, although the writer's exact wording is taken from the Septuagint of Dt. 32:43.

commands even the angels to worship him. It would be idolatry and blasphemy to worship him if he were not the Son
of God. It would be like the folly of those whom this very
same verse, 97:7, denounces for worshipping idols.

But many people would want to challenge the writer's
interpretation. They would argue that in its original context
the 'him' of the command 'Let all God's angels worship him'
refers to God, not to the Messiah, and that the writer is being
unfair to the original sense of the passage. We must take the
objection seriously. A shallow answer would be unworthy.
So let us examine the context thoroughly, first the larger
context and then the more immediate context. Psalm 97 is
one of a closely knit group of psalms that deal prominently
with the problem of evil: why, if there is a God who cares
about justice, does he allow evil people to go on lying,
cheating, oppressing, murdering with apparent impunity?
Psalm 94:2–3 vividly expresses the problem. 'Rise up, O
Judge of the earth,' the psalmist implores, 'pay back to the
proud what they deserve. How long will the wicked, O Lord,
how long will the wicked be jubilant?' Millions of believers
in God in every century have wrestled with this problem.

In contrast to Psalm 94, Psalms 96 and 98 are almost ecstatic
with joy. The reason is, they have the answer to the problem:
the Lord is going to come to judge the earth. In their jubil-
ation they repeat the answer several times. 'Let the heavens
rejoice, let the earth be glad . . . they will sing before the
Lord, for he *comes*, he *comes* to judge the earth', says Psalm
96:11, 13. Not content with having it said once, Psalm 98:9
says it again: 'let them sing before the Lord, for he *comes* to
judge the earth. He will judge the world in righteousness and
the peoples with equity.'

Words could not be clearer. The solution of the problem
is not said to be God's present providential government of
the world. The Psalms, of course, believe in that. But God's
present providential government of the world is part of the
problem. (It still is for us who live in this present period after
the resurrection and ascension of Christ. His ascension has
not solved the problem.) Why is it that God, who even now
exercises providential control over the world, allows evil to
go unpunished and the oppressed to suffer constant injustice?
No, the answer is the coming of the Lord. The Lord will not

remain in his heaven and simply step up the workings of his providential government. The Lord is going to *come* to judge the world.

Notice at this point the obvious. This coming of the Lord which these psalms describe is for them still in the future. (It is still so for us as well.) Admittedly, they are so utterly confident that the Lord will come, set up his reign on earth and bring justice to the world, that in the manner of Hebrew prophets they speak of it as if it had just happened and had now to be announced. 'Say among the nations, "The Lord reigns," ' says Psalm 96:10. 'The Lord reigns', echoes Psalm 97:1. 'The Lord reigns,' re-echoes Psalm 99:1. But they make it quite clear that they are talking of the future: 'for he comes to judge the earth. He *will* judge the world in righteousness . . .'[3]

What then do these psalms envisage as happening at this coming of the Lord? Not the end of the world, obviously. Psalm 96:10–13, using prophetic present tenses, says: 'Say among the nations, "The Lord reigns." *The world is firmly established, it cannot be moved*; (my italics) he will judge the peoples with equity. Let the heavens rejoice, let the earth be glad . . before the Lord, for he comes . . . He will judge the world in righteousness and the peoples in his truth.' In other words, when the Lord comes, he will establish the kingdom of God on earth. The will of God shall be done on earth even as it is done in heaven. Psalm 98:2–4, 6–7, 9, likewise using prophetic perfect tenses, adds to the description of what the coming of the Lord will involve. 'The Lord has made his salvation known and revealed his righteousness to the nations. He has remembered his love and his faithfulness to the house of Israel; all the ends of the earth have seen the salvation of our God. Shout for joy to the Lord, all the earth . . . shout for joy before the Lord, the King. Let the sea resound . . . the world and all who live in it . . . let them sing before the

---

[3] The New Testament uses similarly prophetic language when it looks forward to the establishment of the kingdom of God on earth. It speaks as if it had just happened, though it is in fact forecasting future events. 'We give thanks to you, Lord God Almighty . . . because you have taken your great power and reigned [NIV: have begun to reign]. The nations were angry; and your wrath has come. The time has come for judging the dead, and for rewarding your servants the prophets and your saints . . . and for destroying those who destroy the earth' (Rev. 11:17–18).

Lord, for he comes to judge the earth. He will judge the world in righteousness and the peoples with equity.'

The answer, then, to the problem of evil, according to these psalms, is the coming of the Lord. But that raises another question: how and in what form will the Lord come? According to Psalm 97:5–7 when he comes to reign, 'the mountains melt like wax before the Lord . . . all the peoples *see his glory.*' And the true God being thus revealed, 'All who worship images are put to shame.' But there is a problem. God is invisible. How, then (we repeat), and in what form will the invisible Lord, whom no-one has ever seen, or indeed can see, come and make his presence visible so that all the nations can see him and know beyond dispute that the judgments are his?

The answer to this question is: he will come in the person of the Messiah. 'The Lord, the King' before whom people are to shout for joy at his coming (Ps. 98:6) will be none other than the Messiah of whom God in Psalm 2 has already said: 'You are my Son,' and of whom he also said, 'I have installed my King on Zion.' When Isaiah prophesied, 'Prepare the way for the Lord . . . See, the Sovereign Lord comes with power' (Is. 40:3, 10), John the Baptist claimed that that 'coming of the Lord' referred to Messiah's first coming (Lk. 3:4–18). Similarly, when our psalms speak of the Lord's coming to judge the world and set up his kingdom on earth, they refer to his second coming.

The Lord Jesus interpreted these psalms in the same way. In his parable of the widow and the unjust judge (Lk. 18:1–8), he also dealt with the problem of evil as Psalm 94 does. He recognized that God's apparent inaction in the face of evil tries his people's faith. He assured them, however, that God will soon intervene and see to it that his people get justice. Until that time, he exhorted them, they must continue to pray in faith. But then he added, 'However, when the Son of Man comes, will he find faith on the earth?' Why 'when the Son of Man comes'? we ask. Because his second coming will be the time when God will 'come and judge the earth' and so vindicate the faith of his people who have gone on believing in God and praying throughout the long centuries of waiting.

At last we come back to the writer to the Hebrews and his

interpretation of Psalm 97:7. He says, you remember, that the 'him' in the command 'Let all God's angels worship him' refers to the Messiah. How right he proves to be! But where did he get the idea? He read the whole context! He was no proof-texter! He found that it was talking of the coming of the Lord to set up his reign on earth. He saw that the Lord who *comes* visibly must be the Son of God, the Messiah, and that the coming referred to must be the second coming. That is why he introduces his quotation of Psalm 97:7 with the words, 'And when he again brings his firstborn into the world, he says, "Let all God's angels worship him." '[4]

It goes without saying that the other New Testament writers agree. Paul takes the very words of Psalms 96:13 and 98:9 and refers them to Christ's second coming: God 'has set a day when he will judge the world with justice by the man he has appointed. He has given proof of this to all men by raising him from the dead' (Acts 17:31). Certainly at his second coming all God's angels will be commanded to worship him. 'God . . . gave him the name that is above every name, that at the name of Jesus every knee should bow, in heaven and on earth and under the earth, and every tongue confess that Jesus Christ is Lord, to the glory of God the Father' (Phil. 2:9–11).

Part Three

The second group of quotations

When the Messiah comes to reign, what will his reign be like? And what will he be like as a ruler? And how can we prepare for his coming? Which raises another question. What about the believers of past centuries who have already died? What about us who may be dead before the Lord comes? Shall we and they never see the coming kingdom? Is it all irrelevant as far as we are concerned? The quotations in this second group answer these questions.

[4] Notice my translation. It is possible to translate the Greek, 'And again, when he brings . . .', as though the 'again' meant simply 'and now another quotation'. Many scholars and versions, including NIV, favour this interpretation. But the context of Ps. 97:7 shows that the translation which reads the 'again' as referring to God's bringing Messiah into the world again, *i.e.* at his *second* coming, is the right one. The RV agrees.

4. The permanence and quality of Messiah's reign (Ps. 45:6–7)

'But about [better 'to' as AV/KJV] the Son he (God) says' (Heb. 1:8):

In your majesty ride forth victoriously
  on behalf of truth, humility and righteousness . . .
Let your sharp arrows pierce the hearts of the king's enemies;
  let the nations fall beneath your feet
Your throne, O God, will last for ever and ever;
  a sceptre of justice will be the sceptre of your kingdom.
You love righteousness and hate wickedness;
  therefore God, your God, has set you above your
    companions
  by anointing you with the oil of joy.
. . . at your right hand is the royal bride in gold of Ophir.
Listen, O daughter, consider and give ear: . . .
The king is enthralled by your beauty; honour him, for he is
  your lord. . . .
All glorious is the princess . . .
In embroidered garments she is led to the king;
  her virgin companions follow her . . .
They are led in with joy and gladness;
  they enter the palace of the king.
    (Ps 45:4–7, 9–11, 13–15)

Psalm 45, from which this fourth quotation is taken, is modelled on songs that were sung at the weddings of ancient kings. Were its exact words ever sung at the wedding of some particular king of Judah? If so, we may be sure that what then would have been extreme exaggeration was not spoken by way of oriental flattery, but in the belief that the king, whoever he was, was a temporary precursor of Israel's ideal King, the Messiah. Taken at their face value, its words could apply only to Messiah and his messianic reign.

That 'world to come, about which we are speaking' (Heb. 2:5) will be introduced by Messiah 'riding forth victoriously' at his second coming (*cf.* the description given in Rev. 19:11–21), and destroying the great conglomerations and federations of evil that will rise to their peak at the end of this present age (see 2 Thes. 1:5–2:12). His arrows will 'pierce the hearts of the king's enemies'. The kingdom which he will then inaugurate will be permanent; his reign will be one of perfect justice. It will also witness the consummation of the work of redemption: King Messiah will be married to his 'Bride', the glorified company of the redeemed. The wedding of the Lamb, as the New Testament calls it (Rev. 19:6–10, and notice the sequel in 19:11ff.), will have come. It will be sheer, unimaginable joy; the joy of consummation for which all the ages of history, all the years of life, have been the preparation.

But how can we be sure that this picture of a permanent reign of perfect justice and limitless joy is credible and not just a fairy tale, the produce of religious fantasy? Its credibility depends on two things. First, on Messiah's being human, and secondly, on his being more than human. It is because in his essential nature he is God, Psalm 45 explains, that his government will last eternally: 'Your throne, O God, will last for ever and ever.' And as we have now observed many times, the resurrection of Jesus the Messiah has already demonstrated that he is the Son of God. That demonstrated fact, then, gives certainty and credibility to the psalm's prophetic picture.

The promise that there shall one day be a reign of perfect justice, however, is based by the psalm on Messiah's own personal love of righteousness and hatred of wickedness. That, in fact, says verse 6, is why God has exalted him. His rise to the throne, then, is based not simply on the absolute power of his deity – in virtue of which he can do anything he pleases – but on his perfect moral character and practical righteousness: 'You have loved righteousness and hated wickedness; therefore God, your God, has set you above your companions.'

People generally are obsessed with power rather than with moral integrity and truth. When the Lord Jesus told Pilate, 'You are right in saying I am a king. In fact, for this reason I was born, and for this I came into the world, to testify to the truth,' Pilate replied, 'What is truth?'; and then tried to bring the conversation down to what he thought was a more realistic level. 'Don't you realise', he said, 'I have *power* either to free you or to crucify you?' (Jn. 18:37–38; 19:10). All of us can remember examples – and not merely from the remote past either – of world leaders who worshipped power and sought to build their world-empires on its basis. And we observe with a shudder that the present space-race is more concerned with power than with truth.

Jesus was different. His passionate concern for truth, his love of righteousness, his hatred of wickedness – these are matters of historical fact, not of pious fantasy. The records of his life have been open to scrutiny for centuries, and still issue the challenge, 'Can any of you prove me guilty of sin?' (Jn. 8:46). If to love God with the whole heart, mind, soul and strength is the first and greatest commandment of God's law, and to love one's neighbour as oneself is the second, the Lord Jesus fulfilled both, in his life and superabundantly in his death. The records show that in his life on earth he possessed supernatural power, and used it on occasions. But the records also show that he saw, more clearly than any, that this world cannot be turned into a paradise of justice and peace simply by the exercise of power, even of divine power. The problem of human sin and guilt must be faced and dealt with. What future of justice and peace could be achieved by acting as if the world's past and present sin did not matter, and brushing it under the carpet? Christ certainly would attempt no such thing. He loved righteousness. Divine justice must be upheld.

But to use divine power to insist on divine justice, as Christ will do at his second coming – that would mean the execution of sinners. In that case how many human beings would survive and enter the paradise of peace? And Christ loved sinners, and had come to save them and bring them to repentance and make them, like the dying thief, fit subjects for paradise.

There then was the problem. He hated sin and wickedness with all his heart. It must be exposed for what it is and suffer God's wrath without any excuse. But he loved us sinners. Some way of forgiveness must be found. But then he loved righteousness. If God was going to justify sinners, then that way of forgiveness must allow God to remain perfectly just while justifying those who have faith in Jesus (*cf.* Rom. 3:26). The answer to the problem was his voluntary acceptance of the cross where 'God made him who had no sin to be a sin-offering [NIV margin] for us, so that in him we might become the righteousness of God' (2 Cor. 5:21).

Having, then, provided a way of reconciliation, forgiveness and salvation for all who will have it, he is morally qualified, when the time comes, to execute the judgments of God that will 'weed out of his kingdom everything that causes sin and all who do evil' (Mt. 13:41). The Lamb who died as redeemer will be found worthy to be judge and to 'open the scroll and its seven seals' and so to purge earth of sin and sinners (Rev. 5–7). It is no idle day-dream: God's kingdom will come; God's will shall be done on earth even as it is in heaven.

Then will be celebrated the marriage of Messiah, the wedding of the Lamb. How shall his Bride make herself ready to share his life and throne? How shall she behave, how adorn herself, so that the King shall desire her beauty (as the AV/ KJV of Ps. 45:11 puts it). 'Honour him, for he is your lord,' is the advice the psalm gives (45:11). He loves righteousness and hates wickedness. His wife, bought by his sacrificial, redeeming death, must do the same. The ancient psalm talks of the bride being dressed gloriously in a gown interwoven with gold (45:13–14). Adding to the metaphor the Revelation says, 'his bride has made herself ready. Fine linen, bright and clean, was given her to wear. (Fine linen stands for the righteous acts of the saints)' (19:7–8).

The reign of Christ and the marriage of the Lamb – these are not myths. They draw ever nearer. The time of preparation is short. Let all who believe see to it that they have many righteous acts to enthrall the King with their beauty on his wedding day.

5. The permanence of Messiah himself and of his subjects

And [to the Son] *he also says* (Heb. 1:8),

In the beginning you laid the foundations of the earth,
    and the heavens are the work of your hands.
They will perish, but you remain;
    they will all wear out like a garment.
Like clothing you will change them
    and they will be discarded.
But you remain the same,
    and your years will never end.

(Psalm 102: 25–27)

There is no doubt about the writer's argument: he explicitly claims that these words in Psalm 102, like the words he earlier quoted from Psalm 45, are spoken not by the psalmist to God, but by God to the Messiah.

Now it is the fact, of course, that the writer has already proved by his earlier quotations that the Messiah is the Son of God. He has therefore already justified his earlier claim that the Messiah is the one by whom God made the universe (1:2). That much is no longer in question. No-one could object, therefore, if our writer now simply took words spoken by a psalmist to God as Creator, and applied them to the Son of God as Creator. But that is not what our writer is doing here. He claims that at verses 25–27 of Psalm 102 it is not the psalmist, in his own voice, addressing God as Creator; it is God addressing Messiah and reminding him that he (the Messiah) is the Creator. What ground has the writer for this interpretation? Only a careful, detailed study of the thought-flow of the whole psalm can give us a satisfactory answer.

The psalm has three parts; let us take each of them in turn.

Psalm 102, part one: title and verses 1–11

(The psalmist cries to God to help him quickly; for his days are fast ebbing away, and if nothing is done he will die before seeing the promised rebuilding of Zion.)

A prayer of an afflicted man. When he is faint and pours out his lament before the Lord.

Hear my prayer, O Lord;
    let my cry for help come to you.
Do not hide your face from me
    when I am in distress.
Turn your ear to me;
    when I call, answer me quickly.

For my days vanish like smoke;
    my bones burn like glowing embers.
My heart is blighted and withered like grass;
    I forget to eat my food.
Because of my loud groaning
    I am reduced to skin and bones.
I am like a desert owl,
    like an owl among the ruins.

I lie awake; I have become
  like a bird alone on a roof.
All day long my enemies taunt me;
  those who rail against me use my name as a curse.
For I eat ashes as my food
  and mingle my drink with tears
because of your great wrath,
  for you have taken me up and thrown me aside.
My days are like the evening shadow;
  I wither away like grass.

'Swift to its close ebbs out life's little day' could aptly be written over the first part of the psalm. The psalmist's days are vanishing like smoke, his very bones burn with fever, his heart is devastated, he has lost the desire to eat, and his involuntary groaning exhausts what little strength he has left. Compounding his suffering are not only the taunts of his enemies, but also a sense of guilt in his own heart, that he is suffering the wrath of God who has taken him up and thrown him aside (verse 10). He suffers not merely as an individual for his own sins. As the second part of the psalm will make clear, Jerusalem city also lies devastated under the discipline of God, and the psalmist feels himself involved in the sin and suffering of his people. Hence the wounding power of his enemies' taunts, who have always scorned the Jews' claim to be God's special people, and now think they see in the sufferings of the psalmist and of Jerusalem evidence that their claims are bogus.

For all his suffering the psalmist has not lost his faith; in the second part of the psalm he is about to express his conviction that Zion will be rebuilt. God has promised it and appointed the time for it (verse 13). That time will come. God continues to exist throughout all generations; no illness or weakness carries him off. When the time comes, he will arise and have compassion on Zion, and fulfil his promise.

That's all right for God and for the people who will be living at that time. God can afford to wait centuries to see his purposes fulfilled. But here is the bitter disappointment and frustration of the psalmist's position. His brief lifespan will soon be over. Unless God helps him very quickly, his illness will prove fatal. Then he will never see what he has believed in, prayed for, and expected all his life through – the rebuilding of Zion. Urgently he prays for immediate help (verse 2). Must he endure the pain, suffering, and discipline of God's displeasure and the taunts of his enemies, and then never witness, share in and enjoy the promised restoration?

How many Jews throughout the centuries must have felt the same way and prayed the same prayer![5]

Psalm 102, part two: verses 12–22

(An anticipation of what it will be like when the appointed time comes and the Lord appears and rebuilds Zion, and all the nations assemble at Jerusalem to worship the Lord.)

> But you, O Lord, sit enthroned for ever;
> your renown endures through all generations.
> You will arise and have compassion on Zion,
> for it is time to show favour to her;
> the appointed time has come.
> For her stones are dear to your servants;
> her very dust moves them to pity.
> The nations will fear the name of the Lord,
> all the kings of the earth will revere your glory.
> For the LORD will rebuild Zion
> and appear in his glory.
> He will respond to the prayer of the destitute;
> he will not despise their plea.
>
> Let this be written for a future generation,
> that a people not yet created may praise the Lord:
> 'The Lord looked down from his sanctuary on high,
> from heaven he viewed the earth,
> to hear the groans of the prisoners
> and release those condemned to death.'
> So the name of the Lord will be declared in Zion
> and his praise in Jerusalem
> when the peoples and the kingdoms
> assemble to worship the Lord.

[5] This is a problem unavoidably bound up with the belief that God is eventually going to establish his reign of justice and peace here on earth within time. If all that Scripture promised was an eternal heaven outside earth's history, to which heaven believers of each generation are successively admitted at death, or finally at the end of the world, the problem would not exist.

We should observe the dimensions of the psalmist's vision. He is not thinking of a few repairs to Jerusalem city that pious people might attribute to God's providential care. He envisages a restoration of Zion, so glorious that all the nations will be obliged to admit that it is the work of the Lord. And they will fear the name of the Lord, for the very good reason that 'the Lord will appear in his glory' in order to rebuild Jerusalem; and in consequence the peoples and the kingdoms will assemble to worship the Lord (verse 22).

It is clear then from the terminology used that Psalm 102 is talking, like Psalms 96, 97 and 98, of nothing less than the visible coming of the Lord, what the New Testament calls 'the glorious appearing of our great God and Saviour, Jesus Christ' (Tit. 2:13). God will rebuild Zion at and by the second coming of the Son of God, the one whose role it always has been, is, and shall be, to reveal God's glory.[6]

But now the psalmist tells us a wonderful thing: when the Lord appears and rebuilds Zion, it will be in answer to the prayers of his destitute people (verse 17). 'Let it be written down here and now', he says in effect (verses 18–22) 'for the benefit of the future generation (that will be alive when the Lord comes) so that the people who are not yet created may (then) praise the Lord.' For they will learn from what is written that the coming of the Lord is not some arbitrary, unexpected, unannounced intervention by God. Generations of God's afflicted and persecuted people have believed it to be promised in Scripture, and have longed and prayed for it.

This then is what the psalmist wishes to be recorded. In answer to the pleas of his people: 'The Lord looked down from his sanctuary on high, from heaven he viewed the earth, to hear the groans of the prisoners and release those condemned to death' (verses 19–20).

How graphic and moving these expressions are! He is not thinking of the distance between heaven and earth in spatial

---

[6] And here incidentally is the background to our Lord's prophecy in Lk. 21:24–28: 'Jerusalem will be trampled on by the Gentiles until the times of the Gentiles are fulfilled. There will be signs in the sun, moon and stars . . . Men will faint from terror, apprehensive of what is coming on the world . . . At that time they will see the Son of Man coming in a cloud with power and great glory. When these things begin to take place, stand up and lift up your heads, because your redemption is drawing near.'

terms, as though it could be measured in light-years. He is thinking how infinitely above earth's affairs is the transcendent God; how infinitely beneath his undisturbed glory is the wretched misery of earth's prisons where people groan as they await execution. Yet the transcendent God has 'looked down', viewed earth's misery, heard the groanings of prisoners, and in response will one day appear and rebuild Zion. It is not – obviously not – that five minutes before the second coming God will suddenly turn his attention to earth, become aware of the groanings of prisoners, and decide to act. God has always looked down, always heard the prayers of his distressed people throughout all the centuries. Their prayers have not been lost (see Rev. 6:9–11; 8:3–5). God will yet 'respond to the prayer of the destitute; he will not despise their plea' (Ps. 102:17). The blood of the martyrs, the groans of innocent prisoners, the plea of the author of Psalm 102 and of millions of believers like him, the as yet unanswered intercessions of Daniel (see chapter 9 of his prophecy), the cries from Auschwitz and Dachau silenced by the gas-chambers – all make it a moral certainty that the Lord will one day appear and rebuild Zion.

But of all the prayers and intercessions that God has ever heard, those surely will prove the most effective that came from the lips and heart of the Son of God incarnate. For the amazing story is this: God has not only *looked* down from his sanctuary on high, but in the person of his Son he *came* down! The same Lord who will one day appear in his glory and rebuild Zion, once was manifested in the flesh, and walked the streets of Jerusalem. He not only viewed earth's pains, injustices and cruelties from on high, but personally came and experienced them. He not only heard the prayers of the distressed, but joined in them. He not only listened to the groanings of prisoners condemned to death, but became a prisoner himself; and though sinless, was numbered with the transgressors, was cut off out of the land of the living as a young man little over thirty-three, bore the sin of many and made intercession for the transgressors (see Is. 53:8, 12). Son of God though the incarnate Messiah was – and the writer to the Hebrews has long since demonstrated that – 'during the days of [his] life on earth, he offered up prayers and petitions with loud cries and tears to the one who could save him from death; and he was heard because of his reverent submission' (Heb. 5:7). One day, not only in response to the prayers of the faithful of all ages, but supremely in answer to the prayers and intercessions of the Messiah, God will bring about the appearing of our Lord Jesus Christ (1 Tim. 6:14–16).

What a vindication of the character of God that will be! What a declaration of his name, a demonstration of the glory of his faithfulness and compassion (Ps. 102:13–16, 21)! What a vindication, before all the agnostics and atheists of the world, of the revelation of God in his word witnessed to by historic Israel and Jerusalem. Prayer too will be vindicated against all those unbelievers and critics who said so often that prayer was useless because either God did not hear (perhaps because he did not exist) or, if he heard, did not care. The appearing of our great God and Saviour, Jesus Christ, will demonstrate overwhelmingly that God both heard and cared. God's name and character will be declared in Zion and his praise in Jerusalem. And the peoples and kingdoms of the world will assemble to worship the Lord (Ps. 102:21; *cf.* Zc. 14:16).

Not surprisingly, then, the mood of this second part of Psalm 102 is much calmer and more hopeful than that of the first part. The psalmist remembers that his prayers too will play their part in the eventual bringing about of the appearing of the Lord and the rebuilding of Zion. And that's not nothing!

And yet it still leaves unanswered the problem of the brevity of the individual's life compared with the centuries of time it takes for God to work out his purposes and fulfil his promises. Psalm 102:19–20 says that 'the Lord looked down . . . to hear the groans of the prisoners and *release those condemned to death*'. Who are they? Doubtless those who are in prison just before the Lord appears in his glory will be released. But what of the millions of the faithful all down the centuries who were persecuted and imprisoned and cried to God for deliverance, and never came out but died in prison? It is all right to say in answer to their prayers God will one day bring about the appearing of the Lord, and release those who are prisoners then. But that is little comfort for those in ages past who prayed for deliverance but were not delivered. (It is little comfort for any who die before the Lord's second coming.) Have they all perished? Will they never see the kingdom for the coming of which they prayed? And if not, how would the Old Testament's hope be any better than Marxism which encourages people to believe in, work for and if need be die for, a coming age of peace, justice and prosperity that by definition (since in Marxism there is no resurrection) they will never see?

This is a big enough question in itself; but as we enter the third part of the psalm, we shall find still bigger questions pressing hard on its heels.

Psalm 102, part three: verses 23–28

(Creation will perish, but the Creator remains the same. Therefore his servants will live for ever.)

In the course of my life he broke my strength;
    he cut short my days.
So I said:
    'Do not take me away, O my God, in the midst of my days;
    your years go on through all generations.
In the beginning you laid the foundations of the earth,
    and the heavens are the work of your hands.
They will perish, but you remain;
    they will all wear out like a garment.
Like clothing you will change them
    and they will be discarded.
But you remain the same,
    and your years will never end.
The children of your servants will live in your presence;
    their descendants will be established before you.

And the first question is this. Granted, there is going to be an age of peace and justice established by God on our earth. Yet our earth is only temporary. One day it will perish. Scripture itself tells us that. So, incidentally, do the scientists. Now the atheist can believe that when this earth is finally destroyed, and all human life along with it, it will be the universe's own impersonal forces that will be ultimately responsible for destroying it. But theists of any kind cannot believe that. They must believe that the same personal God

73

who created the earth and the heavens and all that is in them and on them, will himself destroy them. 'They will all wear out like a garment,' as the psalmist puts it (102:26), 'Like clothing *you will change them and they will be discarded.*'

That being so the next question is this: how could any one in any age, whether the age was bad, good or idyllicly perfect, have a satisfying relation with his personal Creator, if he believed that one day that personal Creator would personally discard him; would (as the psalmist puts it in verse 10) take him up and throw him aside, either now or at the end of the world? Yet if we are creatures of God, as the earth and heavens are, how can we be sure he will not do to us, what he will do to the rest of creation?

Two pressing questions, then, are looking for an answer as we examine the third part of the psalm and try to understand what it was originally intended to ·say.

At first sight it would seem quite resonable to suppose that in this third part of the psalm, the psalmist himself continues to speak in his own person.[7] But if you take it so, you will find on closer inspection that it makes very little and very unsatisfactory sense. Let's try it and see.

First (verses 23–24a), the psalmist pleads with God not to 'take me away in the midst of my days'. Understandably: to die prematurely half-way through life is a bitter thing indeed. Then (verses 24b–27) he reminds God that as Creator his (God's) years have no end. Why this reminder? Is the psalmist simply urging God not to be mean; to remember that he himself enjoys eternal life, and therefore he ought not to begrudge a creature of his the few days that make up half a mortal's life? (Some God, if his creatures need to plead with him like that!) But if that is the psalmist's plea, what lasting comfort and satisfaction could it bring even if God granted it? For the psalmist goes on to observe that one day the whole creation will wear out and perish and the Creator himself will

[7] Psalmists do not always do that, of course. Sometimes, having spoken themselves for several verses on end, they suddenly and without warning, in the manner of a dramatist, introduce another speaker or speakers, speaking in direct, not reported, speech. Take for example the nearby Ps. 95. In verses 1–7a it is the psalmist, inspired by the Holy Spirit of course, who speaks in his own person. But from verse 7b onwards, the speaker changes, and it is now no longer the poet but God who speaks directly to his people.

discard it. Granted, the Creator will outlast his creation and remain the same (verse 27). What comfort would that be to the psalmist, if he as a creature along with the rest of the created world is doomed to be discarded? And how, if that is the case, does the psalmist arrive at his final confident statement (verse 28): 'The children of your servants will live in your presence; their descendants will be established before you.' Moreover, however long they lived, if they were doomed as creatures to perish with the rest of creation, what comfort and hope would that provide them?

Taken in this way, then, the last third of the psalm hardly yields a satisfactory sense. Is there a better and more satisfying way of taking it? Yes, there most certainly is. At verse 23 the psalmist is no longer speaking in his own person either to God (as in verses 1–14) or to his readers (as in verses 15–22). Instead, as an inspired dramatic poet he does at verse 23 what Hebrew psalmists frequently do (see the last footnote for an example): without warning he introduces other characters into his drama speaking in direct (*i.e.* not reported) speech in their own persons.

First, in verses 23–24a it is the Messiah who is introduced, speaking directly in his own person to God as he pleads with him to save him from death.

Then, in verses 24b–28 God is introduced again, speaking directly in his own person to the Messiah in answer to the Messiah's plea.

It is in this way that the writer to the Hebrews understands verses 25–27, at any rate, (he does not quote verses 23–24 or 28): as God speaking to the Messiah and reminding him that he (Messiah) is the Creator. (See Additional Note 2, at the end of this chapter, for a discussion of the Septuagint's interpretation of verses 23–24a, and of how far the writer to the Hebrews may have followed that interpretation). This then obviously proves his case once more that the Messiah is said by God in the Old Testament to be the Son of God. But what sense does this interpretation make of these verses first as a prophecy of the future and then as an answer to the two questions that the psalm as a whole raises?

It makes awesomely wonderful sense. First, these verses now become an inspired prophecy of the sacred conversations that eventually passed between God the Father and his Son when his Son was on earth. Its prophetic words ('In the course of my life he broke my strength; he cut short my days. So I said: "Do not take me away, O my God, in the midst of my days" ') found fulfilment when the Son of God stood on the streets of Jerusalem and said, 'I tell you the truth, unless a grain of wheat falls to the ground and dies, it remains only a single seed . . . Now my heart is troubled, and what shall I say? "Father, save me from this hour"? No, it was for this very reason I came to this hour. Father, glorify your name!' (Jn. 12:24–28).

They found their fulfilment even more when in Gethsemane with loud cries and tears he prayed to the one who could save him from death, and, though he died, was answered by the resurrection.

But in those sacred conversations between the Son and the Father, is there any evidence that the Father spoke to him words such as those of Psalm 102:24b–28? Did he comfort the Son by bearing in upon his consciousness the fact that he (the Son) was the Creator and laid the foundations of the world? Did he remind him that he, the Son, would outlast his creation, and not only so, but that those who believed in him, 'the children of [his] servants' would 'live in [his] presence and their descendants be established before [him]', as verse 28 of Psalm 102 confidently asserts?

We cannot go beyond what we are told. But we do know that when the Son prayed, 'Now my heart is troubled, and what shall I say? . . . Father, glorify your name!', there came in reply a voice from heaven, assuring him that his death would glorify God's name indeed, and be followed by resurrection (see Jn. 12:27–33).

And when we listen to the Son praying to the Father for himself just before Gethsemane we do hear him say: 'And now, Father, glorify me in your presence with the glory I had with you *before the world began.*' Listen to him praying for his disciples and for those who in future generations would come to believe on him: 'Father, I want those you have given me to be with me where I am, and to see my glory, the glory you have given me because *you loved me before the creation of the world*' (Jn. 17:5, 24).

Secondly, this interpretation of verses 25–27 makes marvellous sense of these verses as an answer to the two questions raised by the psalm as a whole. For now they point forward to the definitive answer to these questions which was eventually given by the incarnation of the eternal Creator in the man Jesus, the Messiah, and by his resurrection and ascension, as a man still, to the glory which he had as the eternal Creator with the Father before the foundation of the world. The Creator is eternal, but the created heavens and earth are only temporary and one day must perish and be discarded. We human beings are creatures. What assurance can we have that the Creator will never discard any human being that by faith has entered into a personal relationship with God? See here the explicit and absolute assurance! The Creator himself has become human, has entered our temporary world of space and time, with authority to give us eternal life; has prayed to be saved from death, to be glorified in the Father's presence with the glory he had with the Father before the world began (Jn. 17:1–5). And his prayer has been answered! God has raised him from the dead; and he has carried his humanity to the very bosom of the Godhead. The eternal Creator who is eternally the same (Ps. 102:27) has for ever become Jesus, the man, 'the same yesterday and today and for ever' (Heb. 13:8). And God the Father has assured him in the words of Psalm 102:28: 'The children of your servants will live in your presence; their descendants will be established before you.' Or in the words of the New Testament: 'God raised us up with Christ and seated us with him in the heavenly realms in Christ Jesus, in order that in the coming ages he might show the incomparable riches of his grace, expressed in his kindness to us in Christ Jesus' (Eph. 2:6–7). For this is what God had in mind when he chose us in Christ before the creation of this temporary world (Eph. 1:4).

And what is more: none of those who have believed in him, and have lived and worked for his coming kingdom, will miss it, no matter in what distant century they lived and died. For those that are Christ's shall be made alive at his coming (1 Cor. 15:22–23); and when the Lord appears in his glory, and sets up his kingdom, them also will God bring with him (1 Thes. 4:13–18).

Part Four

The final quotation

Messiah's present position (Ps. 110:1)

> The Lord [Yahweh] says to my [David's] Lord:
> '*Sit at my right hand, until I make your enemies*
> *a footstool for your feet.*'

The writer is coming to the end of his case. Angels as a group are referred to in Scripture as sons of God; but God, he points out, has never said to any particular angel what in Psalm 110:1 he says to David's Lord, the Messiah. No angel was ever, or will ever be invited to *sit* in the divine presence, and certainly not in the place of honour at the right hand of God's throne. Nor will God stoop to put their enemies as a footstool under their feet. They are but servants. They *stand* in the presence of God awaiting their orders; or they fly to carry out their duty 'to serve those who will inherit salvation' – that is, human beings who, like Abraham, have believed God.

But God has addressed these words to the Messiah, and their implications are far-reaching.

First, if David referred to Messiah as his Lord, then obviously Messiah was not, in David's prophetic estimation, going to be simply a son of his. No oriental monarch, or even any oriental father at all, would ever refer to one of his sons as 'my Lord'. This is the point that the Lord Jesus himself made (Lk. 20:41–44).

Secondly, the fact that God had to issue the invitation, 'Sit at my right hand,' presupposes that there was a time when the Son of God was not sitting there. In other words it presumes his incarnation, life on earth, death, burial and finally his ascension.

The writer has reached the end of his case. He has proved his point up to the hilt. The Messiah is the Son of God, and Jesus is the Messiah. But his last quotation answers another question. Attempt to prove to some people that Jesus is the Messiah and is risen from the dead, and they will ask, 'Why then has he done nothing these two thousand years to put down evil? Where was he when Hitler was destroying six million Jews? How can he be his people's Messiah, if he has not subdued their enemies in all these long centuries?'

The fact is, however, that the timetable laid down in Psalm 110:1 indicates quite clearly that Messiah's ascension was not to be followed immediately by the subjugation of his enemies, or of his people's either. There had to be a period of waiting: 'Sit at my right hand until . . .'. The present apparent inactivity of the Son of God is precisely what the Old Testament itself leads us to expect.

But one day the waiting will be over. The Son of God will come, and eventually all enemies, the last enemy, death itself included, will be destroyed.

Additional note 1

The clause in Hebrews 1:6, 'Let all God's angels worship him,' is nearer in its exact wording to a phrase in the Septuagint of Deuteronomy 32:43 than it is to the clause in the Septuagint of Psalm 97:7. Many therefore suppose that our writer took it not from the psalm but from Deuteronomy. But F. M. Cross (*The Ancient Library of Qumran*, Duckworth, 1958, pp. 135–136) points out that the phrase in the Septuagint of Deuteronomy is additional to what we find in the Masoretic Hebrew text. It is based on a different Hebrew text. But that Hebrew text has imported this additional phrase into Deuteronomy 32 from Psalm 97:7, presumably because the last verses of Deuteronomy 32 describe the same occasion as Psalms 96 and 97, the coming of the Lord to avenge his people. So the original biblical passage on which our writer's phrase in Hebrews 1:6 is based is Psalm 97:7, even if his precise wording is based on the Septuagint's translation of the verse in the form it took when it was added to some Hebrew manuscripts of Deuteronomy 32:43.

Additional note 2

It is very interesting and very important to notice that the early Christians were not the first to see that Psalm 102:24a–28 is spoken by God to the Messiah. The Septuagint translation of the Psalms pre-dates Christianity by 100–200 years. Its rendering of the third part of Psalm 102 has God as the speaker all the way through from verse 23 to the end. It reads as follows:

> 23He [God] answered him in the way of his strength:
> 'Declare to me the shortness of my days;
> 24Bring me not up in the midst of my days.
> Your years go on through all generations.
> 25In the beginning, O Lord, you laid the foundation
> of the earth . . .' (and so on to the end of the psalm).

The Septuagint translation of verses 23–24a is based on the same consonants as in the Masoretic text; but the translators have supplied those consonants with different vowels. They have understood God as asking Messiah in verses 23–24a to recognize that God's set time for the restoration of Jerusalem (see verse 13) is but a short time away, and not to demand God to act prematurely while the time of waiting is still only half-way through. God then goes on to remind Messiah that he (Messiah) is the Creator and that his years are eternal. He can afford to wait. Finally he assures him that his servants' children will continue to live in his presence.

Now it is clear that the writer to the Hebrews follows the Septuagint translation of verses 25–27, for in verse 25, when he begins his quotation, he has God addressing the Messiah as 'O Lord', just as the Septuagint does, whereas the vocative, 'O Lord', is not present in the Masoretic text of the Hebrew. Did the writer to the Hebrews also accept the Septuagint's interpretation of verses 23–24a which attributes their words to God, rather than the interpretation we have followed, which reads their words as Messiah's prayer to the Father, with the Father's reply beginning at verse 24b? If it could be shown for certain that he did, we would certainly follow him in his following of the Septuagint and abandon our own interpretation. But we cannot tell for certain, since the writer to the Hebrews begins his quotation only at verse 25, and therefore we cannot say what he thought of the Septuagint's interpretation of the previous verses. The writer to the Hebrews, we know, believed in a suffering Messiah who needed to pray to be saved from death, and actually died. Did the translator(s) of the Septuagint Psalms? What we can say for certain is that the early Christians did not invent the idea that verses 24b–27 are spoken by God to the Messiah. The idea was already current in Jewish circles, in Alexandria and perhaps also in Palestine, a century – perhaps two centuries and more – before Christianity was born.

Further study might well begin with F. F. Bruce, *The Epistle to the Hebrews* (Marshall, Morgan and Scott, 1965), pp. 23–23, and S. Lewis Johnson, Jr, *The Old Testament in the New* (Zondervan, 1980), pp. 81–90.

Questions

Part One

1 What programme for the salvation of the world do you think the Old Testament holds out?

2 Suppose you were in conversation with a Jew who thought that the idea that the Messiah is God incarnate is (a) blasphemous and (b) an invention of early Christians like Paul. What Old Testament passages would you refer to in order to show him that the deity of the Messiah is taught in the Old Testament?

3 What does it matter whether Jesus was born of the seed of David or of someone else? Read 2 Timothy 2:8 and Romans 1:2–3 and comment on the references to David in these verses.

4 Why is it important for us as Christians
(a) to know the Old Testament;
(b) to believe that it is as equally God's Word as the New?

5 Why does the writer constantly contrast our Lord with angels in his first chapter?

6 How many of the Old Testament passages cited in Hebrews 1 to prove the deity of the Messiah can you quote by heart?

Parts Two, Three, Four

1 Do you agree that to see the full meaning of many of God's promises in the Old Testament you have to read them in the light of the fact of the resurrection of Jesus? Cite examples.

2 If the resurrection of Jesus vindicates his claim to be

the Son of God, what evidence would you cite for the resurrection itself?

3 Is it fair to say that the cross of Christ exposes the rebelliousness of *every* human heart against God?

4 In what sense and to what extent is Christ's teaching about his relation to the Father unique, compared with the teaching of (a) the Old Testament prophets, (b) any of the world religious leaders you know about?

5 (a) What is meant by 'the problem of evil'?
(b) Why is it that the continuing existence of evil in the world is more of a problem to believers in God than to atheists?
(c) What would you say to someone who said, 'If there is a God and Jesus is his Son, why don't they put a stop to all evil in the world?'
(d) Give a mini-sermon on Matthew 13:24–30, 36–43.

6 What do you understand by 'the wedding supper of the Lamb'? How does one get ready for it?

7 Both the Bible and scientists say that our world is only a temporary phenomenon. How does that affect the question of the purpose and meaning of human life?

8 Would it make any difference to you if Jesus Christ were not the Creator incarnate?

9 What is 'eternal life'? How and on what terms do we receive it?

10 In what ways do you think that angels serve those who will inherit salvation?

4

THE HUMANITY AND
SUFFERINGS OF CHRIST
Hebrews 2

Chapter 1 of the letter to the Hebrews has filled our minds with the glories of the deity of Christ. Chapter 2 is about to do the same with the glories of his humanity and of his sufferings. But before it does so, the writer issues the first of his solemn warnings: it is possible to miss salvation and to be eternally lost!

'How?', you say. 'Surely people must commit some desperately outrageous sin to be lost eternally?'

So they must. But let us be clear in our minds what that sin is. It is to hear God speak, then to do nothing about it, to neglect or ignore it.

When God spoke to the nation of Israel and gave them the law, he did so through the agency of angels (see Acts 7:53; Gal. 3:19). The law contained, as we know, the commandment to observe the sabbath. Soon after it was given, a man was found gathering sticks on the sabbath. The man knew the law, he could not claim ignorance. They put him in custody and consulted God about what should be done. God replied that the man should be taken out of the camp and stoned to death (Nu. 15:32–36).

I wonder how we react to that. Do we find ourselves saying, 'That was excessively severe. After all, it was only a simple act, a mere gathering of sticks, innocent in itself. What harm did it do?'

That is to miss the point completely. Almighty God had spoken. Never mind that he had done so through the agency of angels and through Moses as mediator. It was God who had spoken. For a creature straight away to turn round and neglect or ignore what God had said, no matter how small the issue involved, was a direct affront to almighty God. If people still think that such an attitude was a mere peccadillo, they have lost their hold on reality.

That is easily done. In our modern world, where everybody's opinion in religion is ranked equal with everybody else's, it is perilously easy to treat God and his Word as simply one authority among many, to be consulted if thought desirable, but not necessarily to be followed. And perilously easy, too, to come to feel that God would be unreasonable, if he got upset because people sometimes preferred to follow their own ideas, or some other authority, rather than his Word. But if God is God, unbelief, disregard, neglect of his Word, is the cardinal sin of sins. When God spoke to Israel, therefore, through the agency of angels, he had to teach people that they could not disregard his Word with impunity: 'the message spoken by angels was binding, and every violation and disobedience received its just punishment (2:2).

Now God has spoken again, and this time not indirectly through the agency of angels, but directly in the person of his Son. This time he has spoken, not simply to restate his law but to proclaim his gospel. Not to warn innocent people not to break his law; but to offer a salvation, staggering in the dimensions of its mercy and grace, to people who have flouted his Word and broken his law times without number. God has not only given the message: the messenger is God, and God is the message. It tells the almost incredible story that God 'the Incarnate Maker has died for man his creature's sin'. It offers not only reconciliation and pardon, but eternal life through spiritual union with the Son of God, and participation in the joys and glories of his eternal kingdom. 'How shall we escape', asks the writer, 'if we ignore such a great salvation?' (2:3). Our original sinfulness was bad enough. Compounded by disregard of the offered salvation, it would be a certain recipe for disaster.

Neglecting salvation

There are, of course, many people who have never heard of this salvation. The writer is not for the moment concerned with them, but with those that have heard. Theirs is the greater danger. And the danger is, not so much that upon hearing it they might reject it out of hand; but that having heard it and understood it, they might not do anything about it. It is not enough to have heard the gospel. We must do something about it. We must believe it, and take our stand on it personally and act on God's word.

A girl may enjoy hearing her boyfriend repeat how much he loves her, and what he will do for her if only she will consent to be his wife. But hearing him say it over and over again is not enough. If she is ever going to be his wife, she must believe him, and respond to him, and say 'Yes' to his proposal, and accept him as her one and only husband, and deliberately say 'I will' and mean it, and accept unquestioningly his 'I will', and take his pledged word for it and act on it.

So it is with us and the Saviour. We must take God with deadly seriousness when he says that we need salvation and cannot save ourselves, and that only Christ can save us. We must abandon trust in all else and put our faith solely in Christ. When he says to us personally, 'Do you believe in the Son of Man?' (Jn. 9:35), we must accept his pledged word in response: 'Whoever comes to me I will not in any way whatever turn away' (Jn. 6:37, literally). And we must proceed to live and act upon his word, as if it were true – because it *is* true, because *he* is true.

The gospel was at the beginning announced by the Lord Jesus and confirmed to us by those who heard him (2:3–4). That in itself was guarantee enough of its truth and reliability. But not content with that God also testified to it by signs, wonders and various miracles and gifts of the Holy Spirit distributed according to his will (2:3–4). Here, then, was no arbitrary deification of some holy book written by some self-appointed and tyrannous religious leader. All three persons of the Trinity were involved in the announcement and authentication of the gospel. How could we escape if we neglected it?

The danger is, let me repeat, not that people reject it out of hand – though many do that. There is a more insidious danger: that having heard we do not pay careful attention to what we have heard, and as a result, eventually drift away. The Greek word for 'drift away' carries a suggestive metaphor. In calm weather a boat can sit idly by the quayside in the harbour for hours without being properly tied up. But let bad weather come, and the boat can drift away and be lost, all because it was never actually moored.

The first readers of the letter to the Hebrews had certainly heard the gospel and had taken their place alongside it. But then the bad weather had set in and a prolonged storm. What was happening now? Was it that, tossed up and down by the swell from their recent persecution, they were stretching their mooring ropes to the limit, but with no danger of the ropes giving way (see 6:19)? Or were they beginning to drift away from the gospel because they were never properly tied up in the first place; because, like their ancestors who will be brought to our notice in chapters 3 and 4, they heard the gospel but never combined it with faith (4:2); because they heard about salvation but neglected it? If so, how would they escape? The warning had to be urgent. Pay attention to what you've heard! Lay hold of eternal life! Make sure you are anchored and securely tied up! Don't drift!

Such a great salvation

But the writer has more for his readers than stern warnings and exhortations. He was astute enough to know what was causing their tendency to drift. There was first the shame of being associated with the man Jesus of Nazareth, the shame of his humble beginnings in Nazareth, the shame above all else of his crucifixion. In those days the cross was not the universally respected symbol that it has since become. Crucifixion was the ultimate disgrace a human being could suffer. Indeed, among the Jews, for anyone to be hanged on a tree was to be under God's curse (Dt. 21:23).

Secondly, there was the instinctive feeling, which many people still have, that salvation and 'being saved' are somehow mean little ideas. Religion itself, of course, has not always been above reproach. True religious discipline on the other hand can command widespread respect just like moral concern and philosophical endeavour. But 'salvation' and 'being saved' are ideas which often embarrass even the most sincerely religious people. They are associated in their minds with the mystery religions of the ancient world or with the multifarious cults in modern times. They may appeal to certain gullible temperaments, but the average person dismisses them as self-evidently bogus, and the satirists find them easy targets.

The writer will deal with both these problems. He will show them that there is nothing to be ashamed of either in salvation or in the Saviour who has made it possible. Salvation, as he describes it, certainly concerns individuals at the personal level. But it is far from being a little individual private matter. When he talks of 'such a great salvation', he is thinking of God's programme for 'the world to come' (2:5), a programme that will one day liberate creation itself from its bondage to decay, and put it under the perfect control of redeemed men and women, who themselves have been reconciled to their Creator, have become children of God through faith in Christ Jesus, and have been trained and matured into moral and spiritual conformity with the Son of God (*cf*. Rom. 8:18–30). He is talking of releasing men and women from the sense of non-significance and non-worth that haunts so many of them; from the feelings of fear and futility that afflict them and make life a kind of bondage; from the violence, desecration and disease that degrade and humiliate their bodies. He is talking of restoring to people the vision and the hope and, one day, the reality of attaining that noble purpose for which God originally created mankind.

It is not the worst thing you can say about people, but it is perhaps the saddest, that many of them have no real hope. And without hope life becomes a dead end. 'There's no future in it,' as people say. They have lost their youthful idealism and good spirits. They do not believe in God; they know of no satisfying goal and purpose for their lives or for the world to aim at, nor of any credible Messiah-figure who could bring either them or the world to that goal. They are, as the New Testament puts it, 'separate from Christ . . . without hope . . . and without God in the world' (Eph. 2:12). Consciously or unconsciously they resign themselves to the idea that life is in the end absurd; and they put as brave a face on it as they can.

But if many people have lost their hope, God has not given up hope for mankind! In the world to come about which the writer to the Hebrews now speaks (2:5), God's original purpose will be fully achieved. Indeed, in the man, Jesus, that purpose is already far advanced towards its fulfilment.

What is man?

For what is man? That is a question which has often been asked; but it has never received a more noble answer than that given in the Hebrew Old Testament:

> What is man that you are mindful of him,
>   the son of man that you care for him?
> You made him a little lower than the heavenly beings
>   and crowned him with glory and honour.
> . . . you put everything under his feet.
>   (Ps. 8:4–6, quoted in Heb. 2:6–8)

The psalmist is reaffirming, of course, the Creator's own declared purpose in Genesis 1:26–30. Human beings are not pure spirit as angels are; they are part spirit and part animal. As originally created, therefore, they are lower than angels. But man was not made, as so many ancient mythologies and religions taught, to be the menial slaves, or the playthings, of capricious gods who were themselves the mere products of the conflicting masses and forces of primeval chaos. Nor is man a mere particle of the rational but utterly impersonal material the universe is made of, as so many modern theories teach. Our human love and reason and aesthetic sense, our ability to look forward, to hope and to plan, are not illusions doomed to be shattered by mindless matter and impersonal forces which one day (however distant) will inevitably destroy all human life, along with the earth, and – crowning irony of it all – won't even know they've done it!

No, men and women were made in God's image, made to be God's viceroys, to subdue the earth and progressively to take over control of it in fellowship with the Creator, to rule it and all its various levels of life and to make of it something glorious for God and for themselves. To grow up from their original moral infancy, to learn to 'think God's thoughts after him', as Kepler would put it, and in partnership with God, as sons with a father, to be masters, and not prisoners, of the matter and forces of the universe.

God crowned man with glory and honour, says the psalmist, and put everything under his feet. And the writer to the Hebrews repeats and underlines the fact. The statement, 'You put everything under his feet,' he comments, means exactly what it says. 'In putting everything under him, God left nothing that is not subject to him' (2:8).

That at least was God's original plan. But we do not need to be told that the plan seems to have gone wrong somewhere. Nowadays we do not see everything put under man. We find ourselves in a world that is hard and cruel and that seems, in spite of our great advances in science, to be too much for us. Mankind is a slave to the ground, bound constantly to toil by the sweat of his brow to try to clear it of its weeds and pests; but never fully succeeding, always having to fight the same weary battle all over again, and often handicapped by illness and disease. How little is left of the glory that once God gave us! Life is short, disease universal and death inevitable. 'At present we do not see everything subject to him,' says the writer (2:8). We certainly don't. And what is more, the multi-millions of human beings that have been ruthlessly eliminated in the course of this present century alone – and are still being slaughtered – to suit this or that ideology or religion, and to satisfy men's power-lust, are eloquent evidence of the truth of the Bible's assertion that man has fallen under the power of demonic forces and has been perverted.

The man, Jesus

So at present we do not see everything subject to man. But that does not mean that God has abandoned his original purpose. Sin has spoiled everything, and man by his folly and disobedience has thrown away much of his dominion. But God has not admitted defeat. Far from it.

In his original plan man was deliberately designed to be a little lower than the angels. Perhaps that was because the creation of man was God's tactical answer to rebellion that had broken out in the spirit realm to which angels naturally belong. Who knows? But when Satan very early on successfully corrupted God's viceroy, man, and set him on a course of disloyalty and rebellion against the very God in whose image he was made, the wisdom of God's strategy in making man a little lower than the angels eventually became apparent.

Angels, in their proper state, do not marry or produce offspring. Man can do both. And that made possible God's long-planned strategic move by which he had himself born into our world as a man, so that as man he could defeat the enemy and bring to victorious fulfilment God's original purpose for mankind.

And already, says our writer, we see the first stage of that purpose fulfilled. 'We see Jesus' (2:9). Note his name: it is his human name, a Hebrew name, given him by human parents under the direction of an angel.

'We see Jesus, who was made a little lower than the angels . . .', just as the first man Adam was. He has taken on flesh and blood and has become what angels never were or will be . . . human. See him, then, lying as a baby in a crude manger in an obscure village called Bethlehem, apparently helpless. But don't suppose it is anything to be ashamed of! This is a tremendous leap forward for mankind. It is the first step on the way to mankind's redemption and triumphant glorification!

Suffering the way to glory

And so the first stage in the programme has already been completed: the man, Christ Jesus, has been born. But so has the second stage. For see him now: he is already crowned with glory and honour.

I think I hear the Hebrew Christians sigh. 'Yes, that is true. He suffered on the cross and was rejected and shamefully treated. But in spite of it all, yes, it's true – he is now crowned with glory and honour.'

'Oh, but cheer up,' says the writer, 'it is not that way. He is crowned with glory and honour *because of*, not in spite of, the fact that he suffered death. Do you not see that because man threw away his dominion, and lost his glory by sin, the only possible way that man could reach that glory again was by suffering? Instead of the cross being a mistake, instead of those sufferings being a tragic accident, they have been in God's hand the way of bringing Messiah himself to his crowning with glory and honour: *On account of* the suf-fering of death he is crowned with glory and honour. Cheer up! His sufferings are something to be gloried in.

There is in them the evidence of divine strategy.'

Not only is he himself crowned with glory and honour because of the suffering of death; by God's wonderful grace this has been the means of securing reconciliation for everything. When he went into death and tasted its bitterness, he tasted death for everything. And because of that a day will eventually come (of which the apostle Paul speaks in his letter to Colossians, 1:20–21), when all things, both that are upon earth and that are in heaven, shall be reconciled to God. God will be presented with a heaven and earth freed from sin, cleansed and reconciled in every part, an honour to God and a pleasure to man for ever. It shall all be done by this very means of Christ's suffering, because the man, Jesus, tasted death for everyone.

Why did Christ suffer?

'Look again,' says the writer, 'I know you are feeling the pressure of suffering with Christ. I know you feel the shame of a Messiah who has been crucified. But what other way could God have done it? How else would it have been fitting for God to bring many sons to glory?'

'Why', says someone, 'could God not have used his power? Could God not have sidetracked the cross? Could God not have sent those twelve legions of angels and by force have rescued his Son and Peter and all the rest of them and have transported them to glory without suffering?'

Well, God certainly had the power to do it; but would it have been a fitting thing for God to do? No! Bringing many sons to glory is a task that God must do, if he does it at all, in a way that befits his holiness, dignity and love.

Merely introducing a sinner into celestial glory by a sudden act of divine power would not change his rebellious and selfish heart and turn him into a saint, any more than suddenly introducing a tiger into your home will turn it into a civil, gracious and well-mannered guest. The sinner must first be brought to repentance and forgiven; the rebel be reconciled to God; the mere human creature be born again and become a child of God. And if the person concerned is going to have an *abundant* entrance into the eternal kingdom (see 2 Pet. 1:11, AV/KJV), and there carry an 'exceeding and eternal weight of glory' (see 2 Cor. 4:17, AV/KJV), some process, long or short, of preparation, training and refining is absolutely indispensable; and suffering will be an inevitable part of the process.

In order to bring his many sons to glory, then, God had first to provide them with a source and leader, a pioneer and pathfinder, of their salvation. And then God had to allow him to be qualified as their leader by first suffering himself. As the pre-incarnate Son of God he enjoyed equally infinite power as his Father. But how much did he know then about suffering from personal experience? And how, without that personal experience of suffering, could he ever understand and sympathize with his people in their suffering?

In saying this, of course, the writer is not laying down conditions which he demands that God shall fulfil. Inspired by the Holy Spirit he is relaying to us how God himself felt about it all. And what a glorious insight into the character of God it gives us! Possessing infinite power he had the right, as Creator, to treat us in any way he pleased. But having decided to bring us to glory through a pathway of suffering, his infinite compassion insisted that it must be done not just anyhow, but in a way that would be fitting, even if it meant the suffering of his Son.

Christ not ashamed of us

There is nothing therefore in the sufferings of Jesus for any Christian, Jew or Gentile, to be ashamed of, either in God for allowing them, or in Christ for enduring them. We should not hide the fact that he suffered, but advertise it worldwide.

But the writer has something more to say about our Lord's amazing condescension. It is so wonderful, even if we read it at a superficial level; so wonderful in fact that if we are not careful, we might fail to notice that he is saying something even more wonderful than at first sight we thought he was:

'Both the Sanctifier and those who are being sanctified', he points out, 'are all of one; and for this reason he is not ashamed to call them (his) brethren' (2:11, my translation).

The first wonderful thing is that he is not ashamed of us. (He will be of some people; see Lk. 9:26. Let us see to it that we are not among them.) But why is he not? Any one of us, knowing ourselves as we do, could surely think of a thousand and one reasons why we might expect him to be ashamed of us. If, in spite of that, he is not ashamed to call us his brothers, that must surely set us asking, 'Why not?'

Well, you say, he is not proud, as we are; so that's why he is not ashamed of us.

Well said! Of course he is not proud, for pride is sinful and Jesus is sinless. But when you've said that, you have only said the obvious. What Christian did not take that for granted? Besides, although it is true, it is not the reason the writer gives for Christ's not being ashamed to call us his brothers. The reason is: 'Both the Sanctifier (that is, the Lord Jesus) and those who are being sanctified, (that is, we who trust him) are all of one: *that's the reason why* he is not ashamed to call us his brothers.'

But if that's the reason, then what does it mean? The difficulty lies with the phrase 'are all of one'.[1] Most, but not all, modern translators and commentators feel that the word 'one' refers to God, and that what our writer is saying is this: Jesus is the Son of God, and we who have received him have become sons of God (see Gal. 3:26). He and we therefore have the same Father, and are in the same family. And that is why Jesus is not ashamed to call us his brothers.

Now in and of itself this is a true and wonderful fact: Jesus is the Son of God; we who trust him are sons of God; and that for us is a source of eternal worship and joy. But it is hardly this particular fact to which the writer wants to draw our attention here, for if it were, see what it would do to his argument. It would now run something like this: We once were mere creatures of God. But now as sons of God we are so exalted that even the second person of the Trinity, the Son of God himself, is not ashamed to call us his brothers. In other words, the reason given for his not being ashamed of us would not now be his condescension to our level, his solidarity with us as human beings, but our exaltation to his level. And this would not fit the context at all. The whole of 2:5–18 is talking not about the deity of the Son of God (as chapter 1 was), but about the manhood of Jesus; not of our

---

[1] NIV, 'are of the same family'; NASB, 'are all of one Father'; NEB, 'are all of one stock'; RSV, 'have all one origin'.

elevation to his level, but of his condescension to ours.[2] Verse 10 has been talking not of his eternal Sonship but of his sufferings; and verses 14 and 17 are about to point out how, in order to become exactly like us (apart from sin), he shared our 'flesh and blood', that is, he became truly human and shared our humanity.

Why, then, is it that the one who was the pre-existent, eternal Son of God, the second person of the Trinity, is not ashamed to call us his brothers? Because, when he does so, the term 'brothers' is not empty religious rhetoric, or pious sentimental exaggeration: it is absolutely genuine, and means exactly what it says. There is no pretence in it. He has become as truly human as we are (though not sinful: sin is no necessary part of humanity). He has experienced human joys and human sorrows. He knows from having suffered it, what it is to be hungry (Mt. 4:2), tired (Jn. 4:6), thirsty (Jn. 19:28), sorrowful at the death of a loved friend (Jn. 11:35), and broken-hearted in the face of blind, unreasoning rejection (Lk. 13:32–35). He knows what temptation is, and he knows what death is more than we who trust him ever will.

When, therefore, he calls us his brothers, it is not empty talk. He is not afraid that anyone will ever compare his circumstances and experience with ours and accuse him of hypocrisy for daring to call us his brothers. The term represents reality. He is not ashamed to call us brothers because he and we are genuinely 'all of one'.

We must, of course, be careful to notice exactly who it is that the writer says are 'all of one'. He is not saying that because our Lord has become truly human, he calls every human being his brother. People nowadays constantly quote our Lord's words 'Inasmuch as ye have done it unto one of the least of these my brethren, ye have done it unto me' (Mt. 25:40, AV/KJV), as if they meant to say that every man, woman, boy and girl on the face of the earth, all the unregenerate, all the deliberate atheists, religious hypocrites, crimi-

[2] Though we are sons of God through faith in Christ, it would not be true to say that we have been raised to his level of sonship. As the second person of the Trinity, his sonship will be for ever different from ours. In speaking of our common Father, he did not say, 'I am returning to our Father,' but, maintaining the distinction between his relationship to God and ours, 'to my Father and your Father' (Jn. 20:17).

nals, child-molesters, cheats, liars and murderers, are one and all brothers of the Lord Jesus. It is not true of course. Our Lord himself was very careful to indicate precisely who his brothers are: 'My mother and brothers are those who hear God's word and do it' (Lk. 8:21). And the writer similarly phrases himself very carefully: 'The one who sanctifies and those who are being sanctified', he says, 'are all of one.' He is talking of Christ's identification and solidarity with his redeemed people. He died to make them holy; he lives to perfect their sanctification.

A prophetic psalm

This solidarity of the Messiah with his redeemed people, so the writer proceeds to show, was in fact both prophesied and prefigured in the Old Testament. The writer quotes Psalm 22:22 which says,

> I will declare your name to my brothers;
> in the congregation I will praise you.

This psalm is composed of two parts: the dark night of suffering, of forsakenness and of prayer heard but unanswered (22:1–21), and the morning, bright with answered prayer, with praise in the congregation and with the proclamation of God's righteousness to future generations (22:22–31). King David wrote the psalm; but the description both of the night and of the morning go beyond whatever it was he personally experienced. He wrote as a prophet; the psalm is messianic, and in due course the Lord Jesus repeated its words at Calvary.

'My God, my God, why have you forsaken me?' (Ps. 22:1; Mt. 27:46). Christ's life had been utterly perfect and sinless, whereas Israel's had been warped and sinful. In spite of that, when they cried to God, they were heard and answered; but when he cried he was not heard – or at least, being heard, he was not answered.

In his heart he knew why he was forsaken. It was because he insisted on taking his place alongside his brothers; because he refused to be separated from them in spite of their sin, weakness, frailty and rebellion against God. He bore their sins in his body on the tree, and for their sakes was forsaken by God. As the apostle John puts it: 'having loved his own which were in the world, he loved them unto the end' (13:1, AV/KJV).

World history has never seen a darker night for mankind than when the man, Jesus, mankind's representative, suffered the wrath of God against human sin, and was forsaken. 'He was delivered over to death for our sins' (Rom. 4:25).

But he 'was raised to life for our justification' (Rom. 4:25). The dark night of forsakenness gave way to the dawn of resurrection and to the noonday splendour of the ascension. Earth was now to be exchanged for heaven, suffering and shame for glory, the cross for the throne and the crown. The man Jesus was about to be invited to sit on the right hand of the Majesty on high. Would not that loosen somewhat the ties that bound him to his disciples? Would not the glorified Son of Man now feel a little ashamed before the majestic angels of God to acknowledge his humble followers on earth as his brothers?

Never! On the very threshold of the ascension he said to Mary: 'Go . . . to my brothers and tell them, I am returning to my Father and your Father, to my God and your God' (Jn. 20:17); and in the bright morning of the second half of Psalm 22 we hear the glorified Messiah announce: 'I will declare your name to my brothers; in the congregation I will praise you' (22:22). And still wherever his people meet, there he is among them, revealing the Father's name to them (Jn. 17:26, AV/KJV) and leading the response of their praise.

Here then rises the irrepressible and inexhaustible fountain of our hope for mankind. As the last two verses of Psalm 22 puts it: 'Posterity will serve him; future generations will be told about the Lord. They will proclaim his righteousness to a people yet unborn – for he has done it.'

A prophetic prefigurement

But there is another reason for Christ's solidarity with his people, and therefore another basis for hope. The writer to the Hebrews explains it by quoting the words of the prophet Isaiah. Let us read his words in their full context so that we can understand the situation that led Isaiah to speak them, and then how they apply to the Lord Jesus.

The Lord spoke to me . . .

The Lord Almighty . . . will be a sanctuary;
   but for both houses of Israel he will be
a stone that causes men to stumble
   and a rock that makes them fall.
And for the people of Jerusalem he will be
   a trap and a snare
Many of them will stumble;
   they will fall and be broken,
   they will be snared and captured.
Bind up the testimony
   and seal up the law among my disciples.
I will wait for the Lord,
   who is hiding his face from the house of Jacob.
I will put my trust in him.

Here am I, and the children the Lord has given me. We
are signs and symbols in Israel from the Lord Almighty,
who dwells on Mount Zion (Is. 8:11–18).

Isaiah was appointed by God as a prophet in the year of
King Uzziah's death (see Is. 6). The nation's affairs, both
spiritually and politically, were at a very low ebb. For three
generations no king of Judah had died a natural death: one
after another they had been assassinated. And when Uzziah
died, he died in a leper house in disgrace for a presumptious
sin against God (2 Chr. 26:16–21). The coalitions which the
ten tribes of Israel were making with other nations against
Judah, were keeping the king and people in a constant state
of alarm (Is. 7:1–9); and on the horizon stood the growing
threat of the Assyrian empire.

In vain did Isaiah assure the people of Judah in the name
of God that if only they would repent and believe God, he
would fulfil his promise to David, maintain David's royal
line, and eventually send the Messiah (Is. 7:1–17). In vain did
he assure them that one day Messiah would sit on David's
throne, the nation would be restored and reunited and death
banished, and the other nations would come flocking to
Messiah's banner and be treated to the delightful banquet of
his messianic kingdom (Is. 25:1–9). To the king and people
of Judah it all sounded like utterly unpractical daydreaming.

97

They preferred to rely on their own diplomacy and international alliances. The results were disastrous. The very Assyria with whom they sought alliance eventually took the ten tribes of Israel away into captivity. A century and more later for similar persistence in sin and unbelief, Judah found themselves removed into exile by the Babylonians and their capital, Jerusalem, destroyed.

The fact was that in Isaiah's day, the nation's sin and rebellion against God had become chronic (Is. 1:2–9). They could no longer repent; their faith in their God-given role in history, to be the nation through whom the Saviour of the world would come, was virtually non-existent. Their very God who would have been a sanctuary to them was becoming 'a stone that causes men to stumble, and a rock that makes them fall'. Unable to believe him, they would reject his word and bring on themselves calamitous consequences.

Isaiah was not only a prophet foretelling the coming of the Messiah, he and his circumstances were a prefiguration of what the times of the Messiah would be like. Jesus proved to be *par excellence* 'the stone that caused men to stumble, and the rock that made them fall' (see Lk. 20:18; Rom. 9:33; 1 Pet. 2:8). Israel's leaders rejected his call to repentance, and pooh-poohed his claim to be the Messiah. The masses, initially impressed by his teaching and miracles, deserted him when they found that he was not prepared to lead them in a war of liberation against the Roman imperialists, and that the deliverance he was offering them was a spiritual salvation. So Jesus was executed as a fraud and imposter, and the nation went its own preferred way of worldly-wise politics. In less than forty years they were hijacked by right-wing freedom-fighters, forced to join in a revolt against Rome, and were crushed. Their temple was destroyed, and Jerusalem trampled on by the Gentiles. In AD 135, after a similar revolt, Jerusalem was reconstituted a Gentile city, and remained so until recently.

But Isaiah was a prefigurement of Christ, not only in the gloom of his circumstances but also in the fact that in him and his disciples God lit an inextinguishable beacon of hope for the nation and eventually for the world. As he stood there in the midst of national apostasy but surrounded by his believing disciples (his 'children' as he called them), Isaiah's faith in God and God's purposes ran high. 'I will put my trust in him,' he declared, 'for look at me and these children that the Lord has given me. We are signs and symbols in Israel from the Lord Almighty, who dwells on Mount Zion' (*cf*. Is. 8:17–18). It was God who had given him these 'children', who had opened their eyes to see the truthfulness of his God-given prophecies. And if God had caused them to believe the prophecies, it was a sure sign and pledge that God would one day fulfil them.

Let's allow ourselves to digress a moment, and think what Isaiah might say to us now, if he could, about the way his faith and hope have been vindicated! He prophesied that when Messiah came, he would first be rejected by his nation and executed; that God however would make his life a vicarious sacrifice for sin; that after his death, he would live again and see his spiritual offspring. Through his death people would find healing of life's deepest unease: the guilt of sin and alienation from God. They would come to see that the Messiah was pierced for their transgressions, crushed for their iniquities; that though they had gone astray like lost sheep, the Lord laid on him the iniquity of them all. Through his punishment they would find peace and reconciliation with God (see Is. 53).

It is a straightforward fact of history that the birth, death and resurrection of Jesus have given us a world figure who fits Isaiah's predictions with unfailing accuracy. But more than that. Through the death and resurrection of Jesus untold millions have actually found the healing Isaiah talked of: healing of the heart's deepest wounds, the removal of the plague of guilt, the end to alienation from their Creator, to feelings of hostility and rebellion towards God; reconciliation, peace, and the enjoyment of God's love, and bright hope for the future. This *is* the beginning of the promised new 'age to come'! This *is* the very dawn of heaven. The healing of the human heart is the necessary prelude to the healing of the universe.

But to return to Isaiah. His confidence was based on the fact that God had given him his disciples. It was God who had opened their eyes and brought them to faith. 'Here am I, and the children God has given me.' It was exactly how Jesus would speak of his disciples centuries later. It was this that prompted in him such affection for them and solidarity with them; and created in him such unshakeable confidence that all God's promises for their ultimate glorification would be fulfilled. 'I have revealed your name', he said in his prayer to his Father, 'to those whom you gave me out of the world. They were yours; you gave them to me and they have obeyed your word' (Jn. 17:6; see margin).

Humanly speaking, Christ's disciples were neither wise nor learned, and they were certainly not powerful. They were, on Christ's own admission, mere children. Yet in them the divine miracle had taken place: God had been pleased to reveal himself to them through the Lord Jesus. 'I praise you, Father,' he said, 'Lord of heaven and earth, because you have hidden these things from the wise and learned, and revealed them to little children' (Lk. 10:21).

This, of course, is what had to happen again, millions and myriads of times, if ever, as Isaiah promised, the earth was going to be full of the knowledge of the Lord as the waters cover the sea (Is. 11:9). God is not a mere subject, like mathematics or physics, that can be 'proved' to anybody who is sufficiently intelligent to follow logic. God is a person. He is known only as he lets himself be known and reveals himself directly to people. But the very fact that God had revealed himself to Christ's disciples not only filled Christ with joy (Lk. 10:21) and created an unbreakable bond of unity, love and life between him and them. It filled him with the certainty that God would continue to reveal himself to multitudes more, and he prayed for all those multi-millions who all through the centuries would believe on him through the testimony of the original few disciples (Jn. 17:20–23).

And there is yet another way in which Isaiah and his disciples were a prefigurement of the Messiah. In the midst of all the apostasy and impending doom, Isaiah and his believing disciples were a God-given pledge that one day God in his faithfulness would restore the whole nation. They were, to use Isaiah's metaphor, the stump of the tree of Israel, which, when the tree itself was cut down, would continue to live and eventually grow up again (Is. 6:13). 'Here am I, and the children God has given me,' said Isaiah. 'We are signs and symbols in Israel from the Lord Almighty, who dwells on Mount Sion.' At the primary level, this pledge, these signs and symbols, were fulfilled in Israel's return from the exile in Babylon. At the highest level, they still await fulfilment.

But listen to Paul arguing in the same way about the Lord Jesus and his Jewish believers. Faced with Israel's hardening unbelief, increasing apostasy, and the impending doom which as we know began to fall in AD 70, Paul asks: 'Did God reject his people? By no means! I am an Israelite myself, a descendant of Abraham . . . God did not reject his people, whom he foreknew' (Rom. 11:1–2). Paul's argument is the same as Isaiah's. The number of Jews who, like Paul, had had their eyes opened by God to see that Jesus was the Messiah, was comparatively small. They were only a mere remnant of the nation. But the very fact of the existence, by God's grace, of such a remnant was a pledge that one day the nation as a whole would be saved, reconciled to their Messiah and to God. Then would take place scenes of unprecedented joy: it would be a veritable resurrection of the dead (Rom. 11:15–16).

The conquest of death

But if the 'children', that is, Christ's disciples, were going to be able to look forward to the age to come with confidence and eager anticipation, then they had to be delivered from the fear of death.

Death is still an enemy. Say what we will, we shrink from it, and from the pain and sorrow, disease and disgust, that so often accompany it. But it is not the process of dying that holds the most terror, but what happens afterwards; for death carries its real sting in its tail. Ever since the devil induced man to disobey God, and through that one man's disobedience sin entered the world, and death through sin, the 'sting' of death, as Scripture describes it, has been sin (1 Cor. 15:56). For after death comes the judgment. Scripture affirms it and conscience inwardly knows it and fears it, whatever people say outwardly. It is no use, when someone has died as he lived – unbelieving, unrepentant, unforgiven, unregenerate – to pretend that, after all, sin does not matter, and all will be well with him. 'The power of sin is the law,' Scripture adds. God's law will never say that sin does not matter, either here or in the world to come. How could it? Death is not some kind of fairy wand that magically transforms the impenitent sinner into a glorious saint. Die an unforgiven sinner and you remain an unforgiven sinner for ever (Rev. 22:10–11).

It is this fear that has led multitudes of people, from the most primitive to the most sophisticated, to invent and practise all kinds of rites and rigorous disciplines, designed to lessen the punishment and suffering that they fear awaits them on the other side of death. And all to no effect, except that it has added another slavery to the original bondage of the fear of death.

It is this fear that has led multitudes of others, like the ancient Roman poet, Lucretius, to try to prove that nothing awaits man after death. Death ends all. Cold comfort this, if it were true, for those who are suffering cruel injustice and have no hope that they will ever get their just rights in this life; for in this case they must believe that they will never get justice. Cold comfort, too, for people born with a major physical handicap. They can see what life could be like without the handicap. They must exist in pain with no prospect of relief or enjoyment in this life; and now, if this theory is true, with no prospect of anything better, of anything at all after death.

Others therefore have the opposite fear: not that there *is* something after death, but that there *isn't*. They fear that this life is everything; that death ends all enjoyment, because it ends all. Simply to keep alive physically, therefore, they have been prepared to let go all that lifts human life above mere animal existence: honour, loyalty, truth, moral rectitude, and faith. What a bondage the fear of death has been and still is for multitudes of people.

In this situation the only way Christ could save us was first by becoming human like us so that he could die; and then not by miraculously coming down from the cross and escaping death, but by deliberately remaining on it and dying. For by death he suffered the penalty of our sin to set our conscience free from guilt and therefore free from the fear of facing God's wrath after death. And by dying and rising again he showed us that his sacrifice for us was accepted and that we who trust him are accepted in him; that the reign of sin and death is broken, and the devil robbed of his power. The believer may know with absolute certainty that to die is to depart and to be with Christ which is far better (Phil. 1:23); that to be absent from the body is to be immediately at home with the Lord (2 Cor. 5:6–8); that at the resurrection he will have a new and glorious body, like the body of the risen Saviour (Phil. 3:20–21); and that one day death itself will be done away with for ever (1 Cor. 15:26).

What Christ was obliged to do

And now we come to what in its way is the most staggering statement in this whole second chapter: the infinite Son of God, second person of the Trinity, creator and heir of all things, was actually obliged to be made like us his brothers in every way. He had to be (2:17).

At first sight it seems a shocking thing to say. Surely the Son of God was always free and was never obliged to do anything? Certainly he was under no obligation to save us. No-one made him do it. Had he left us to perish in our sinful rebellion against God, we would have had no ground whatever for complaining that he had failed in his obligations towards us. When he stooped to take hold of our hands to help us (2:16), he did so voluntarily (see Jn. 10:18).

Yes, but (explains our writer) once he embarked on the task of helping us, there were certain things that that task itself obliged him to do, if it was to be done perfectly. Once he started, it was unthinkable that he should do it less than perfectly. So for this reason 'he *had to be* made like his brothers in every way' (2:17). There could be no stopping short; he had to go the whole road.

We were not superior, angelic, spirit beings, or even majestic, but fallen, angels. We were the descendants of Abraham, says the writer – and, he might have added, weak and sinful into the bargain, and subject to constant temptation. Supreme above all our other needs would be the necessity first of being *made* right, and secondly of being *kept* right, with God.

For that purpose he would have to become our high priest in order to make propitiation (NIV atonement) for our sins, to place us and maintain us in the favour of God. He would have to be faithful to God, of course. There must be no lowering of God's standards, no excusing of our sin, no

103

fudging of the reality of our guilt, no objecting to the rightness of God's holy wrath. At the same time he would have to be merciful towards us. He must himself die instead of us, must offer himself as a propitiatory sacrifice for our sins, and rising again, must act as our constant intercessor before God. He would have to be merciful towards us, able to understand the suffering involved in temptation, by experiencing it himself. Yet he would have to be faithful to us: covering our failings by his sacrifice; but not allowing us to think that yielding to temptation does not matter. On the contrary; he would fortify our wills and strengthen our power to resist temptation. For all these many reasons, if he were realistically going to help us, he would have to become like us in every way (except of course, sin) and become human.

Knowing, then, what he would be obliged to do if once he started, nevertheless he took hold of our hand to help us and was made in all things like his brothers. He came and lived in poverty, and toiled in the smelly streets of ancient eastern cities. His own disciples were often more comfortable than he; they had their homes: he had nowhere to lay his head. All of us, without exception, fare far better than Christ often did. We shall all have a bed tonight, I suppose. He often slept rough and lived hard, so that he would be able to sympathize with all his people and be accessible to the humblest of them. And at the end he died for us.

How can we keep from worshipping a Saviour like that? Be ashamed of his manhood? Be ashamed of his sufferings? Be impatient with our own suffering for his sake? How could we be? His very suffering is his glory – and ours too; for it is the royal road by which he will bring redeemed mankind to their destiny of sharing universal dominion with God's perfect man.

Questions

1 What was 'the message spoken by angels' (2:2)? What makes the gospel more important than that message? Why do some people slip away from it?

2 What do you understand by the phrase 'the world to come' in 2:5? Would you prefer the translation 'the age to come'?

3 What have you learned from this chapter about God's original purpose for man?

4 To what extent has that purpose been achieved in Adam and his descendants? And to what extent in Christ? Has everything already been put under Christ's feet? (Consult 10:13.) If not, when will it be?

5 In what sense did Christ have to be 'made perfect' through sufferings? And what for (2:10)?

6 Why is Christ not ashamed to call those who trust him his brothers?

7 What do *you* think the point and relevance of the quotations in 2:13 are?

8 In what sense did Satan hold the power of death? And in what sense has he been destroyed? (2:14).

9 Why did Christ have to be made like his brothers in every way? (2:17).

10 How does Christ help us when we are tempted?

5

ENTERING GOD'S REST
Hebrews 3 – 4

A warning and its context

Chapters 3 and 4 of the letter to the Hebrews go together because they contain one of the solemn warnings for which this letter is famous. In fact they contain the longest of all these warnings. It is all the more important then that we quietly and diligently seek to understand the terms that the Holy Spirit uses, in case we either fail to apply this Scripture as forcefully as it ought to be applied, or apply it in the wrong direction.

First of all notice the setting of this warning. Just before it begins, the Holy Spirit speaks to us of the priesthood of the Lord Jesus Christ (2:17; 3:1). Then, when the warning is finished, he again reminds us of our great high priest who can sympathize with our weaknesses (4:14–16). So, as we come to consider this warning, we are to keep in mind our merciful and faithful high priest. Let him lead us. Let us stand by his side and hear these words from his lips. He will tell us what to do and what to avoid. Then, when we have listened to the warning, let it guide us back to him again. However much it may make us feel our weakness, let that very weakness drive us to him who can sympathize with our weakness and is ready to grant us his ever present help.

In chapter 1 we thought together of the Lord Jesus in his deity, the divine spokesman of the divine message. In chapter 2 we thought of him in his manhood qualified to be our high priest, and not ashamed to call us his brothers. Now as 'holy brothers, who share in the heavenly calling', we are asked to fix our thoughts on Jesus as the apostle, the divine spokesman of chapter 1, and also on him as the High Priest of chapter 2.

What shall we think about him? Consider him, says the passage, who was faithful to the one who appointed him as also was Moses in all his house. Now it is perfectly legitimate to translate the Greek here by a past tense: who *was* faithful. But it is equally legitimate – and more appropriate, surely – to translate it by a present tense: 'Consider him *being* faithful.' Consider not only that he *was* faithful in some past time when he came as an apostle and brought us God's message and delivered it faithfully; but consider him still, now that he acts as our high priest, being faithful to God, who appointed him, in all God's house.

Christ compared with Moses

To give us some idea of our Lord's faithfulness to us, the Holy Spirit compares our Lord with Moses. We notice that the phrase he uses of Moses, 'who was faithful in all God's house', comes from a context where Miriam and Aaron had joined the ranks of those who were grumbling against him (Nu. 12:1–8). Israel was never slow, it seems, to grumble against Moses: their food and water supply and even his personal and private affairs, such as his getting married, all became reasons for grumbling against him, even though at that time he was the captain of their salvation. But in all this Moses' grace shone brightly. He was, says Scripture, more humble than anyone else on the face of the earth (Nu. 12:3). I wonder how he ever managed to keep his temper. He had given his life for this nation. He might have been at that very moment reclining on soft cushions in the palace in Egypt. Yet there he was amongst this race of ill-mannered and uncouth ex-slaves, doing his very best for them, and getting in return constant naggings and grumblings on every side.

What was it that kept the man so faithful to Israel? It was his faithfulness to God who had appointed him to his house. Moses had been sent to Israel as God's apostle with the message of deliverance from Egypt. Moses thereafter acted as the mediator between Israel and God, and saved the people by his intercessions. In spite of all their grumblings and mistakes and personal insults, Moses remained faithful to the task that God had given him. 'Consider, holy brethren,' the writer says in effect, 'you who share a heavenly calling, consider, as you pursue your pilgrimage from earth to heaven, the apostle and high priest whom you confess. How many times we have grumbled and murmured! But let us consider him being faithful in spite of it, constantly and ever faithful; consider that he will always be faithful every step of the pathway home.'

Moses broke down at last, in spite of his faithfulness. There came a day when the Israelites so angered him by their ungrateful complainings, that he erupted: 'Listen now, you rebels,' he shouted at them, 'must we bring you water out of this rock?' And with that he struck the rock with his staff instead of just speaking to it as God had told him to do (Nu. 20:9–12).

That act of impatience cost Moses his entry into the promised land. It seems hard on Moses, doesn't it? But God had appointed Moses to look after Israel, and if Moses could not do it without losing his temper and so misrepresenting God to the people, then Moses must be set aside. And God has appointed us a captain of our salvation, and made him responsible for seeing us through this world home to glory. Thank God we can count on his faithfulness and know that he will never fail, never once lose his patience or his temper with any of us, but will fulfil his God-appointed task to the very end. He will save to the uttermost all who come to God by him.

The warning

There are many other respects in which Jesus is superior to Moses, of course, and our writer proceeds to detail two of them. Moses was faithful in God's house: he built the ancient tabernacle for God. But Jesus is God and, as we have seen in chapter 1, he is the builder of everything, including the eternal tabernacle, of which Moses' tabernacle was but a humble copy (see 8:1–5). Secondly, Moses was a servant in God's house; Christ is the Son over it.

But time forbids us to dwell on these details, for our prime task is to follow the writer as he takes this idea of God's house and uses it as a base from which to launch his warning. Moses was appointed over a tabernacle made of wood and gold and linen; God's house nowadays is formed of human beings. 'And we are his house,' says the writer, 'if we hold fast our boldness and the exultant boast of our hope' (3:6, my translation).

We notice the 'if' at once. The writer is obviously not prepared to state as a matter of fact 'We are his house,' and leave it there. He adds an 'if'. In what sense does he mean us to take it? He reinforces this 'if' by using a similar expression in verse 14: 'We have become partners of Christ, *if* we hold fast the beginning of our confidence firm to the end.'[1]

Two statements, then, followed by an 'if'. How shall we take them? Since they are both obviously making the same point, let's begin with the second one (verse 14). Its wording is at first sight a little odd; and if we can come to understand what it is saying, it will cast light on the 'if' of verse 6 as well.

The first part of verse 14 with its perfect tense, 'We have become partners of Christ,' states a fact, something that has already happened in the past; but the second part adds a condition relating to the future: 'if we hold fast . . . to the end'. And the problem is this: how can you make something that has already happened in the past depend on something that has not yet happened in the future?

'Yes,' you say, 'if I have become a partner of Christ, then I have become one, and am one now. How could what I already am depend on what I do in the future? If it said, "We *shall become* partners of Christ, if we hold fast . . . to the end," then, clearly enough, we should not be able to claim that we had become partners of Christ until we reached the end. But as it is, the verse says we have already become his partners. How can it then go and make that present fact depend on a future condition?'

The answer is simple, really. Let's go back to what this verse calls 'the beginning of [your] confidence', that is, the moment when you first believed the Saviour. If in genuine

---

[1] My translation. 'Partners of' rather than 'partakers of' is the better translation of the word here. *Cf.* its use in Lk. 5:7, 'his partners' in the other boat. The rendering in AV/KJV, 'we are made', is of course old English for 'we have been made'. It is a perfect tense, and not a present tense, as it might appear to be to a modern English reader. *Cf.* NIV, 'We *have come* to share in Christ.'

repentance and faith you did truly believe the Saviour, then of course there and then you became one of his partners. And if your faith was true and genuine faith, you need have no uncertainty or doubt: your faith will endure, you will keep the beginning of your confidence firm to the end. Nor is it presumptuous to claim this. One of the reasons why God has graciously provided true believers with a high priest, is so that he might by his constant intercessions pray for them, as he did for Peter (Lk. 22:32), that their faith may not fail. And it will not fail – whatever else fails – any more than Peter's did.

So now the question we must ask is: At 'the beginning of your confidence', did you truly believe the Saviour? Was your faith genuine?

'Yes, of course,' you say, 'I did truly and sincerely and genuinely believe on the Lord Jesus Christ – and if I had not done so then, I would do it right now this very minute.'

Excellent! But suppose I ask for evidence from you that your faith was, and is, genuine and that you have really become a partner of Christ. Suppose I say, as the writer to the Hebrews is saying, 'Yes, you certainly have become a partner of Christ, if as a result of it your life gives clear evidence of it.' What kind of evidence have I a right to expect?

Again, the answer is simple. The mark of true faith is that it does endure to the end. If therefore you did genuinely believe the Saviour and have become a partner of his, I, and everyone else, have a right to expect that you will demonstrate it by 'holding fast the beginning of your confidence firm to the end'. I notice that, according to what you have just said, you not only believed in the past, but you still do believe. Well, keep it up; continue your demonstration that you are a true believer right up to the end. And it is this same challenge that the writer's first conditional clause in verse 6 issues us with: 'We are his house, if we hold fast our boldness and the exultant boast of our hope.'

But at this point another question arises: 'What happens if someone who once professed to believe on the Lord Jesus does not hold fast the beginning of his confidence? Does that mean that he ceases to be a believer? Or that he never was a true believer?'

We need to be careful how we answer this question. All of

111

us at times behave in a way that is inconsistent with our Christian profession; and many of us have gone – and still go – through periods when our faith is decidedly wobbly. It happened to Peter on the occasion we have referred to. We have it on the authority of the Lord himself that underneath, in his heart of hearts, his faith did not fail; and, of course, after his fall he was restored, just as the Lord confidently asserted he would be even before he fell. But imagine standing by Peter's side when he deliberately and repeatedly denied he was a Christian and used all the swear-words he knew to prove it! If we had not heard what the Saviour had said, we would have found it very difficult to know, wouldn't we, whether he was another Judas, who had professed to be a believer but never was one (Jn. 6:64, 70–71), or whether he was a genuine believer who was temporarily acting inconsistently.

But when we have made due allowance for this real-life situation, we must study very carefully the example of a sad, and very famous, case which the Holy Spirit now cites from the Old Testament. In particular we must notice very accurately the terms he uses when he diagnoses what went wrong with the people concerned.

A fearful example

The historical example to which the Holy Spirit now calls attention can be summed up in a few words. The ancestors of the Hebrew Christians to whom our letter is written were once slaves in Egypt. They eventually found freedom, first by being saved from the wrath of God through the blood of the passover lamb; and then by being set free from Pharaoh's tyranny by the supernatural power of God. They were baptized to Moses in the cloud and in the sea (1 Cor. 10:2); they made a start towards the promised land of rest. But few of them ever got there. They so rebelled against the Lord that in his anger he declared on oath that they would never enter his rest. And they never did.

We must be doubly careful. First, to make sure we understand exactly what the Holy Spirit says went wrong, exactly what the cause was why they never got in to their promised rest. And secondly, to see how the writer applies the lesson to his readers and to ourselves.

Let us take first the plain, straightforward statement at 3:19. 'So we see that they were not able to enter, because of their unbelief.' Notice the term. Unbelief. Not worldliness, carelessness, lack of devotion, but unbelief.

'Yes, but that could apply to any one of us,' you say, 'to any true Christian in fact. Any believer can at times be guilty of unbelief. Peter was when he stepped out of the boat and began to walk on the sea towards the Lord, but suddenly lost his faith and began to sink. Suppose the Lord challenges me to do some work for him and gives me a promise to encourage me, but then I find that I haven't faith enough to believe the promise. Isn't that unbelief? And wouldn't that disqualify me from entering into the rest which God offers me?'

Well, certainly unbelief is unbelief; but we must notice exactly what it was these ancient Hebrews did not believe. We find that in 4:2: 'For we also have had the gospel preached to us, just as they did; but the message they heard was of no value to them, because those who heard did not combine it with faith.' And then again in 4:6, 'those who formerly had the gospel preached to them did not go in, because of their disobedience'. These statements could not be plainer: it was the gospel which they did not believe. They heard it; but it did them no good because they never did believe it.

What the gospel is

Now unless we get the right idea of what the gospel was in their case (and what it is in ours) we shall find it difficult to understand this statement that they never did believe the gospel. We shall be inclined to argue that after all they did leave Egypt and they were baptized to Moses. They must have believed the gospel, or at least part of it, otherwise they would never have come out of Egypt. It was only the later parts of the gospel, that is the report of the spies (Nu. 13:27) and especially Joshua's and Caleb's report (Nu. 14:6–10), that they failed to believe and so came to disaster.

But that's just where we make a big mistake. The gospel preached to the Israelites did not consist of two or three separate parts so that they could believe and accept one part without necessarily believing and accepting the others. Moses did not go around saying, 'Look, the main thing is to escape

113

the wrath of God on passover night, and then to escape from
bondage to Pharaoh in Egypt. That's the gospel God offers
you. So let's keep things simple. The main thing is to get out
of Egypt and into the wilderness. After that you might like
to consider taking some of God's advanced courses, such as
walking in fellowship with God through the desert and then
finally entering into the inheritance in the promised land.
But those advanced courses are optional. You don't have to
take them if you don't want to. So decide that later. For
the moment just believe the simple gospel and get out of
Egypt.'

No, of course not. Moses did not preach the gospel like
that, for there was no such gospel to preach. The gospel was
that God had come down to redeem them; and redemption
meant being delivered from the wrath of God through the
blood of the passover Lamb, being set free from the power
of Pharaoh, being accepted as God's own people, leaving
Egypt, crossing the desert and entering their inheritance in
the land of promise. It was all one indivisible package. They
could not believe and accept the first part but reject the rest.
It was all or nothing; and this was made clear to them from
the very start (see Ex. 6:6–8).

As we know, they all professed to believe the gospel and
left Egypt. But when they got in sight of the promised land,
they deliberately and persistently refused to go in. So what
did that show? That they had believed the gospel, but not
the rest of God's word? Or that they had believed some parts
of the gospel but not other parts? No! To say that would be
to reduce the seriousness of the Holy Spirit's verdict. He says
that the message they heard was of no value to them because
they did not combine it with faith. They did not believe the
gospel.

And 'we also', the writer adds, 'have had the gospel
preached to us'; and we need to make sure that we have
understood what the gospel is and that we have believed it.
And then we ought to be very careful how we present it to
others. We should not give people the impression that the
gospel is solely concerned with offering us forgiveness of sins;
and that after that there are some optional courses such as
progress in holiness, and eventual conformity to Christ and
entrance into our great heavenly inheritance. The hope of the

gospel stored up for us in the heavens is an integral part of the gospel, and the early Christian preachers used to make this plain to their unconverted audiences right from the start in the course of their initial evangelism (see Col. 1:5). The gospel is one indivisible whole. You believe it all, or nothing. To profess to have believed the gospel, and then subsequently to refuse, deliberately and persistently, to make progress in the path of holiness and to enter into the great inheritance stored up for us 'in the heavenly realms in Christ Jesus' (Eph. 2:6) is very serious. It would cast grave doubts on whether we had ever really believed the gospel at all.

The meaning of 'disobedience'

But perhaps you have an objection. 'It's all right,' you say, 'for you to quote 3:19 and 4:2 and to claim on the basis of these verses that those who did not get into the promised land were people who did not believe the gospel – in other words, complete unbelievers. But look at 3:18 and 4:6; these verses give another reason. It says that the people who did not get in were those who *disobeyed*. And what is more, 4:11 warns us to be careful not to follow their example of disobedience. Surely you are not going to say that it is impossible for a true believer ever to be disobedient. All of us disobey the Lord sometimes; and these verses surely warn us that a true believer could disobey the Lord so seriously as to lose his salvation.'

Well, no, I am certainly not going to say it is impossible for a true believer ever to be disobedient. Sadly, all of us disobey this or that commandment of the Lord from time to time, either because we do not know his Word well enough to realize that we are breaking it, or because we think that some of his commandments are not important, or because temptation or self-will overwhelms us. And, if we do not repent of it, it will lead to discipline in this life (see 1 Cor. 11:30–32) and loss of reward (NB 'reward', not 'salvation') in the next (see 1 Cor. 3:11–15). That is serious indeed, and I have no intention of undermining its gravity.

But our task at the moment is to examine what kind of disobedience it is to which the Holy Spirit refers here in chapters 3 and 4 of Hebrews. The Greek word for 'disobedience' in 4:6 and 4:11 is *apeitheia*. Including these two occasions it occurs seven times in the New Testament.[2] Its related verb, *apeitheō*, 'to disobey', occurs in Hebrews 3:18 and 11:31, and fourteen more times in the New Testament, sixteen times in all.[3] The related adjective, *apeithēs*, 'disobedient', does not occur in Hebrews; but it occurs in six other places in the New Testament.[4] Twenty-nine occurrences, then, of the noun, verb, and adjective, and not once is any one of them ever used to describe the disobedience of a true believer. Always when these words are used, the disobedient are those who reject God, reject his law, reject his gospel and refuse to believe either him or it.

Let's leave aside the occurrences in Hebrews 3 and 4 for the moment and take some examples from other contexts. In 11:31, the writer observes that Rahab the harlot 'by faith . . . was not killed with those who were disobedient'. And who were these disobedient people that were killed when the Israelites destroyed Jericho? True and genuine believers who had recently been overcome by some temptation or other? No, of course not. Rahab had heard of the true God and what he was doing through Israel; and she believed and showed her faith by welcoming the spies (see Jos. 2:8–13). Her fellow-citizens in Jericho had heard as much about the true God as she had; but by contrast they had refused to believe and repent; and whereas she was saved, they perished.

Take one typical example from Acts. At 14:1–2 we read that Paul and Barnabas 'spoke so effectively that a great number of Jews and Greeks believed. But the Jews who [literally] *disobeyed* stirred up the Gentiles and poisoned their minds against the brothers.' Who then were these Jews who disobeyed? True and genuine believers who were in poor spiritual health and were guilty of disobeying one of the Lord's commandments? No, far from it. They were Jews who, when they heard the gospel preached, 'refused to believe', as NIV puts it.

Or take Paul's argument in Romans 10. He longs, so he says, for his fellow-nationals to be saved, and it grieves him

[2] Rom. 11:30, 32; Eph. 2:2; 5:6; Col. 3:6; Heb. 4:6, 11.
[3] Jn. 3:36; Acts 14:2; 17:5 (text uncertain); 19:9; Rom. 2:8; 10:21; 11:30–31; 15:31; Heb. 3:18; 11:31; 1 Pet. 2:7–8; 3:1, 20; 4:17.
[4] Lk. 1:17; Acts 26:19; Rom. 1:30; 2 Tim. 3:2; Tit. 1:16; 3:3.

that the majority are not. Then why are they not saved? Paul lists a number of reasons, and ends by quoting the words of God: 'All day long I have held out my hands to a disobedient and obstinate people' (verse 21; Is. 65:2). Here too 'being disobedient' means refusing to believe the gospel. And there is no salvation for anyone who refuses to believe the gospel. Listen to the gospel of John: 'Whoever believes in the Son has eternal life, but whoever [literally] *disobeys* the Son will not see life, for God's wrath remains on him' (3:36). 'Disobeying the Son', then, is the opposite of 'believing in the Son'. It denotes, not a believer who is temporarily misbelieving, but a downright unbeliever; which is why the NIV translates the phrase 'whoever rejects the Son'. And Peter warns us of the seriousness of doing that: 'What will the outcome be', he says, 'for those who do not obey the gospel of God?' (1 Pet. 4:17).

It would be tedious at this stage to work through all the places where this word is used. But one last example is for our purpose specially illuminating. In the letter to Titus, 1:15–16, Paul remarks: 'but to those who . . . do not believe, nothing is pure. . . . They claim to know God, but by their actions they deny him. They are detestable, disobedient and unfit for doing anything good.' In the context he has been talking of false teachers. Now he speaks of people who 'claim to know God'. But their profession is false, says Paul. They do not believe; they are disobedient. The two terms, we notice, are virtually synonymous.

With that we come back to our passage in Hebrews, and we notice that our writer uses these same two terms. The ancient Israelites professed to believe when they came out of Egypt; but their subsequent rebellion and refusal to enter Canaan showed that they had never truly believed the gospel. They 'disobeyed', he says in 3:18. 'They were not able to enter, because of their unbelief', he adds in 3:19.

'Yes,' someone may say, 'but you are not being fair to these ancient Israelites. Admittedly they rebelled against God and Moses after they had travelled a long way through the desert and had come to the borders of the promised land. And certainly they refused to believe Caleb and Joshua when they assured them that God would give them the land. So, quite clearly, they had completely lost their faith by that time.

But it is not fair to say that they never were believers. They were redeemed by the blood of the passover lamb in Egypt; they were sprinkled with the blood of the covenant at Sinai. It is obvious that they were true and genuine believers to start with, and only later lost their faith or threw it away, and so perished.'

God's verdict

Well, the best thing we can do to settle the question is to consult God himself. Will he agree that to start with in Egypt and for some time after that they were true and genuine believers and only later on lost their faith? Here is God's own verdict: 'How long will these people treat me with contempt? How long will they refuse to believe in me, in spite of all the miraculous signs I have performed among them? . . . not one of the men who saw my glory and the miraculous signs I performed in Egypt and in the desert but who disobeyed me ten times – not one of them will ever see the land I promised on oath to their forefathers' (Nu. 14:11, 22–23).

According to God, then, in spite of having seen all the miracles in Egypt at the beginning and thereafter in the desert, these people had shown consistent unbelief and disobedience all the way along the line, and in addition contempt for God himself and for his glory. They had left Egypt amid a good deal of excitement and religious fervour; but as for genuine personal faith in God, quite clearly they never had any. The subsequent happenings in the desert merely exposed what had always been true of them underneath.

Psalm 106 delivers the same verdict. Israel gave no thought to God's miracles in Egypt, and rebelled at the Red Sea (v. 7). God saved them, in spite of that, for his name's sake (v. 8). The undeniable evidence of the miracle at the Red Sea induced in them a superficial, temporary faith (vv. 9–12), as our Lord's miracles did in some of his contemporaries (Jn. 2:23–25). But soon afterwards they reverted to their normal pattern of lack of understanding, ingratitude, unbelief, rebellion and outright idolatry (vv. 13–43).

The warning applied

Thus far we have been considering the case of the Israelites in the desert; but now we must listen while our author draws from it a warning for the people to whom he is writing.

'Ah,' you say, 'there can be no doubt about them, at least. They must have been true believers because at the beginning of chapter 3 the writer addresses them as "holy brothers, who share in the heavenly calling".'

Well, certainly, if they did genuinely believe the gospel when they heard it, they could be absolutely sure that they would be eternally saved. Look what the writer says in 4:6 and contrast that with what he says in 4:3. 'Those who formerly had the gospel preached to them did not go in,' he says, 'because of their disobedience' (4:6). By contrast, 'we who have believed enter that rest'. There is no doubt about it. Where a person has once believed truly and genuinely – (notice the tense: 'we who *have* believed') there is no uncertainty about it, that person enters in. This is one of God's glorious affirmations of unvarying and unbreakable certainties. Just as two and two make four, not sometimes but always with unfailing constancy, so God's Word affirms that 'we who have believed' do 'enter that rest'. We can be as sure about it as we can about that other affirmation; 'Whoever believes in the Son has eternal life' (Jn. 3:36).

Only, as we saw earlier, the writer urges his readers to make sure that they have truly believed the gospel, that they are genuine believers, that they have not simply gone along with the crowd under the power of religious fervour without ever having come to personal faith in the Lord Jesus. If they have not personally believed, or if they are unsure of it, let them believe now. It is still open to them to do so, and he quotes Psalm 95:7 again (3:13, 15) to assure them that their day of opportunity has not passed. 'Today if you hear his voice, do not harden your hearts.'

'See to it,' he urges them, 'that none of you has a sinful, unbelieving heart that turns away from the living God'; and to that he adds a special warning. Sin is a deceiver, and without an unbeliever realizing it, it can harden his heart.

The cardinal sin

All sin, of course, is bad and, if continued in, can harden the heart; but the sin which the writer has in mind here, as the context makes abundantly clear, is the sin of unbelief, the sin of hearing the gospel but rebelling against it (3:16), the sin of refusing to enter the promised land, for which God was angry with Israel for forty years (3:17); the sin of disobedience and unbelief (3:18–19). Do notice that all those who came out of Egypt by Moses were guilty of this rebellion, all, that is, except people like Caleb and Joshua (3:16). As we have seen, right from the start they never did believe the gospel; but this sin of unbelief deceived them and eventually so hardened their hearts that they outwardly rebelled against God, rejected Moses' leadership and talked of appointing another captain and of returning to Egypt (Nu. 14:2, 4).

Unbelief, refusal to believe, is of course the cardinal sin, so much so that sometimes in Scripture the term 'sin' is used in the sense of failure or refusal to believe the gospel. So, for instance, our Lord says in John 16:8–9 that when the Holy Spirit comes 'he will convict the world of sin . . .[5] of sin because they do not believe in me'. In other words he is speaking not of individual sins which true believers commit from time to time (and for which there is forgiveness when the believer confesses his sin), but of the basic, cardinal sin of not believing the Saviour.

And this basic sin is very deceptive and can so easily harden a person's heart. It happens all too often that people drift into church membership without any personal experience of the Saviour, or are swept into a profession of faith on the wave of some emotional or ecstatic experience without having been genuinely born again. As time passes by, and the fervour dies away, they come to realise that Christ and his word and his work mean little or nothing to them, because in fact they have never had any personal experience of regeneration, they are not believers. But instead of being alarmed, owning up, seeking the Saviour and personally receiving him, they allow this sin of unbelief to deceive them into thinking that as long as they keep up external appearances of being decent and

[5] So the Greek. The NIV is a paraphrase here.

religious, their lack of personal experience of Christ and salvation does not matter. Eventually their unbelief so hardens their hearts that no preaching of the gospel could ever awaken them to their peril or lead them to repentance and faith in the Saviour. What a tragedy!

Entering God's rest

What then is this rest into which all who have once believed are said to enter? Is it something present or something future?

For the ancient Hebrews, entering their rest meant entering Canaan under Joshua's leadership, destroying all their enemies and settling down at peace in their God-given inheritance in a land flowing with milk and honey.

The Christian's 'inheritance', says Peter, which 'can never perish, spoil or fade', is 'kept in heaven' for us 'who through faith are shielded by God's power until the coming of the salvation that is ready to be revealed in the last time' (1 Pet. 1:4–5). In this sense entry into our rest is still future. And here the wonderful thing is that God's statement in 4:3 assures all who have genuinely believed, that not only do they already enjoy forgiveness and acceptance with God, but they will also most certainly enter that great rest above one day.

That does not mean, however, that we have to wait until we die or until the Lord comes, before we can begin to enjoy our heavenly inheritance. We can here and now by faith enter into some of its blessings. The ancient Israelites' entry into Canaan took place in two phases. From the very moment they entered under Joshua's leadership they began to enjoy the fruit and corn of the land; but their possession and enjoyment of their inheritance was restricted by the fact that they had to fight their many enemies who were entrenched in the land. But at last the time came when all their enemies had been destroyed and the Lord gave them rest on every side; then they were able to take complete possession of their inheritance and enjoy it to the full (Jos. 21:43–45).

In the same way when the Lord comes we shall enter fully into the possession and enjoyment of our inheritance; but even now, as the apostle Paul explains, God has 'raised us up with Christ and seated us with him in the heavenly realms in

Christ Jesus (Eph. 2:6), though at present we still have to 'struggle . . . against the powers of this dark world and against the spiritual forces of evil in the heavenly realms' (Eph. 6:12).

With the ancient Israelites it was, we may remember, the necessity of facing the enemies and fighting them that proved the last straw: confronted with this prospect their unbelieving unregenerate hearts broke out in open rebellion against God and they refused to enter the first phase of the conquest. In vain Moses, Joshua and Caleb pointed out to them that they would not have to fight in their own strength. God was faithful: he would give them the victory, he would give them the land. They were unwilling to face the enemy, and point blank they refused to go in. And, of course, refusing to take part in the first phase of the conquest, they could never take part in the second, never enter at last the rest that God finally gave to his people.

And now we remember the Hebrews to whom our author was writing. Because of their profession of faith in Jesus as the Messiah they had been called upon to stand their ground in a great contest in the face of suffering (10:32). If they could have gone to heaven at once (as the dying thief did) and entered into the final rest without having to face conflict and suffering, they would have been happy enough. As it was, faced with the challenge to suffer and fight in the wars of the Lord, some of them were wavering. Let's hope they soon regained their courage and continued the fight.

What then about us? It will be glorious in heaven; and entry into that great, eternal, rest and inheritance is given to every believer as a completely and genuinely free gift. The rest is God's rest, says the writer (4:3–5), quoting God's phrase, '*my* rest', from the psalm. Just as God did all the work of creation and then rested, so the work on which the eternal rest is built is God's work. We are invited to accept it by faith and share God's rest. But until we finally enter, we must face the enemy and fight. It is the mark of true believers that by God's grace, strengthened by his Spirit, under the captaincy of the Lord Jesus, they are prepared to do so.

Of course there must have been times when under the pressure of conflict and persecution the early Christian felt sorely tempted to give up the fight and try to enjoy a kind of rest by going back to Judaism. After all, God had eventually given their ancestors rest under Joshua in the literal land of Canaan. Wasn't that enough? Wasn't that a big enough inheritance? Why should they trouble themselves about this eternal rest and inheritance in heaven which the Christian apostles preached? Why not be satisfied with their inheritance in this world and not worry about the next?

'Ah, but then', says the writer, 'the rest and inheritance that God gave Israel under Joshua was never the final rest and inheritance which God had in mind for his people. If it had been, God would not have spoken centuries later (in Psalm 95) about another great sabbath of rest which his people, though already in Canaan, were invited to enter.'

The rest Joshua gave them then was at best only a humble prototype of the great eternal rest. Thank God for that! When God talked of 'his rest', open to his people, his promise was not exhausted by the gift of the little land of Palestine in the Middle East. There was far more to it than that. His promise will not be finally fulfilled until every believer has entered God's own rest in the eternal world (4:6–10).

If we are believers, then, we shall resist the temptation to give up the fight, to settle down in this world as though success and attainment in this world were everything. The hope stored up for us in heaven, the hope of one day being fully like Christ, the thought of our inheritance above, will keep us moving on the road as pilgrims, staying in the fight as warriors, and purifying ourselves as saints, even as he is pure (1 Jn. 3:2–3).

Facing God's scrutiny

With that we come to the all-important question: have we personally believed the gospel? Are we believers?

We must answer that question now, not so much to one another, but before the one to whose eyes the deepest recesses of our souls are open to view. Our account is with him (4:12–13). Our behaviour will tell him, whether it tells anybody else or not, whether in our heart of hearts we have believed. Everything is naked and open to his sight; he discerns between our spirit and our soul, and is a critic of the very thoughts of our hearts. He reads us now this very moment as we search our own hearts. Are we really believers? Or are we merely temporary fellow-travellers among the genuine people of God?

Our resource in Christ

Has this put doubts or fear into your mind? There is no need to fear, for we have a high priest, now passed through the heavens, but who once lived in our world. He was tempted in all points as we are, knows the weakness of his people, and bids us come to him. Do we feel uncertain and insecure? Then let us come boldly.

'But,' you say, 'I have sinned today; see all my weakness and my broken resolutions; I want to be a Christian, but I have been a miserable failure. How dare I come?'

Come boldly in spite of it all. You need not come cringingly. Come and stand openly at his mercy seat. He knows and sees all; but come boldly, and you will find mercy for every failure. We richly deserve his judgment, but come boldly to him and you will find his mercy for all past mistakes and his grace to bring you through every difficulty and land you safe in your eternal inheritance. Only keep near to him, and none shall perish; only believe him and rest on him, learning never to trust your own efforts, and you shall find rest of heart now, and enter that great rest above.

Questions

1 In what sense is Jesus both apostle and high priest?
2 Why, do *you* think, is the great warning of 3:7 – 4:13 sandwiched between two passages which talk to us about the Lord Jesus as our high priest?
3 What is the point of the comparison between Christ and Moses in 3:2–6?
4 What in your opinion was the spiritual history of the ancient Israelites who refused to enter Canaan? Were they (a) originally true believers who later lost heart and fell to temptation, or (b) people who had never really believed the gospel?
5 Read 4:2,6 again. Then say (a) what the gospel was which

Moses preached to the Israelites, and (b) what the gospel is nowadays.

6 Read 4:3–9 again. How does the writer prove to Jewish readers that even after God gave Israel rest in Canaan, there still remained a bigger rest to be enjoyed?

7 Hebrews 3:7 – 4:11 is virtually a sermon, in which the writer first cites his text (3:7–11) and then expounds it. How many major 'points' does he make based on the actual wording of his text? Would modern preachers be wise to follow this example of expository preaching?

8 Have you believed the gospel?

9 Are you certain that you will enter God's eternal rest?

10 In what sense do believers have to fight in this present life in order to enjoy their inheritance?

6

OUR HIGH PRIEST AND THE COST OF OBEDIENCE
Hebrews 5:1 – 6:3

Let's take our bearings. We have just worked our way through Hebrews 3 and 4 and found that they contain a very solemn warning. When we eventually encounter chapter 6, we shall find it contains another warning. It will not be so long as the one in chapters 3 and 4; but it is the most famous – and perhaps the most feared – of all the warnings in the letter. It speaks of people who have sinned in such a way that it is impossible to bring them back again to repentance.

Now, many genuine believers with sensitive consciences have read this warning, and without understanding exactly what it is saying, and taking little notice of the context in which it comes, they have jumped to the conclusion that they have, or might have, committed this irreversible and unpardonable sin. Instead, therefore, of being filled with comfort and encouragement at the thought of their high priest and of his gracious ministry towards them – which, according to the writer (see 8:1) is the main point of these middle chapters in Hebrews – they have become haunted by fear and anxiety. Their zeal and effectiveness for the Lord have been diminished, and in some cases their physical and psychological health has been undermined.

It is no cure for this kind of trouble to shut one's eyes to the warning in chapter 6 or to pretend it does not really mean what it says. When we come to it we shall face it as squarely and as honestly as we can. But if we have any respect for the Word of God and for the inspiration of the Holy Spirit, we shall carefully observe the proportion which he himself has imposed on the details of his message in these central chapters of Hebrews. If we start at 5:1 and work our way through to

8:1, and if we get the impression the Holy Spirit intended us to get, the main thought that will grip us will be: 'I have a high priest! Thank God, I have. And such a high priest at that!' (7:26; 8:1).

Many of us have too small an idea of our Lord's high priesthood. We speak of him in that capacity as though he held a sinecure, as though we should be saved anyway, even if he did not minister as a high priest. But that is not true. We would all be lost if we did not have a high priest who constantly and incessantly intercedes for us. We began our spiritual path when we realized that his sacrifice put away all the guilt of our sin. We look back to that with joy. But there is more to his saving ministry than that. As chapters 3 and 4 have reminded us, it is not enough to begin the path of spiritual pilgrimage. Beginning would all be in vain if we did not continue all the way through our spiritual journey and enter our heavenly inheritance at last. How then shall we continue? How can we be sure of entering in at last?

The answer is: we have a high priest! In spite of our failures in the past, through him there is mercy for us at God's throne: we need not abandon our confession of faith. In spite of the temptations ahead, he understands what temptation means, and through him there will be grace to help us in our time of need. He is able to save us completely (7:25).

What is more, our high priest has himself gone through the heavens, says 4:14. He has sat down at the right hand of the Majesty in heaven, says 8:1. That is, he has already entered and arrived in the heaven towards which we are making our way. He has gone before us (so NIV) not merely because he started out before we did and therefore has arrived first. He has entered heaven on our behalf as our official forerunner, or precursor, announcing to all concerned that we are coming on behind, and by his ministry as our high priest guaranteeing our eventual safe arrival (6:20).

If this then is the main point of these central chapters, our main task will be to make certain we understand it and all its far-reaching implications. To help us do so, the writer will now point out what was required in Israel's ancient high priests if they were going to minister effectively to the people; and then he will show us how Christ meets, and more than meets, those requirements.

The duty and qualifications of any high priest

First of all, his duty. Any ordinary human high priest, whoever he might be, 'is selected from among men and is appointed to represent them in matters related to God, to offer gifts and sacrifices for sins' (5:1).

If his duty on behalf of those he represents is to offer gifts and sacrifices for sins, it is obvious that the people he represents are sinners, people who have gone astray through ignorance (5:2). Their ignorance might be very trying and their sins obnoxious. But their representative before God must be able to deal gently with them. The word translated 'deal gently with' means 'to control and moderate his feelings' towards them. He must never lose his temper with them (as Moses once did with Israel, and thereby earned God's severe censure on himself, see Nu. 20:7–12). He must not be indulgent on the one hand, nor heartlessly severe on the other. However much they might tax his patience he must always treat them with kind consideration, mercifully remembering their weaknesses. And in this of course he can be greatly helped by simply remembering his own weaknesses. The people are not the only ones to sin! He too sins, and has to offer sin-offerings to cover his own sins as well as theirs.

And secondly his appointment. Granted he can come up to these requirements, that does not automatically confer on him the right to claim the office of high priest. Nor can he appoint himself. To become high priest a man has to be called by God to that office. Even Aaron had to wait for that call.

Christ's right to priesthood

What right then has Jesus to claim the office of high priest? A Hebrew Christian might well ask himself the question, and his unconverted Jewish friends certainly would. In Israel it was not enough for a man to be physically, mentally, morally and spiritually suited to being a high priest. According to the Old Testament law relating to priesthood – and both non-Christian and Christian Jews accepted that law as laid down by God – the high-priesthood was like an hereditary

129

monarchy.[1] To be high priest you had first to belong to the correct tribe, the tribe of Levi; and then in addition you had to be a member of the right family within that tribe and physically descended by the right line of descent from the original high priest Aaron. That is what is meant by being a high priest 'after the order' or 'in the line' of Aaron. Any attempt by anyone from some other tribe or some other family within the tribe to become high priest carried the death penalty (Nu. 18:7). So when at one stage Korah, Dathan and Abiram (the last two not even of the tribe of Levi) rebelled against the established order and attempted to seize the priesthood, God took unprecedented steps to show his displeasure: the earth opened and swallowed them up (Nu. 16:20–35). How then could Jesus of the tribe of Judah claim to be high priest?

Christ's divine appointment

The answer is, of course, that Jesus has not arrogated this office to himself (5:5). As Messiah, Son of God, he has been appointed high priest by God. Nor is it that his followers, out of excessive devotion, have dreamt up the idea that God has appointed him high priest. The Old Testament itself announced that Messiah would be appointed to that office. Indeed, the very one who said to him 'You are my Son; today I have begotten you' – and the announcement is recorded, as we have seen, in Psalm 2 – said in another psalm, namely Psalm 110:4, 'You are a priest for ever, in the order of Melchizedek.'[2]

This announcement that Messiah would be a high priest after the order not of Aaron but of Melchizedek showed that Messiah would not disregard the Old Testament law and attempt to get himself installed illegally as a high priest in Aaron's line. This was a point of great practical importance for the early Christians. In the course of comparatively recent (post-Maccabean) history, the nation had been bitterly divided when, for political reasons, men who were not of the correct line according to the law had nevertheless assumed

---

[1] After the loss of the monarchy, the high-priesthood became in fact more and more a political as well as a religious office.
[2] For a fuller discussion of Melchizedek, see pp. 160ff.

office as high priest. Jesus, by contrast, never attempted to minister even as an ordinary priest, let alone as high priest, in the temple at Jerusalem. When he became high-priest, it would not be in connection with the Jerusalem temple and its Aaronic order of priests at all.

At the same time the announcement carried another far-reaching implication. The Aaronic high-priesthood was like an hereditary monarchy in another respect. Just as by definition there cannot be two monarchs at any one time ruling over the same people, so according to the Old Testament there could not be two high priests presiding over the nation, one of Aaron's line and another belonging to some other order. The announcement in the Psalms that the Messiah would one day be appointed high priest after a different order, that of Melchizedek, carried a startling implication: when that happened, the earlier law relating to the Aaronic priesthood would have to be cancelled, and the Aaronic high-priesthood made obsolete. But this is a topic that the writer will deal with more fully later (see p. 163). For the moment let us consider another implication of staggering significance.

Only remember what we are talking about. We are discussing an office invented for the purpose of looking after ignorant and straying people (not of course 'disobedient' people in the sense we were thinking of in our last chapter) and designed to bring them, in spite of their weaknesses and wanderings, safely through their spiritual pilgrimage home to God's heaven. How important is this office of looking after such ignorant, wayward weaklings? To our astonishment we discover that it is an office of immeasurable majesty. It is doubly so. First, because of the transcendent glory of the one who confers the office: he is the almighty God. And secondly, because of the unique relationship with God of the one on whom the office is conferred. The proclamation of conferment brings both together. It is the very one, observes our writer, who said to Messiah, 'You are my Son; today I have begotten you,' who also says, 'You are a priest for ever, in the order of Melchizedek.'

Contemplate too the indescribable majesty of the appointment ceremony. In our third chapter, we followed Psalm 2's graphic depiction of the triumph of our Lord's resurrection and ascension: Jesus, as God's King installed by God on

131

God's holy hill of Zion, declaring before the entire universe the divine decree: '[The Lord] said to me, "You are my Son, today I have begotten you." ' Now we listen as the composer of Psalm 110 takes over as commentator on this same awesome occasion. We hear first the Lord God almighty address the words of the invitation to the ascended Lord Messiah: 'Sit at my right hand until I make your enemies a footstool for your feet' (Ps. 110:1). And then as the ceremony proceeds, we hear the Almighty utter the great oath of appointment: 'The Lord has sworn and will not change his mind: You are a priest for ever in the order of Melchizedek' (Ps. 110:4).

'Priest for whom?' we ask; for instinct tells us that if induction into this office is attended with such exalted ceremony, the office itself must be of cosmic significance, its objectives infinitely important, and its beneficiaries blessed beyond all possible calculation. 'For whom is he priest?' we repeat.

And the answer comes back 'For those who have trusted the Saviour.'

'What for?' we ask.

'To save them from their ignorance and wandering, to save them completely, and to present them faultless at last before the presence of his glory with exceeding joy (*cf.* Jude 24, AV/ KJV).

Christ's divinely certified qualifications

But it is not enough for a priest to be divinely appointed; he must have the necessary experience and qualifications. And chief among those qualifications is that he must have the experience and ability to deal gently with the ignorant and erring because he understands their weaknesses. Of what use is a high priest, even if divinely appointed, if he does not understand us well enough to understand why we need his ministry?

And here you might think that our Lord's divine Sonship and sinless character unfitted rather than fitted him to be our high priest. An ordinary merely human high priest, as was earlier pointed out, would not find it too difficult to deal gently with the ignorant and erring. A sinner himself, he was constantly obliged to offer sin-offerings for his own sins.

He could hardly fail therefore to understand the people's weaknesses that involved them in so much sinning and himself in so much sacrificing for them. But our Lord was sinless. Never once did he have to offer a sin-offering for himself. How then and in what sense can he understand our weaknesses? The answer is to be found in his incarnation.

First, he understands by personal experience the weakness that is inherent in being human – not in being a sinful man, but in being a man at all, even at man's very best. He was hungry and thirsty; he felt tired and sleepy. He felt the need for companionship and the distress of loneliness and rejection. He felt pain and sorrow. These things were not sinful but an essential part of what it means to be human. Son of God though he was, and ever continued to be, he became really and genuinely human.

And in the second place, Son of God though he was, he learned by experience the cost of obeying God in a fallen and sinful world like ours.

We must be careful with the translation here in 5:8 'Although he was a son . . .' (or something similar), say many translations. But the verse is not implying that he was one son among many, or that he was a son of God in the sense that a believer is a son of God, and that in spite of it, he learned obedience. It would make no sense to say of us that *although* we are sons, we have to learn obedience. It is precisely *because* we are sons, and not illegitimates, that we are disciplined by the Father (12:7–10). And if the verse were saying that Christ is a son just like us, there would be nothing remarkable in his learning obedience through suffering. The wonder is that being the unique Son of God with right of command over every created being and force in the entire universe, nevertheless, Son though he was, he learned obedience, and learned it by suffering.[3]

Moreover, as the eternal Son of the Father, he did not have to be taught to do the Father's will. He did not have to learn *to obey*. He had always obeyed flawlessly. But doing God's will in heaven is nothing but joy and gladness; and if as the pre-incarnate Son he had confined himself to heaven and left

[3] For a most helpful comment on the translation of this verse, see F. F. Bruce, *The Epistle to the Hebrews* (Marshall, Morgan and Scott, 1965), pp. 102–103.

our world unvisited, he need never have learned, or paid the price of, obedience to God in this ungodly world. And who could have been surprised if he had done so? Who could have complained?

But then how could he have learned what it costs to obey? And if he did not learn that by experience himself, how could he understand what it costs us to obey him?

And so he came and lived in our world and learned. Strong, sinless as he was, courageous to stand in the face of the bitterest opposition and the most painful physical and mental suffering, the experience nevertheless brought him to loud crying and tears. Let us recall Gethsemane. I know that when we stand in its dark shadows, we stand in a mysterious place, the juncture of the human and divine. We must take the shoes off our feet. The ground is holy. Worship rather than analysis becomes us. But when our Lord prayed, 'Abba, Father, everything is possible for you, Take this cup from me. Yet not what I will, but what you will' (Mk. 14:36), he said what he meant and he meant what he said. There was no insincerity. He was not pretending that he did not want to drink the cup when all the while he did. And it certainly was not osten-tatious-stage-show calculated to heighten the effect when later he would give in and say 'Your will be done'. In utter sincerity with bitter anguish and tears he cried to God to spare him having to drink that cup.

But the Father's will was that he drink it. So he willed God's will and drank the cup, unreservedly, unresentfully, to its last drop – and discovered by experience the cost of obedience. 'Son though he was,' says Scripture, 'he learned obedience from what he suffered.'

Scripture is not ashamed to let us know that when he faced the cost involved in obedience, his prayers were accompanied by loud cries and tears. His tears were not sinful, were not, as sometimes they are with us, the expression of frustration at not being allowed to have our own way. His heart was submissive to God and his prayers were heard and answered because of his reverent submission to God's will. But the cost and pain of drinking the cup, of 'being made sin for us' – how could he pretend he enjoyed it? Or pretend he did not feel it? To be crucified on the false charge of being a heretic and blasphemer, and then to have God himself forsake him

(Mk. 14:33–34; 15:34) – how would he not weep?

But his prayers were answered. The night of suffering was followed by the morning of resurrection and by God's vindication of his faith. Qualified now by his obedience and suffering, Christ has become the source of eternal salvation for all who obey him, and officially designated by God to be our high priest.

His obedience and ours

'For all who obey him'. We should notice the term: not simply 'for all who believe him', but 'for all who obey him'. We must heighten our ideas of Christianity. From the very start we are called to yield Christ the obedience of faith (Rom. 16:26). It is not that we are to obey a code of laws in order to be saved. We do not earn or merit salvation by our obedience. But we are saved on the condition that we receive him as Lord. He is the author and source of eternal salvation. There is no insecurity or doubt. Salvation cannot be cut short half way: it is an eternal salvation. But he requires all who desire the eternal salvation to commit themselves utterly and implicitly and without question to him as their Lord as well as their Saviour. To all who do so he is prepared to accept total responsibility for their eternal salvation. He will do all; he will save them for ever. But they must be prepared to commit all implicitly to him.

Some will object that we are making things too hard, and imperilling the doctrine of salvation by grace. They urge that all we have to do to be saved is to believe in Jesus as our Saviour. Do that and we are eternally secure. Then after that we can make up our mind whether we wish to go further and become loyal disciples of Christ by receiving and obeying him as Lord.

That is not true, as we saw in the last chapter. The gospel preached to the ancient Israelites in Egypt was not: 'All you have to do if you want to escape from Egypt and enter the promised land is to shelter behind the blood of the passover lamb. After that you can decide whether or not you wish to commit yourself completely to Moses as your captain and follow him and God across the desert.' No salvation was offered to Israel that did not require them to commit themselves unconditionally to Moses' captaincy right from the start.

And so it is with us. We are required right from the very start to yield ourselves in principle to the complete lordship of Christ. Certainly it is altogether by grace and through faith in Christ, who was 'lifted up' on the cross for us, that we are born again. But we are not born again into the kingdom of God on the understanding that once we are inside the kingdom, we shall still be free to make up our minds whether we intend to obey the King or not.

It is true of course that having committed ourselves in principle to the lordship of Christ at the moment of our salvation, we often falter in our practical obedience. But then the Holy Spirit will do for us what he did for the first readers of our letter. He will take us back to our original confession, and if that confession was genuine, we will repent and seek his grace and strength to work out in practice the obedience we originally professed.

It goes without saying that such obedience can sometimes be hard. We should not under-estimate the difficulty and cost of obedience. But then that is why we have a high priest fully qualified to minister to us, because he learned what obedience involves by what he suffered.

An unfortunate condition

But now we – or rather the writer of the letter – meets a difficulty. His readers had been professing Christians for a considerable time, so long indeed that they might reasonably have been expected to be able by this time to teach others. Unfortunately, they had remained spiritual babies. Far from being able to teach others, they needed someone to teach them the elementary truths of God's Word all over again. Like infants they needed to be fed with milk not solid food. And being infants they had no experience of the Word of righteousness and no practice in training their spiritual perception to distinguish between what was spiritually good and what was spiritually bad.

Now, however, they were in a critical situation of testing and trial and they desperately needed to know as much as ever they could about the high priest in the order of Melchizedek. But the writer fears that it will be too much for them to take in. If so, it would be cruelly sad; for these were the very things they needed to know to bring them safely through their crisis.

It is always so. If we remain infants and are careless about our spiritual growth and education, all may go fair for a while; but let the storm rise and the crisis come, and we shall find that the very things that we need to know and to grasp hold of to keep us and bring us through the storm, we shall not know, and therefore shall not be able to grasp hold of. These Hebrews were being tried to the limit, their faith was being sorely tested, basic faith without which they would not have been believers at all. If only they had been able to understand something of the ministry of their high priest!

We remember that Peter found himself in a similar situation. How it must have buoyed up his spirit, even when he went out and wept bitterly at his dismal failure, as he thought again and again of the Lord's gracious promise, 'I have prayed for you, Simon, that your faith may not fail' (Lk. 22:32). And Peter came round, with all that that meant, to face his fellow disciples again, to face the Lord again, to face the public again, after such a dismal defeat. Peter came round, and he owed it to the fact that he had a high priest, and knew it. Let us be sure, when the sun shines and things go easily and we feel like singing all the day long, that we take care to store our minds and hearts with the riches of God's holy Word that in the evil day we may be able to stand, and, having done all, to stand.

But these Hebrews not only did not know much if anything about their high priest and his ministry; the writer fears that even when he proceeds to tell them – as he does in chapters 7 and 8 – they will find it difficult to take in. Why? Not so much because, as the NIV puts it, they were slow to learn. Many of us, even when we are doing our best to keep both ears open and are keen to learn, find learning and grasping the point a rather slow business, though we get there in the end. No, the reason why it would be difficult for these people to take in what they were told about Jesus as the great high priest was that they had become sluggish in hearing, that is, they were not too keen to hear what they were told.

They had not always been like that; but they had become

so. When they first heard the gospel, and accepted it, they may not have realized fully its implications: that it would make their Judaism with its earthly high priest, and its order of priests distinct from the laity, its repeated sacrifices offered to secure forgiveness, its incense and vestments – it would make all those things obsolete, and would require them eventually to abandon them. And so they received the gospel with joy. But now that its implications were beginning to dawn on them that they could not have *both* Jesus as high priest and head of the church *and* Aaron or any other man on earth as high priest and head of the church, they were not keen to hear too much about it. Instinctively they would fear that if they learned too much about Jesus as the high priest in the order of Melchizedek, it would face them with decisions which they did not wish to take. So they would prefer to dub this teaching about the Lord's high-priesthood as 'advanced', 'too difficult for ordinary people like us', and stay comfortable behind the protection of ignorance.

Professor F. F. Bruce describes the situation well. 'Their sluggishness showed itself in a disposition to settle down at the point which they had reached, since to go farther would have meant too complete a severing of old ties. To such people the exposition of the high-priestly service of Christ, with the corollary that the old order of priesthood and sacrifice had been abolished once for all, might well have been unacceptable; the intellect is not over-ready to entertain an idea that the heart finds unpalatable.'[4]

Pressing on to perfection

What will the writer do then? Will he say to himself, 'Ah well, with their background these people, understandably, are not too keen to hear about the Lord's high priesthood; so let's keep off the topic and concentrate on things on which non-Christian Jews and Christian Jews can agree'? Certainly not!

There are such things, of course, and he proceeds to list them (6:1–4). He calls them 'the elementary teachings about Christ' (NIV), or more literally, 'the doctrine of the first prin-

[4] *Op. cit.*, pp. 108–109.

ciples of the Christ' (*i.e.* the Messiah). Look closely at the items in the list: repentance from acts that lead to death, faith in God, instruction about baptisms (note the plural: it is not talking about Christian baptism – there is only one Christian baptism – but about the significance of Jewish ablutions), and about the laying on of hands, the resurrection of the dead and eternal judgment. There is nothing in this that an ancient Jew (other than a Sadducee) could not accept. And Christian Jews accepted these things too. They, as well as non-Christian Jews, called on people to repent and exercise faith in God. They too preached the resurrection of the dead and warned of eternal judgment. These things lay at the very foundation of their evangelistic preaching.

But notice at the same time that there is nothing distinctively Christian about the items in this list. There is no mention that Jesus is the Christ, no mention of his deity or atoning sacrifice or priesthood, no reference to his personal resurrection or to his second coming. No true Christian, therefore, would or could be content with this list, as it stands, as a statement of the way of salvation. The items in the list are foundational: but a foundation is no use at all unless it is built on. To get a house, or whatever it is you want, you must go beyond the foundation; not abandon it, but build on top of it. To be content with its foundation, to keep re-laying it, but to refuse to go further and build on it, would be to make a nonsense of having a foundation at all.

The writer, therefore, cannot possibly allow his readers to settle down with these foundational things that are common to Judaism and Christianity. The foundation was good. But now that the Lord Jesus has come there is no salvation without or apart from his deity, his sacrifice, his resurrection and ascension, his present high-priestly ministry, his second coming, his exercise of the final judgment. To insist on settling down with the foundation and refuse to go on to full acceptance of the Lord Jesus, his once-and-for-all sacrifice and his priestly ministry – that would spell disaster. They must go on; and if they are true believers they will. And if we are true believers, so shall we.

Questions

1 What part does Christ's ministry as high priest play in our salvation? How important a part is it?

2 How would you prove to a Jew the validity of Christ's priesthood? What Old Testament passages would you refer to?

3 In what sense did the Son of God 'learn obedience from what he suffered'? And why did he have to?

4 When it says that Christ has become the source of eternal salvation for all who *obey* him (5:9), does that contradict the doctrine of salvation by grace.

5 Why was it so important to get the readers of the letter to go beyond the things that are common to Christianity and Judaism?

7

ON TO PERFECTION
Hebrews 6:4–20

In our last session we saw how vitally important it was that the Hebrew Christians should not rest content with those things that are common to Judaism and Christianity. They must leave those elementary things and move forward.

But let us now notice what it is they are to move forward to. 'Let us go on unto perfection,' says the AV/KJV. 'Let us . . . go on to maturity,' says the NIV. Both translations can claim to be correct; but the question is: What does the writer mean by the term 'perfection' or 'maturity'? What kind of perfection or maturity is he talking about?

What is 'perfection'?

The larger context will tell us. These words 'perfection' and 'perfect' (adjective and verb) now begin to occur quite frequently in the flow of the argument. Here are some of the occurrences.[1]

Hebrews 7:11: 'If *perfection* could have been attained through the Levitical priesthood (for on the basis of it the law was given to the people), why was there still need for another priest to come – one in the order of Melchizedek, not in the order of Aaron?' Or again, Hebrews 7:18–19: 'The former regulation [*i.e.* about Aaron's dynasty of priests] is set aside because it was weak and useless (for the law *made nothing perfect*), and a better hope is introduced, by which we draw near to God.'

---

[1] A full list would be: noun, *teleiotēs*, 6:1; noun, *teleiōsis*, 7:11; adjective *teleios*, 5:14; 9:11; verb *teleioō*, 2:10; 5:9, 7:19, 28; 9:9; 10:1, 14; 11:40; 12:23. These words do not of course always have exactly the same connotation in every instance.

The topic is clear enough: it is priesthood. And the contrast is clear enough too. The writer is not contrasting two different priesthoods in Christianity, one less, and the other more, mature. He is contrasting Christ's priesthood with Aaron's. Aaron's priesthood was not evil: but it was weak and useless in the sense that it could not make anything perfect. But Christ's priesthood can. The readers therefore are to leave Aaron's priesthood behind and embrace Christ's.

Look at Hebrews 8:2. Here we are told that our Lord, now ascended, 'serves in the sanctuary, the true tabernacle set up by the Lord, not man'. And 9:11 adds that 'he went through *the greater and more perfect* tabernacle'.

Again the topic is clear enough. It is not a question of two Christian tabernacles, one more mature and perfect than the other. The contrast is between Judaism's sanctuary on earth and the heavenly sanctuary in which our Lord now ministers. In calling this latter 'the *true* tabernacle', the writer is not implying that Judaism's earthly sanctuary was false. But it was at best only 'a copy and shadow of what is in heaven' (8:5). The heavenly sanctuary into which Christ now admits his people (see 10:19–22) is 'more perfect' because it is the real thing. So when he urges his readers to 'press on to perfection', he is urging them to leave behind Judaism's earthly sanctuary with its lights, incense, vestments, altars and laver with its holy water, and in their worship of God to draw near in spirit into this more perfect, spiritual and heavenly sanctuary into which Christ has gained us admittance.

Take one more example. At 10:1 our writer points out that Judaism's sacrifices, repeated though they were endlessly every year, could never make perfect those who drew near to worship. But what they could never do, Christ's sacrifice has done. Says 10:14, 'By one sacrifice *he has made perfect* for ever those who are being made holy.'

Once more it is not a question of two stages within Christian experience, one less, and the other more, mature. It is a question of Judaism's many sacrifices and Christ's one sacrifice. Judaism's sacrifices had to be constantly offered all over again because they could not make 'the worshipper perfect as far as his conscience was concerned' (so 9:9, literally). Christ's sacrifice never needs to be repeated because it can and does make perfect – has, indeed, made perfect – all who trust him.

Press on to perfection? Why of course! Who wouldn't? Who would want to stay with Judaism's imperfect priesthood and inadequate sacrifices that could never give you a conscience permanently at peace with God, when you could enjoy the benefits of the perfect sacrifice and priesthood of Christ?

Yet the readers of the letter were faltering. They had originally professed to believe that Jesus was the Messiah, risen and ascended to heaven. But for some time now they were obviously beginning to sense the implications of really believing Jesus to be the Messiah. Jesus was also high priest. You couldn't have two high priests. If you were going to accept Jesus as high priest, you must let Judaism's high priest (and all the rest of its priesthood) go. Jesus' death was the perfect sacrifice for sin. You couldn't base your acceptance with God *both* on his perfect sacrifice *and* on Judaism's inadequate sacrifices. If you accepted Christ's sacrifice, you needed none other; and to carry on offering further sacrifices would be an insult both to him and to God.

The alternatives

They had to choose, then, either to stay with Judaism or to press on to the perfection of Christ's sacrifice and salvation. What would they do? What did their faltering mean?

It was a momentous question. To realize oneself to be a sinner; to repent; to believe Jesus to be God's Messiah; and then, in spite of some faltering, to go on from that to discover with ever deepening understanding and increasing delight that Jesus is the true high priest who supersedes all others, that his sacrifice perfects the conscience and makes all other sacrifices obsolete – that is wonderful indeed. That *is* salvation.

On the other hand, to realize oneself a sinner; to repent; to profess to believe that Jesus is God's Messiah; but then to reject his priesthood and his sacrifice and to cling to Judaism's priesthood and sacrifices – that would be to make a nonsense of the whole way of salvation. It would be worse, infinitely worse, than the ancient Israelites who came out of Egypt but then refused to enter the promised land.

Which of these two alternatives would correctly describe the readers of our letter? The writer eventually states (6:9) that in his heart of hearts he really thinks that they belong to the first alternative; he thinks there is evidence in their past lives that they are genuinely saved. They will therefore eventually respond to his exhortation. They will overcome their faltering. They will go on to perfection. Hence his tactics. In spite of their apparent reluctance to hear about our Lord's high-priesthood and its implications, he is determined to press on and tell them about it.

But suppose after all they did belong to the second alternative – and he admits in 6:9 that he has spoken as if he thought they did, even though in his heart he thought differently – what then? Will he, rather than offend them, content himself with general moral and spiritual truths such as both Christians and Jews can accept? No! Of course not. He is concerned for people's salvation; and if they reject Christ's priesthood and sacrifice, there is no salvation for them. He cannot and will not tone down the gospel and concentrate simply on general moral and spiritual truths which everybody, non-Christian and Christian, can accept.

Well then, will he try to bring them back to repentance again? They would certainly appear to need it. To profess to believe that Jesus is the Messiah, to profess to repent of his execution by the nation, and yet subsequently to reject his deity, his once-for-all sacrifice and his high-priestly ministry – that would be a contradiction in terms. It would show that whatever they had professed in the past, they did not now believe that Jesus was the Messiah. They must have gone back on their profession of repentance and faith.

So try to bring them back to repentance again? 'No,' says the writer, 'it's no use attempting the impossible. People like this it is impossible to renew to repentance.'

The impossibility of renewal to repentance

These are exceedingly solemn words; but whatever we do, we must not reduce or minimize their meaning. When the writer says of some people that it is impossible to bring them back to repentance, he means 'impossible', nothing less. What kind of people are they, then? And what exactly is it they have done?

It is often said that they are true believers who have grown cold in heart, have lost their first love (Rev. 2:4), have made some wrong decision or other and have wandered away from the Lord. Such things do unfortunately happen to true believers. But how could it then be said that it is impossible to bring them back to repentance? Is it a fact that if you make a mistake, or at some point in your Christian life you grow cold and worldly, you can never be renewed to repentance on that score? Of course not. If it were, it would make a farce of Christ's ministry as our great high priest. In his famous letters to the seven churches (Rev. 1 – 3), in which he has to rebuke his people for leaving their first love, for immorality, for serious disloyalty and false doctrine, Christ nevertheless constantly calls on his people to repent (Rev. 2:5, 16, 21; 3:3); and he certainly would not do that, if it were impossible for them to repent of these things anyway. Who has never grown worldly at times and cold? Who could claim that he had always behaved consistently with his faith? Let me be the first to confess I have not; and I owe it to the Lord's high-priestly ministry that I have been brought back to repentance many times. And so, I suspect, it is with many Christians.

So let us notice exactly what it is that the writer says it is impossible to do. He does not say that it is impossible for God to forgive them. God will forgive anyone who truly repents and believes. But these people will not repent; and there can be no forgiveness without repentance.

Now whatever else is involved in repentance, its basic element is what the Greek word for 'repentance' means: a change of mind. So what the writer is saying is that you will never get these people to change their minds again. Why not? And over what?

Well, in the first place they have already been enlightened once (6:4).

'There you are,' you say, 'they were saved, then. They must have been, if they were enlightened.'

But wait a minute. Is being enlightened the same as being saved? Surely not. John 1:9 says that the true light sooner or later enlightens (it is the same Greek word as in our passage here in Hebrews) everyone. Does that mean that everyone is then saved? Sadly, no. To be enlightened is certainly a necessary part in the process of being saved; but it is not the same thing as being saved. It is all too possible to be enlightened, and then to shut one's eyes against the light, and to do it knowingly and deliberately. There is no salvation for those who do that.

It is indeed an exceedingly serious thing to do, which in turn is what makes 'being enlightened' such a solemn matter. If being enlightened is followed by repentance and faith, it is salvation and glory. If it is followed by persistent rejection of Christ, it is fatal, and eternally fatal.

Take, as an example, Saul of Tarsus, that terrible persecutor of the early Christians. Talking subsequently of his unconverted days, he says, 'I was shown mercy because I acted in ignorance and unbelief' (1 Tim. 1:13). At first sight it is difficult to see how he could claim to have acted in ignorance. After all, he was a highly educated man, and was acting, you might have thought, with the utmost deliberation and resolve. And so, of course, he was at one level. 'I was convinced', he said, 'that I ought to do all that was possible to oppose the name of Jesus of Nazareth' (Acts 26:9). But at another level he was acting in complete ignorance: he had not yet been enlightened. And that was the reason, he explains, why he was shown mercy, *because* he acted in ignorance and unbelief.

But then he was enlightened by the risen Christ, dramatically so. Happily he was not disobedient to the heavenly vision, as he put it (Acts 26:19). But if he had been, he could no longer have claimed to be acting in ignorance.

'Yes,' you say, 'but the people envisaged in Hebrews 6 have not only been enlightened. It says they have tasted the heavenly gift, have shared in the Holy Spirit and have tasted the goodness of the word of God and the powers of the coming age (6:4–6). That surely implies that they have gone beyond being enlightened, and have actually been born again.'

Well, not necessarily so at all. Let us notice the terminology the writer uses here, and try to get at its meaning by putting it in its historical context.

He talks of tasting the powers of the age to come. Now that is language which we Gentiles scarcely use. You would,

146

I imagine, think me a bit odd if I asked you, 'Have you tasted the powers of the age to come?' But such language would make immediate sense to Jews of New Testament times. They thought in terms of two ages, the present age and the coming age of the Messiah. The present age was full of evil; the coming age of the Messiah would be an age of millennial bliss and happiness.

Now when Jesus came and claimed to be the Messiah, the Jewish nation, led by their rulers, crucified him. They did it, we should have thought, with their eyes open. In spite of all his unique miracles, they deliberately put him to death. Yet Peter, when he talked to them after the resurrection, said, 'Now, brothers, I know that you acted in ignorance, as did your leaders' (Acts 3:17). In ignorance? Yes. They had not yet been personally enlightened by the Holy Spirit. They were in darkness when they did that foul deed. So there was mercy for them, even for the crucifixion of Christ, if they would have it; and Peter called on them to repent, and assured them that upon repentance they would receive the gift of the Holy Spirit (Acts 2:38).

Moreover, to authenticate the gospel and demonstrate that Jesus was indeed risen from the dead the apostles were empowered to do outstanding miracles: a congenitally lame man was healed (Acts 3), as were the sick and the demon-possessed, so much so that people laid their sick relatives on beds in the streets that as Peter passed by his shadow might fall on them and they be healed (Acts 5:15–16). Later in Acts we are told that God did extraordinary miracles through Paul: 'handkerchiefs and aprons that had touched him were taken to the sick, and their illnesses were cured' (19:11–12).

What tremendous evidence this was and how irrefutable, that Jesus was indeed the Messiah. These mighty signs and wonders, as Peter pointed out, were nothing less than anticipations of the time when God would restore everything as he promised long ago through his holy prophets, in a word foretastes of the Messianic age to come. That age would dawn with the second coming of Christ. Meanwhile Israel must repent and turn to God (Acts 3:17–26).

The multitudes, then, that were physically healed certainly had evidence that the prophets' promises were true, God's word was good. Their healing was effected by the power of the Holy Spirit. They tasted the powers of the age to come. They had overwhelming evidence that Jesus was the Messiah. Does that mean that they were all saved? that the moment Peter's shadow fell on them and the Holy Spirit healed them, they were simultaneously born again? that Paul's apron, when they touched it, effected not only physical healing but spiritual regeneration? Hardly! They had been given a share of the Holy Spirit and had received tremendous physical benefit from it; but receiving physical benefit through the power of the Holy Spirit is not the same thing as being born again spiritually.

Some of them, however, received undeniable *spiritual* benefit from the Holy Spirit. He enlightened them. Like Saul of Tarsus, in spite of seeing many miracles performed, they had continued to reject Christ. But they acted in ignorance – until the moment came when the Holy Spirit by his direct and personal operation enlightened them. Now their eyes were opened and they knew through the Holy Spirit's illumination that Jesus was the Messiah. They had partaken of the Holy Spirit, they had tasted the heavenly gift in a real and wonderful way.

Does that mean that having been enlightened, they all went on to believe in the Lord genuinely, and to be saved? Sadly, no. Some were like the Jews mentioned in John 8:31–58. They believed on Jesus, says Scripture, so we must not say they didn't. But what was their faith worth? An hour or so later, when they discovered what Jesus actually taught, what his salvation would imply and what truly believing on him would mean, they rejected his teaching out of hand. He then pointed out that they were not children of God. They were of their father, the devil – were, and always had been. And at that they picked up stones and drove him out of the temple. So it was after the resurrection: some who professed to believe, subsequently fell away.

But if having once been enlightened a Jew (or anyone else for that matter) deliberately rejects Christ, what is his position? In the first place he can no longer say he is acting in ignorance. He has lost the ground on which mercy could be shown him.

Secondly, he now takes upon himself personally the responsibility for crucifying the Son of God. The nation

148

crucified him, denying that he was the Son of God. But they did it in ignorance. This man personally, not now deceived by the priests, nor any longer in ignorance, but having felt the power of the Holy Spirit, with his eyes enlightened, knowing all the facts, nevertheless deliberately takes on himself the personal responsibility for crucifying the Son of God (6:6). That is what is means for such a person to cling to, or go back to, Judaism.

You cannot belong to Judaism and accept the deity of Jesus; and if he is not the Son of God, then he deserved to be crucified. If he is the Son of God, you cannot remain in Judaism. It has to be one or the other. Those who go back personally declare that they agree with the crucifixion of Jesus Christ. Of such people God himself has plainly said that it is literally impossible to renew them again to repentance.

What it means to reject the Holy Spirit

But God is not hard. Please observe what God actually says. He does not, I repeat, say that it is impossible to forgive their sins. He does not say that he is not prepared to forgive them. That is not the point at all. He says it is impossible to get them to change their minds after this. You will never get them to repent, or to have anything to do with Christ.

'But', you protest, 'that's saying a lot, isn't it? How do you know?' For this simple reason. The only thing that could possibly bring them to repentance is the Holy Spirit's power. Once they have felt that and have deliberately rejected it, there is no other power in God's universe that could possibly reach them. The Holy Spirit, after all, is God. Reject him finally and knowingly, and there is nothing else that could save you.

Take the illustration that is given. Here is a piece of land. The rain comes down from heaven, moistens the earth and causes it to produce a useful crop. That's excellent: it receives God's blessing. Here's another piece of land. The same rain, of exactly the same quality, comes down and waters it; but sadly the ground produces only thorns and thistles. What can we do about that? 'Oh,' you say, 'I should give it a little bit more rain.' But that won't do any good. The more rain, the more thorns. What can be done? Nothing can be done. Once a person has had his eyes opened by God's Holy Spirit, has seen the truth, has perhaps made intellectual profession, and then has gone back and rejected it all deliberately – when someone has once done that there is no more hope. I don't doubt that God would save them if he could; but God himself has no power greater than that of the Holy Spirit by which to renew them to repentance.

Let me pause to apply the lesson to anyone who may be reading this book. If the Holy Spirit has enlightened you, and you see the truth, and you know what you ought to do, but you have not yet taken the step of placing your faith in Christ and of yielding him the obedience of your heart, then do it now; in case you end by finally rejecting the Holy Spirit, and then never wish any more to be saved, and are lost eternally.

The evidence of true faith

'But, beloved, we are persuaded better things of you, and things that accompany salvation' (6:9, AV/KJV). How this shines out like the sun after the dark clouds have passed!

We heave a sigh of relief for them, they were not so bad after all then. No, thank God they were not. The writer has been talking like this because it was natural for him to be concerned; but in his heart of hearts he has come to a better conclusion about them: 'I think there is evidence in your life that you are genuinely saved, even though I have been speaking as if I thought you were not saved!'

For 'God is not unjust, he will not forget your work and the love you have shown him as you have helped his people and continue to help them' (6:10).

We listen intently. We felt relieved just now when he informed them that he thought they were saved. But listen, whatever is he saying now? – 'I think you are saved, for God is not unjust: he will not forget your *work*'? 'I thought we were saved by faith and not by works,' you say. 'And if so, what would it matter if God did forget our works? Should we be any the less saved?'

We are confusing two different things. The writer is not talking of the *ground* and *condition* of their salvation: *that* is solely by faith. He is talking of the *evidence* of their salvation, the evidence that they are true believers. And of course the only evidence we can have that a person's faith is genuine is that person's works. 'Show me your faith without deeds,' says James – but of course it can't be done – 'and I will show you my faith by what I do' (Jas. 2:18).

Quite so. But it is not enough for you to show me or for me to show you that our faith is genuine. God requires us to show *him* by our works that we are genuine believers. And if we have no works by which to show him, or if the evidence of our works is hopelessly inconsistent, that is serious.

It is a very great comfort, therefore, to hear what the writer says to his readers. The evidence of their behaviour and works had not been too good recently. On the other hand, when they first professed to trust Christ, the evidence of their works had been very good indeed. And, says the writer, God is not unjust: he will not forget that past evidence.

It has sometimes been suggested that if a believer walks worthily and fights valiantly for the Lord all his life and then at the last makes an unfortunate slip and falls, that one fall disqualifies him for ever. Such a statement is a libel and a slander upon the justice of God. It is not so. God is not unrighteous to forget the evidence that we have provided at any time that we are genuine. He will remember every piece of genuine evidence that there ever was.

That's no reason, of course, for letting ourselves get slack. Ahead lies the great inheritance. If we claim to have the hope that one day we shall enter into all that God has promised us there, we must keep on pressing forward towards it. The great spiritual pilgrims like Abraham maintained the momentum of their pilgrimage right to the end. And they have now entered into the promised inheritance. We must be like them (6:11–12). As the apostle John puts it: 'Everyone who has this hope in him', that is, in Christ, 'purifies himself' – keeps on purifying himself – 'just as he [Christ] is pure' (1 Jn. 3:3). Not only ought to, but does – if he really and truly possesses the hope that he professes to have.

The security of our hope

'But', says someone perhaps, 'if what you say is true, it completely knocks the bottom out of our sense of security.'

'How is that?'

'Well, we always thought that we were justified solely by faith; and while we knew we ought to live as Christians should, yet we knew, or thought we knew, that in the end it didn't really matter what our works and behaviour were like, because – well, after all, we had been justified by faith without works. But here you are saying that our works really matter, because we have to convince God by our works that we are genuine believers. That's a different story altogether. If that were true, how could we ever feel secure? And besides, it doesn't make sense. God can see our hearts. He knows whether we are true believers or not. So why does he need us to show him by our works that we are? Other people, of course, need to be shown some good works before they can see our faith is genuine. But not God, surely. At least that's what we have always been taught: we are justified by faith before God, and by our works before other people. But if, as you say, we have to be justified by our works before God . . .'

'Then you could never be sure of your acceptance with God, I suppose? All your security would be gone?'

'Precisely.'

Well now, this is very interesting, because if it is security that we are interested in, these next few verses, 6:13–20, are one of the strongest statements in the whole of the Bible of the utterly unbreakable security that every believer may constantly enjoy.

It starts by citing the experience of Abraham. God made him a tremendous promise: 'Surely blessing I will bless thee, and multiplying I will multiply thee' (6:14, AV/KJV), or as the NIV puts it, rather less vigorously, 'I will surely bless you and give you many descendants.' Now God cannot lie. So when God makes a promise, his bare word ought to be enough for anyone to rest on with unshakeable confidence. But on this occasion God was not content simply to make the promise; he swore an oath as well: 'By myself have I sworn . . . that in blessing I will bless thee, and in multiplying I will multiply thy seed' (Gn. 22:16–17, AV/KJV). He did it, the writer explains, not simply for Abraham's sake. He did it for the sake of all those who down the centuries would inherit the benefits of this promise, that is, all those who would truly believe in God and in his Son, Abraham's seed, Jesus Christ our Lord. And he did it because he wanted us to have as strong encouragement as he could possibly give us in the knowledge that his purpose to bless us is utterly unchangeable. 'God did this so that, by two unchangeable things' (that is, his promise and his oath) 'in which it is impossible for God to lie, we who have fled to take hold of the hope offered to us may be greatly encouraged' (6:18) or 'may have a strong encouragement' (RV).

What a hope Christians have! They have cast their anchor not in their fluctuating moods or feelings, or in their varying circumstances, or in anything else in this changing world. Christ himself as their precursor has taken their anchor right through into heaven itself and embedded it in the immovable ground of the presence and throne and character of God (6:19–20).

Justified by works

At this point there remains one question. At what stage in his spiritual experience did God make Abraham this promise and confirm it with an oath?

'That's easily answered,' you say, 'it was when Abraham offered Isaac on the altar to God, as it tells us in Genesis 22.'

Quite so. But that was on the occasion when, according to James (2:21–24), Abraham was justified by his works.

'Ah,' you say, 'I thought there was a snag in it somewhere.'

No, there is no snag in that, at least as long as we remember what being justified by works means. Some people imagine that being justified by works is the opposite of being justified by faith. It isn't, of course; it is, as James points out (2:23), the fulfilment of being justified by faith. So let us look at Abraham's experience once more.

'Abram believed the Lord,' says Genesis 15:6 early on in Abraham's career, 'and he [God] credited it to him as righteousness.' His faith was genuine. He was justified there and then. If he had died the next day, he would have gone straight to heaven.

But the following chapters show that at first Abraham's genuine faith was mixed up with a certain amount of dross. He thought, for instance, that faith in God's promise to give

153

him a son meant really that it depended on his and Sarah's efforts and scheming whether that promise would be fulfilled or not. So he produced Ishmael. But he had to learn that that was wrong. His efforts would not fulfil God's promise. What God had promised was a gift that would be given by God's grace and miraculous power, not by his and Sarah's struggles and schemings.

At length the promised seed, Isaac, was born; and in a very real sense all God's promises to Abraham and all Abraham's future were centred in Isaac. But now there was a danger that Abraham's faith for the future would come to rest partly in Isaac instead of resting solely in God. And that would never do. For his own sake, if for no other reason, Abraham must learn that no one can enjoy total security for the future unless his faith is solely and utterly in God and God alone.

And so, if I may reverently paraphrase the situation, God came to Abraham and said, 'Abraham, when I first promised to give you a son and offspring as numerous as the stars, you said you believed me. Was that true? Did you really mean it?'

'Oh, yes,' said Abraham, 'of course I did.'

'Well, what does your faith for the future rest in now?'

'In you, of course,' said Abraham.

'Are you sure it rests only and altogether in me, and not partly in me and partly in Isaac?'

'Oh, not in Isaac,' said Abraham, 'in you and only in you.'

'Then, Abraham,' said God, 'I ask you to demonstrate that your faith is in fact in me and in nothing and no-one else. Please give me Isaac.'

And Abraham gave up Isaac on the altar to God and demonstrated by this act that his faith was totally and altogether and solely in God. He justified his profession of faith and showed it was genuine; he was justified by his works. And God's reply was 'Now I know – not now Sarah knows, or your servants know, or the Philistines know – now *I* know that you fear God, because you have not withheld from me your son, your only son' (*cf.* Gn. 22:11–12). With that God gathered up all his previous promises, renewed them and confirmed them with a mighty oath, that Abraham and all others whose faith is in God alone might enjoy the 'strong encouragement' of absolute, unchangeable and eternal security.

Our minds go back to the readers of the letter. Some time before they received it they had professed to believe in Jesus as Son of God, Messiah and Saviour. Now God was coming to them as he came to Abraham. Was their faith for salvation and for eternity in Christ as high priest or in Judaism's Aaronic priesthood? in Christ's sacrifice or in Judaism's sacrifices? partly in Christ, his priesthood and sacrifice, and partly in Judaism's priesthood and sacrifices? or only and altogether in Christ, his priesthood and sacrifice?

Only in Christ? Good, for only in him is there salvation, only in him is security. But now they must act. Now they must justify their profession of faith by their works. Now they must give up Judaism's priesthood and sacrifices and so demonstrate before God and other people that their faith was indeed in Christ alone.

As we listen to God speaking to them, we may be sure that God will one day come to us who profess to believe in Christ and Christ alone for salvation, and ask us to give up everything that is inconsistent with his deity, his sole high-priesthood and headship of the church, and his once-for-all sacrifice for sins.

Questions

1 'Let us . . . go on to maturity' (NIV). 'Let us press on unto perfection' (RV). What is meant by 'perfection' or 'maturity' in this exhortation (6:1)?

2 Is being enlightened the same as being saved (6:4)? Why or why not?

3 What does it mean to 'taste the powers of the coming age' (6:5)?

4 Does 6:4–5 necessarily describe a regenerate person? Give reasons.

5 What does it mean to 'crucify the Son of God all over again and subject him to public disgrace' (6:6)?

6 Why is it impossible to bring back to repentance those who are guilty of (5) above?

7 On what is the believer's security for the future based (6:13–20)?

8 What do you understand by 'being justified by works'?
   Illustrate it from Abraham's experience and indicate how
   it would apply to us today.

THE SUPERIOR PRIESTHOOD
Hebrews 7

The seventh, eighth, ninth and tenth chapters of the letter to the Hebrews are taken up with long and detailed explanations of how Christ's priesthood is better than Aaron's, his new covenant better than Aaron's old one, his sanctuary better than the one which Moses made, and his one sacrifice for sins infinitely better than ancient Judaism's endless sacrifices.

At first sight all this might seem a little remote from us in modern times, at least for those of us who were not brought up in Judaism. Even they, one suspects, might find some of it a little remote, since modern Jews have no high priest, and centuries have passed since they offered animal sacrifices. But in reality these chapters deal with matters that are extremely relevant to our present understanding of what Christianity really is and of what it stands for.

First of all, they will heighten our appreciation of the work of Christ and the blessings of salvation. Some of us are so familiar with these things that if we were not careful we might take them for granted too. A glimpse back into Old Testament religion will make us aware, by contrast, of the tremendous blessing, assurance, freedom and peace which we enjoy in Christ.

And then there is a second point. Incredible though it must seem to us nowadays, in the second and third centuries, Christendom – in spite of the letter to the Hebrews! – forgot or forsook many of the great freedoms which we have in Christ, went backwards and began to model itself on ancient Judaism. Professor F. J. A. Hort remarks: 'The whole of Church History is full of beliefs, practices, institutions, and the like, which rest on misconceptions of the true nature of the Gospel dispensation, and are in effect a falling back after the coming of Christ to a state of things which His coming was intended to supersede, a return, as St. Paul would have said, to the weak and beggarly elements.'[1]

Any tourist, for example, will know that Europe is full of mediaeval church buildings arranged inside just like the ancient Jewish tabernacle or temple. There is the chancel, the most holy part, divided off by a chancel-screen from the nave, the less holy part; just as the most holy place in the tabernacle was divided off from the holy place by the veil. The effect, if not the intention, on the minds of generations of people was nothing short of disastrous. Instead of reminding them, as Hebrews will presently remind us, that every believer has freedom, here and now on earth, to enter the Most Holy Place, that is the immediate presence of God, by the blood of Jesus (19:19–22), it taught believers to 'stand afar off' as if unfit to come too near into the most holy part of the church building on earth, let alone into the presence of God in heaven. And it reinforced the false idea that no-one can be certain here on earth whether or not he or she will be finally accepted by God into heaven; the best we can do is to hope.

Thank God that in more recent times many of these things have been changed. But perhaps we should not take it for granted that all Christian believers have even now completely escaped from these lapses into Old Testament forms, ceremonies and ways of thinking. As we read these next chapters in Hebrews, we might be wise to check if all our beliefs and practices are truly Christian or if they are in some respects still interlaced with borrowings from ancient Judaism.

The prototype priest, Melchizedek

The writer then in chapter 7 sets out to win the faith, love and allegiance of his readers exclusively for Jesus as their high priest, and away from Judaism's Aaronic high priest. The first obstacle that he must overcome is, of course, the horror that this would raise in his readers' hearts. It was not simply that they had been brought up from childhood to reverence

---

[1] *Judaistic Christianity* (Macmillan, 1904), pp. 1–2.

their nation's high priest. It was, as we saw in Chapter Six, that the high-priesthood in Judaism was a divinely ordained institution. To abandon it would at first seem to a pious Jew to be unimaginable rebellion against the Most Holy.

How will the writer get round the problem? By appealing to the Scriptures themselves. First, as we have already seen, he points to the Old Testament where God announced to Messiah, 'You are a priest for ever, in the order of Melchizedek' (Ps. 110:4). And then he appeals to sacred Scripture again, to the place where the inspired record describes this ancient priest whom God himself appointed as a prototype of our Lord. The passage is Genesis 14, and he points to a number of highly significant details in the record:

1 Melchizedek blessed Abraham, not Abraham Melchizedek.
2 Abraham gave tithes to Melchizedek, not Melchizedek to Abraham.
3 Melchizedek's name means 'king of righteousness', and he was king of Salem which means 'peace'.
4 He is without father or mother, without genealogy, without beginning of days or end of life, but made to resemble the Son of God.
5 He remains a priest perpetually.

The last two items will seem very odd to us unless we realize what the writer is doing and what his presuppositions are. Far from disregarding the authority of holy Scripture (as many Jews might imagine from his claim that Judaism's priesthood was now to be abandoned), he believes that all Scripture is inspired by God; that the human author of Genesis was guided by the Holy Spirit in his selection of the material for his book; and that therefore not only what he includes is significant, but what he leaves out as well.

In Genesis we are normally told of the genealogy, birth and death of each of the great patriarchs and servants of God. But this great priest of God Most High, Melchizedek, has none of these details recorded. He suddenly appears in the record and just as abruptly disappears again. We are not told who his parents and ancestors were, or when he was born or when he died. All this information is withheld, so the writer believes, by the Holy Spirit in order to make the record of this priestly prototype of our Lord point to actual features in the Son of God who in reality had no beginning of days nor end of life. Moreover, he points out, nowhere in Scripture are we told that this ancient priest Melchizedek died, or that his order of priesthood was superseded. As far as Scripture is concerned his order of priesthood has no end. And that is highly significant; for, as will soon be pointed out, the Old Testament did indicate that Aaron's order of priesthood would be superseded by another order.

The writer, then, has picked out and listed these five features in the Genesis record of Melchizedek, and he will now proceed to show how they apply to our Lord's priesthood which is said to be 'in the order of Melchizedek'.

The superiority of the order of Melchizedek

First of all he calls his readers to consider the greatness of Melchizedek's position: 'Just think how great he was' (7:4). It is obvious why he does this. Jews in general reverenced their high priest with an adulation almost approaching the ecstatic. (Not all did, of course; but those who did not, usually objected not to the office itself but to the fact that in their opinion the reigning high priest did not meet the biblical requirements for the office.) The high priest held the primacy among all other priests. He wore the ineffable name of God on his mitre. He alone was allowed to enter the Most Holy Place on the day of atonement. Even his vestments were thought to possess atoning power, and he was accompanied by the most impressive ceremonial. The effect on ordinary Jews both in Palestine and abroad can be judged by this description from an ancient Jew, who in all likelihood never personally saw a high priest but obviously possessed an almost delirious admiration for him and for his office: 'The total effect' of the high priest dressed in his ceremonial vestments ' . . . arouses awe and emotional excitement so that one would think he had passed to some other world. I venture to affirm positively that any man who witnesses the spectacle I have recounted will experience amazement and astonishment

indescribable, and his mind will be deeply moved at the sanctity attaching to every detail.'[2]

If the readers of our letter felt anything like this emotional
attachment to Judaism's high priest, the problem was: how
could the writer loosen these emotional ties and transfer his
readers' awe, reverence and loyalty to the Lord Jesus?

First of all he points out that even ancient Melchizedek,
according to the Jewish Scriptures themselves, held an
immeasurably more important office than any priest of
Aaron's line, since he was demonstrably a more important
person and a more exalted servant of God than even Abraham
himself. That's not to deny that Abraham was great. He was
after all chosen by God to be the founder of the Hebrew
race. Personally favoured with a direct vision of God (see
Acts 7:2), he had already received from God the promises
that indicated the unique and glorious role which he and his
descendants were to play in the history of the world and of
redemption. Yet Abraham, so says inspired Scripture, paid
tithes to Melchizedek, not Melchizedek to Abraham, and so
acknowledged the superiority of Melchizedek's office. Melchizedek in turn blessed Abraham, not Abraham Melchizedek, which in the protocol of the ancient world indicated
beyond all dispute that Abraham was Melchizedek's inferior
(7:7).

It would not have been so significant if at the time Abraham
had been merely a private individual. But he wasn't. He was
already founder of the nation, patriarchal head of all the great
office-holders such as Moses, Aaron, David and Elijah, that
were to spring from him. When therefore in his official
capacity he paid tithes to Melchizedek, he was acknowledging
not only for himself but on behalf of all his descendants, high
priests of Aaron's line included, the superiority of Melchizedek's office over all others (7:5–10).

The writer therefore is not denying that Scripture originally
gave to high priests of Aaron's line an exceedingly important
and exalted office. What he is pointing out is first that that
same Old Testament attributed to Melchizedek an even more
important and more exalted office, and secondly that the Old

---

[2] Pseudo-Aristeas, *Letter to Philocrates*, edited and translated by M. Hadas,
New York, Harper and Brothers, 1951, sect. 99.

Testament itself declares that Messiah's priesthood is after the order of Melchizedek and not of Aaron.

Why cling to what at best was a second-rate order of priest, when now every believer, however humble, has the right of direct access to the high priest of the supreme order?

The Old Testament priesthood superseded

But at this point one can imagine a Jewish convert responding by saying: 'Look, I totally accept that the priesthood of Christ is better than Aaron's. But surely that does not mean that we must necessarily give up Aaron's priesthood. If you buy a new car, you know, you do not necessarily get rid of the old one. You may do, but you don't have to. Why can't we have both: the priesthood of Christ in heaven, and the Aaronic priesthood in the temple on earth?' Many of his fellow-converts, I imagine, were wishing it could be so. Life would have been easier for them; the break with Judaism would not have been so severe, the reproach of being a Christian not so heavy.

It can't be done, says the writer, and that for a number of reasons. First, the appointment of Messiah as a priest in the order of Melchizedek exposes the inadequacy of the Levitical priesthood. You see, he says, if perfection could have been attained through the Levitical priesthood, there would not have been any need for another priest to be appointed according to a different order (7:11). But the very announcement of this new priest belonging to a different order exposes the fact that the old order was weak and useless (7:18).

You can, I'm sure, see the point. A Model T Ford may still be able, with frequent stoppages, to get you round the block. But if you're thinking of flying round the world you'll have to leave the Ford and take to a jet aeroplane. The Ford is just not up to the job. Even when it was brand new, it could never have flown. It does not belong to a high enough order of machine.

On the basis of the Levitical priesthood, the nation was given the law. But how effective was it? What good did it do? For all the good intentions of Aaron and his sons, they never accomplished what we require a priest for. They never really brought anybody into close contact with God. They could not. The Israelites always stood at a distance, waiting afar off; they were never allowed to come near to God. When God was giving his law upon Sinai's top, the ordinary Jewish commoner was commanded under dire threats to keep away. If so much as a beast touched the mountain it had to be stoned (12:18–21). Equally on the great day of atonement, though the people gathered round the tabernacle, they gathered in fear, they kept outside. Although they had a high priest, the high priest could not bring them – dare not bring them – into the presence of God. And the reason was that the law, in spite of all its elaborate rules and regulations regarding the priesthood and the sacrifices, made nothing perfect (7:19). What use then all its vestments, powerfully aesthetic rituals, and colourful ceremonies, if it could not do that? So the former regulation had to be set aside, and a better hope introduced 'by which we draw near to God' (7:1). And what an infinitely better hope this is that has given us a high priest who can actually bring us into the immediate presence of God, in spirit now (10:19–22) and in body at his second coming (9:28).

Secondly, says the writer to his Jewish converts, you cannot keep the Levitical high-priesthood along with the high-priesthood of Christ. The two are incompatible.

The Old Testament laid down the most stringent rules controlling the priesthood (see Nu. 17–18). Not only could no one be a high priest unless he was of the tribe of Levi, a member of the right family within that tribe, and physically descended by the right line of descent from the original high priest, Aaron. In addition, as we saw earlier, the high priest as spiritual head of the nation was like an hereditary monarch. There could not be *two* high priests, *two* spiritual heads of the people of God, at one and the same time. The law of God forbade it. When, therefore, in later centuries God announced through the psalmist that he was going to appoint Messiah, of the tribe of Judah, as high priest and spiritual head of his people, it implied that when it happened, the earlier law would have to be annulled. And now, that Jesus has been raised from the dead, the writer argues, and has been appointed as the high priest of his people, the old law and with it the whole institution of the Levitical priesthood has in fact been changed. The appointment of our Lord to be high priest does not conflict with the old law, for the simple reason that the old law has been cancelled. You can write across it 'Finished, obsolete, out of date, done away with for ever'.

But just as in Israel there could not be two high priests, two spiritual heads of the people, so in Christianity. That we can see, if with the writer, we consider the terms under which Christ has been appointed high priest and head of the church, and what it means that he is 'in the order of Melchizedek'. The appointment of high priests in ancient Israel was surrounded and governed by what our writer calls 'a law of a carnal commandment', meaning, as the NIV puts it, 'a regulation as to his ancestry – he had to be of the correct line of descent – and more than that: the regulation naturally enough had to lay down what should happen when the high priest died. That is all completely irrelevant in our Lord's case. He is never going to die again. Raised from the dead and declared to be the Son of God, he has also been declared to be a priest for ever. His life is not merely without end; it is actually indestructible, indissoluble. And it is on this basis of an indestructible life that he has become high priest. The record of the historical Melchizedek was carefully arranged by the author of Genesis, as we noticed above, to prefigure this wonderful fact. The terms of the divine appointment explicitly proclaim it: 'You are a priest *for ever*, in the order of Melchizedek' (7:15–17).[3] And it goes without saying that if these are the terms and conditions for being high priest and head of the church, no-one other than Christ could match them.

So our Lord's appointment sets aside completely the rules and regulations relating to the old Levitical priesthood and – do let us notice it – makes obsolete the institution of Levitical priesthood itself. Let us grasp the fact: 'The former regulation is set aside' (7:18). It is God himself who says so through the inspired writer. Admittedly, from the third century AD onwards some have argued (and some still do) that while our

[3] From that we gather that being in the *order* of Melchizedek does not mean, as it did with Aaron's order, that our Lord's high-priesthood depends on his being physically descended from Melchizedek; it means that his priesthood is after the *pattern* of Melchizedek's.

Lord's high priesthood is outside the Levitical order altogether and is unique, it is perfectly all right for the Christian church to copy the Levitical order in its services and church government here on earth and to divide the people of God into laity, priests and (earthly) high priest as was done in ancient Judaism. But it will not do. When God has set it aside, it would be an affront to him if we reintroduced it.

And let us grasp the reason why it has been set aside: 'because it was weak and useless (for the law made nothing perfect)' (7:18–19). If we disobey God and reintroduce this weak and useless system into the church, it will have the same effect as it had in Judaism; it will put the people once more at a distance from God while higher ranks of supposedly more holy intermediaries come between them and the Saviour.

The oath of appointment

Now comes another distinguishing feature of our Lord's superior priesthood. The announcement of our Lord's appointment was accompanied by an oath: 'The Lord has sworn and will not change his mind: "You are a priest for ever." ' No oath was sworn when Judaism's Levitical priests were appointed. So what is the significance of the oath at our Lord's appointment?

First, 'because of this oath, Jesus has become the guarantee of a better covenant' (7:22). How much better, we shall see in a moment when we move into chapter 8 of the letter. It is enough to notice here two of the covenant's provisions. It undertakes to write God's laws on our hearts and it promises absolute peace with God on the understanding that God will never again remember our sins, that is he will never again raise the question of the guilt and penalty of our sins. The provisions in this covenant are so magnificent that naturally we want to know how we can be sure that they will in fact be carried out. The answer is that Jesus is himself the guarantee. He is personally responsible for seeing that all the terms of the covenant are carried out. By his death he paid the cost of the forgiveness promised by the covenant. Now he lives for ever to see to it that God's laws are written on our hearts. He is, as Melchizedek was, king of peace – look

165

at the absolute and eternal forgiveness he guarantees us. He is also, as Melchizedek was, king of righteousness – he guarantees to write God's laws on our hearts. The oath assures us that he is a priest for ever. He will never be withdrawn, will never die and leave it uncertain whether the terms of the covenant will continue to be honoured and fulfilled. The oath gives us therefore an eternal guarantee. The covenant is secure as long as Christ shall live.

More. Because he will never die, he will never have to hand over his priesthood to someone else. Judaism's priests did, of course. One of them might undertake your cause; but he might well die and have to leave your affairs to somebody else to deal with. Not Christ. Once he undertakes your cause, he will never have to hand it over to some other priest. He is himself able to save you completely because he always lives to intercede for you (7:23–25).

And finally the oath has appointed as our high priest one who is not only perfectly qualified, but also perfectly equipped and therefore perfectly efficient and effective. The priests appointed by the law were hardly this. They were weak at best (7:28). Suppose you came with your pressing needs and got one of them to deal with God on your behalf. First of all, or half way through, he might well have to stop looking after you and put himself right with God and offer a sacrifice for his own sins. Even suppose you managed to get the high priest himself in all his dignified and gorgeous robes to agree to look after you; he might easily in the meantime suffer some accidental physical or ceremonial pollution or defilement which temporarily prevented him from acting himself and obliged him to call in a deputy. And not even the best of them could offer a sacrifice which was sufficient for you for all time. They offered a sacrifice one day, and then if they wanted to keep you right with God, they had to offer another one the next day, and next week, and next year. And when you came to die and they had performed for you all the rites and ceremonies they knew, they still could not guarantee that God would immediately accept you into his heaven. And they could not accompany you on your passage from this world to the next. You were on your own then! How weak they were and how impossibly weak and ineffective all their rites, ceremonies, ablutions and absolutions were!

How different is Christ! See how well qualified he is. Never at any time did he know the weakness of sin or have to offer a sin-offering for himself. He was always holy, blameless and pure, and is now set apart from sinners. During the days of his life on earth he knew the weakness that is inherent in being a man with a natural (though sinless) body. But now he is exalted above the heavens, his body a spiritual body. He knows no weakness or frailty. His eyes never slumber, he never grows weary in his praying, he always persists energetically in his ministry. And see how well equipped he is. The sacrifice of himself at Calvary once and for all is sufficient to cover every sin of every believer until, as William Cowper put it, 'all the ransomed church of God be saved, to sin no more'. As the almighty Son of God he has been perfected, that is fully equipped to be perfectly effective, for evermore (7:26–28).

And when – or if – we come to die, we shall not be on our own. Our high priest has already entered heaven, so that for us to be absent from the body will mean to be instantaneously with the Lord (2 Cor. 5:6–8), where he is seated at the right hand of the throne of the Majesty in heaven (8:1).

Questions

1 What does Scripture mean when it talks of an 'order' or 'line' of priests? Could any one join an order of priests in Old Testament times?

2 What are the practical implications for us that our Lord's high-priesthood is in the order of Melchizedek?

3 Why had ancient Judaism's Levitical priesthood to be set aside?

4 What does Scripture mean when it says that Jesus has become the *guarantee* of a better covenant (7:22)?

5 In what sense has our Lord been 'made perfect for ever' (7:28)?

6 Expound in your own words the claim of 7:26 that 'such a high priest meets our need'. Do you feel free to approach him directly? Or do you feel that you need some mediator to approach Christ for you?

9

THE SUPERIOR COVENANT
Hebrews 8

The writer has now reached a convenient place in his message where he can pause and sum up what he has been saying about our high priest so far. He has been talking mainly of his appointment, and qualifications, and he sums it all up thus: 'The point of what we are saying is this: We do have such a high priest, who sat down at the right hand of the throne of the Majesty in heaven, and who serves in the sanctuary, the true tabernacle set up by the Lord, not by man' (8:1–2).

Now we are about to turn from considering the nature and qualifications of our priest – 'such a high priest' (8:1) – to consider the nature of his ministry: the sanctuary in which he ministers (8:2), the sacrifice on the basis of which he ministers (8:3–4), and the covenant as the mediator of which he ministers (8:6). And as you might expect, the writer is going to argue that our Lord is superior to ancient Judaism's priests, not only in his person and qualifications, or only in the exalted rank of his office, but also in the place, nature and conditions of his ministry.

Chapter 8 will show that his ministry is also better than theirs in respect of the covenant which, as priest, he mediates. Aaron's priesthood was there to work the terms of the old covenant. The Lord Jesus in his priesthood puts into operation the terms of the new covenant (8:6–13). His ministry, so chapter 9 will show, is better in regard to the place in which it is performed. Aaron's priests performed in the tabernacle, and the tabernacle was only a shadow of the reality. Our Lord Jesus performs his ministry in the true tabernacle, which the Lord pitched and not man. Then chapter 10 will show that his ministry is better than that of the Old Testament priests in regard to his sacrifice. They offered animal sacrifices; he offered the sacrifice of his body. They offered many sacrifices; he needed to offer only one. Their sacrifices had to be constantly offered; his sacrifice has finished the work and never needs to be repeated or offered again.

It is on the first of these topics that our writer is going to concentrate to begin with. But before he does so, he cannot resist talking briefly about the place in which our Lord now ministers. And that is understandable; for, having spoken in chapter 5 about our Lord's installation as high priest, it is only natural that he should think for a moment of the place in which he is installed. That place is heaven, of course. But the writer cannot content himself with such a brief description. His readers were being asked to leave their temple at Jerusalem with its magnificent architecture, its sacred courts, its Holy Place, and its Most Holy Place – so holy that only the high priest could enter it and that only once a year; their sacred and beloved temple, centre of attraction for world Jewry with its marvellous pageantry of sacrifice and liturgical chanting. For Jews living abroad, to visit the temple was life's crowning experience.

And they have to leave all that? Then what would or could replace it? Why, of course, the sanctuary in which our Lord now serves. And where is that and what is it like? Our Lord has sat down, says our writer 'at the right hand of the throne of the Majesty in heaven'. The tabernacle in which our Lord ministers is 'the true tabernacle', that is, the real thing of which the temple in Jerusalem for all its splendour was only a copy and shadow (8:5). Who wouldn't abandon a mere model, if he could have the real thing? No young man will continue playing with the model cars that meant so much to him us a boy, when he has the opportunity of owning and driving a real car.

But not only so. Listen to this astonishing statement: our Lord has sat down on the right hand of the throne of the Majesty in heaven. Perhaps you would have to be an ancient Jew to see its full significance. In their temple there was the Most Holy Place, and in that Most Holy Place the ark, a symbol of the throne of God. Such was its sanctity that for 364 days in the year no-one was allowed near that throne: a veil hid the Most Holy Place and its symbolic throne from view. Just one day a year their most holy priest was allowed to enter, and for a few moments glimpse what he could of that throne through clouds of shrouding incense. But – sit down on the throne? Mere symbol though it was, never once in all Israel's history did any high priest ever dream of sitting anywhere near it, let alone on it.

But Christ has sat down, not at the right hand of some earthly symbol of God's throne, but at the right hand of the actual throne of the Majesty in heaven. And as if that were not astonishing enough in itself, when the writer comes to the climax of these next few chapters, he will remind us that our Lord as high priest over the house of God invites us even now to come boldly and join him in spirit at that very throne of the Majesty in heaven (10:21–22; *cf.* 4:16).

When the readers of the letter got used to exercising this privilege as believers, they would scarcely be impressed any more when on their visits to Jerusalem some Jewish high priest in the earthly temple, that mere model of the real thing, tried to tell them that the temple was so holy that a mere member of the laity could not be allowed to enter its Holy Place, let alone the Most Holy Place. And it would pull them up with a start to be reminded, as the writer now reminds them (8:4), that if our Lord were still on earth they would not, and according to Old Testament law could not, allow him to enter either, let alone minister there. The implications for a Jewish believer would be obvious.

Our Lord's superior ministry

But not only is the place in which our Lord is installed as high priest superior to the Jewish temple; his ministry is superior to theirs, because he is the mediator of a new covenant infinitely better than the old covenant which the Jewish priests had to operate.

To understand the difference between the old covenant and the new, let us first consider what the term 'covenant' means in this context. We can illustrate the matter by the customs prevalent in the world in the days of Moses. In those times great emperors would draw up treaties with their vassal kings, which would remind these subject kings just who the great emperor was, what benefits he had conferred on them, what behaviour was expected from the vassals, what blessings would accrue to them if they obeyed the emperor, and what punishments they would incur if they rebelled against him. In other words, these treaties spelled out the relationship between the great sovereign and his subjects.

Now these treaties were called covenants, and the old covenant was, so to speak, a treaty between God and the Israelites, which defined the relationship between him as their sovereign and them as his subjects. The covenant specified in ten major commandments and in scores of lesser ones the behaviour God required of Israel, and then detailed the curses that would come upon them if they broke the terms of the covenant, and the blessings that would follow if they kept them.

The old covenant, then, was a two-party covenant. God had his part to play and his conditions to fulfil, and the Israelites had theirs. So it was clear from the start that if the Israelites broke their part of the covenant and failed to meet its demands, they would not only forfeit the blessings that God promised them: they would ruin their relationship with God and bring down his curses on their heads.

And that is precisely what they did! In spite of the fact that they enthusiastically welcomed the covenant and readily undertook to keep their part, Moses scarcely had time to bring the tables of law down from the mountain before the people had broken the most fundamental of all its requirements. God was patient, but Israel constantly and endlessly failed to keep its part and in the end God rejected them: 'they did not remain faithful to my covenant, and I turned away from them, declares the Lord' (8:9).

It ought to be a lesson to us; but unfortunately there are still people even in Christendom who imagine that a true and satisfactory relationship with God can be built on those same terms of keeping the old covenant. They may not express their idea in such theological terms as we have just used; they tend to say something more like this: 'I believe that if I do my best to keep the commandments, to serve God and love my neighbour, I shall be all right, and everything will turn out all right in the end.' But of course it won't. It couldn't. What they call 'doing their best to keep the commandments' turns out, when you examine it, to be not a keeping of them but a failure to keep them, a 25% failure, or more, or less; but always a failure to keep them perfectly. And if they insist on their relationship with God depending on their faulty efforts to keep his law, then God will have no option but to reject them as he rejected Israel.

The new covenant

God himself therefore has scrapped the old covenant and all attempts to build a relationship with human beings on its basis. This is not some new-fangled idea thought up by Christians. God announced his intention of doing so centuries ago through the Jewish prophet Jeremiah. He announced that one day he would make a new covenant with his people. And the very fact that he had to make a new covenant, the writer argues (8:7), shows that there was something faulty with the first one. It was not that its standards were too high. It was that it was a two-party covenant: God had his part to keep and so had Israel. And Israel could not keep theirs but constantly broke it, with disastrous results.

So the new covenant had to be different, radically different, from the old: 'It will *not* be like the covenant I made with their forefathers when I took them by the hand to lead them out of Egypt' (that is, the law given at Sinai). Do let us notice that 'not'; for sometimes we hear it suggested that after all the new covenant is not all that much different from the old. But according to God it is radically and fundamentally different.

In what respects? First in this that the new covenant is not a two-party covenant. That was precisely the trouble with the old; for when Israel could not keep their part, the whole covenant was ruined, Israel lost its blessings and suffered its curses. So the new covenant is not going to be like that. It is a one-party, not a two party, covenant. Look at its terms as they are listed here (8:10–12) and you will see that there is not one thing that God's people are required to do, not one condition that they are called upon to fulfil. The terms of the covenant simply announce, one and all of them, what God will do. He does it all! And since God will fulfil all the terms he has promised to fulfil, the covenant will never be broken,

173

and God's people will never be abandoned or rejected.

God's law within

And then the new covenant is radically different from the old in other respects as well. Look at the first thing God coven-ants to do: 'I will put my laws in their minds and write them on their hearts' (8:10). The point of this promise can be seen if we remember that the ten commandments of the old covenant were written on two tables of stone. That is why they were so ineffective in getting people to do God's will. They were simply external commands written on stone. They told a person what to do, but they could not give him the strength to do it; they told him what not to do, but they could him no power to refrain from doing it. They were in themselves perfectly good and reasonable commands, and if people could have kept them, they would have produced in them most noble characters. But no-one could keep them. Our hearts are weak and sinful, deceitful above all things, as the Old Testament puts it (Je. 17:9), and desperately sick.

Before one could have any hope of keeping God's law in a manner that would satisfy God, one would need to be given a completely new heart, a new nature, a new power. And therefore it is precisely this that the first clause in the new covenant provides for. God's undertaking to write his law on our hearts means far more than helping us to remember it so that we could, if necessary, repeat if off by heart. It means nothing less than the implantation within us of a new nature, the very nature of God in fact (see 2 Pet. 1:3–4). For, as the letter to the Romans puts it, 'the mind of the flesh is enmity against God; for it is not subject to the law of God, neither indeed can it be (8:7, RV); and therefore, if we are going to fulfil God's law, God must create within us a new life that by its very nature does the law of God. John the apostle calls the process by which it is done a 'new birth'; the new covenant calls it 'the writing of God's law on our hearts'.

Knowing God

The next clause in the covenant provides that each believer will enjoy an intimate knowledge of God in his personal experience. It runs: 'I will be their God, and they will be my people. No longer will a man teach his neighbour, or a man his brother, saying, "Know the Lord," because they will all know me, from the least of them to the greatest' (8:10–11).

Knowing God in this sense is not, of course, just a matter of knowing that there is a God. The verb 'to know' is one which the Bible uses of the intimate relationship between a man and his wife (Gn. 4:1, AV/KJV). At the spiritual level knowing God denotes a personal, direct, intimate relationship with God. Second-hand experience of God conveyed through books, or preachers, may have a real and positive value. But it is not enough.

Other people may help us a great deal to understand things about God; but in order to experience salvation, to have God's law written in our hearts, we must know God personally and directly ourselves. A girl may first come to know of her husband-to-be through the glowing reports of some friend, and the friend may after a while introduce the couple to each other. But if ever the girl is to become the man's wife, there must come a point when the friend gets out of the way and the girl enters a direct and personal relationship with the man.

Moreover, failure to enter such a personal relationship with God is spiritually fatal. Our Lord has himself warned us that when at last he rises up and closes the door, and has to bid those on the outside to depart from him, the reason why they will have to depart will be given in these words: 'I never knew you' (Mt. 7:23). That cannot mean that Christ never knew they existed, or never knew who they were; it means that they and Christ never had any direct and personal dealings with each other. And Christ further warns us that the fact that these people will be able to cite evidence of having been religious even above average will not prove an adequate substitute for personal knowledge of the Saviour (Mt. 7:22; Lk. 13:26).

Conversely, of the true believer Christ says: 'I am the good shepherd; I know my sheep and my sheep know me – just as the Father knows me and I know the Father,' and again, 'My sheep listen to my voice; I know them, and they follow me. I give them eternal life, and they shall never perish; no-one can snatch them out of my hand' (Jn. 10:14–15, 27–28).

175

Now the glorious thing about this personal knowledge of God, and relationship with God, is that it is not a something which we have to work up and qualify for by long and rigorous preparatory disciplines. The new covenant offers it as a gift. It is effected by the Holy Spirit in the very heart of every one who trusts Christ. Listen to Paul: 'Because you are sons, God sent the Spirit of his Son into our hearts, the Spirit who calls out, "*Abba*, Father" ' (Gal. 4:6). When we first trust Christ and become children of God, we are still very immature. We are not yet spiritual adults or even full-grown strong young people; we are nothing but spiritual little children. Yet John says of such: 'I write to you, dear children, because you have known the Father' (1 Jn.2:13)

God's forgiveness

The third and final clause in the new covenant runs as follows: 'For I will forgive their wickedness and will remember their sins no more' (8:12).

The stupendous thing about this magnificent clause is that here we have forgiveness of sins written into the terms of the covenant. Consider its significance.

You may well be thinking, 'Yes, I have found since I was converted that I do love to do God's will and that I naturally think about his Word; it is so different from what it used to be before I got converted. Then I loathed doing certain things that God said – now I love to do them. But, for all that, I do not always manage to do God's will. Even when I want to! So what happens then? That's what I want to know. What happens when in spite of all my good intentions I fail? Is everything done for, when I fail?'

Why, of course not, for the final clause of the covenant is this: 'I will forgive their wickedness and will remember their sins no more.' Thank God for the order of this covenant. Drawn up as it is by the most exact lawyer in the universe, its very order is significant. It does not say, 'First I will forgive their iniquities and then I will write my law in their hearts.' It says, 'First I will write my laws in their hearts and in their minds. And suppose that in spite of all that they fail, shall I do with them what I did with Israel and turn away from them? No! This covenant is different: I will be merciful to their iniquities and their sins I will remember no more.'

And here is a very interesting thing which is quite the opposite of what you might expect. When believers in Christ discover this limitless grace of God towards them, and the function of the Lord Jesus as their priest to save them to the uttermost, and the unbreakable terms of the new covenant, it does not make them feel that they want to take advantage of it all in order to go and sin and do as they like. Not if they really belong to Christ. It makes them feel that they want to go out and live always and ever for Christ; it makes them feel that to sin against him would be the blackest ingratitude that they could ever be capable of; it makes them determined always to seek the aid of the high priest, that they may not sin and displease him.

Some will object that if the covenant guaranteed forgiveness so that we could be sure of it in advance, it would be nothing better than the old medieval scandal in which you could buy indulgence in advance for sins you had not yet done but intended doing, and could so proceed to commit the sins with the certainty of being forgiven and therefore with virtual impunity.

The answer to the objection is that it forgets what the first clause of the new covenant says. That clause expresses God's determination to write his laws on the heart of the believer, so that, as Paul would put it (Rom. 8:4), 'the righteous requirements of the law might be fully met in us, who do not live according to the sinful nature but according to the Spirit.' That is, the new covenant does not simply provide forgiveness; rather the very first clause announces that its prime objective is to make us holy by the progressive work of the Holy Spirit in our heart, and guarantees that God will not give up until he has made us perfect, whatever it costs (see 1 Cor. 11:31–32).

Only in this context does the third clause assure us that God's acceptance of us does not depend on our spiritual progress and certainly not on our attaining to perfection. In the school of progressive holiness we will have many difficult lessons to face, and our mistakes and failures will be numerous. But we may find courage and comfort in God's guarantee of complete forgiveness, in the knowledge that we can never lose our acceptance with God, and that the goal of perfection will at last be attained.

Questions

1 What are the three areas in which our Lord's ministry as high priest is superior to the ministry of the Old Testament priests (8:2–6)?
2 What, according to 8:9–10, is the essential difference between the old covenant and the new?
3 Expound the terms of the new covenant and say how they affect our relationship with the Lord.
   (a) What is meant by writing God's laws on our minds and hearts?
   (b) What does it mean to 'know' God?
   (c) Is the *position* of the final clause in the covenant significant? Why or why not?

10

THE SUPERIOR SANCTUARY
Hebrews 9

'Now of course even the first covenant had divinely given regulations in regard to worship and the earthly sanctuary' (9:1, my translation).

It is no part of the case for Christianity to deny the importance or belittle the glory of the old covenant. True enough, in verse 6 of this chapter the author will begin to point out the severe limitations of the old covenant's system of worship. But for all those limitations that system, while it lasted, was exceedingly magnificent. The writer not only admits it, he asserts it. If the Christian system of worship is better – and it is – that is not because the old covenant's system was mean and worthless. Far from it. It was the very best system that God himself could devise and provide – 'until the time of the new order' (9:10), when the incarnation, death, resurrection and ascension of our Lord Jesus Christ would make possible an infinitely superior system.

The tabernacle provided by the old covenant, as the writer has already pointed out, was built at God's command according to a pattern shown by God to Moses on Mount Sinai (8:5). Not the greatest cathedral or basilica in the whole of Christendom could ever claim that!

The old covenant 'had . . . the earthly sanctuary' (9:1, literally). Note the definite article: *the* earthly sanctuary. As far as literal, earthly sanctuaries are concerned, this tabernacle (and its successors, the temples built by Solomon and Ezra) was the only one that God ever ordained to be built. Christianity's system of worship is better than Judaism's precisely because it has no (God-ordained) earthly sanctuaries. The sanctuary in which our Lord ministers (8:2) and into which

Christians are invited to enter for their worship of God (10:19–22) is not on earth at all, but in heaven. Understandably, therefore, God never gave to the Christian apostles any orders or plans for building earthly sanctuaries.

But for ancient Israel God did provide an earthly sanctuary, and it was unique. In its Most Holy Place God condescended to dwell in a way in which he never dwelt in any other man-made temple, shrine or tabernacle anywhere else in the world ever. When the Mosaic tabernacle was erected 'the cloud covered the Tent of Meeting, and the glory of the Lord filled the tabernacle. Moses could not enter the Tent of Meeting because the cloud had settled upon it, and the glory of the Lord filled the tabernacle' (Ex. 40:34–35). Similarly when Solomon's temple was completed, 'the priests could not enter the temple of the Lord because the glory of the Lord filled it' (2 Ch. 7:2). God himself sat 'enthroned between the cherubim that are on the ark' in the Most Holy Place (2 Sa. 6:2).

Carefully our writer describes the main features of the tabernacle; and we must try to get a precise understanding of the technical terms he uses.

The tabernacle building, he points out, was composed of two parts. The first part, the Holy Place, was called 'the first tabernacle'; and it is very important to see that by this phrase, 'the first tabernacle', the writer means the first room in the Mosaic tabernacle (and in all subsequent temples at Jerusalem), otherwise called 'the Holy Place' (9:2), as distinct from the second room in that same tabernacle, otherwise known as 'the Most Holy Place' (9:3) or 'the Holy of Holies'. He does not mean the first sanctuary, built by Moses, as distinct from subsequent sanctuaries built by Solomon, Ezra and others. At the entrance to the first tabernacle hung a curtain called the first veil. Another curtain, which our writer calls the second veil, divided the first tabernacle from the second, that is the Holy Place from the Most Holy Place. Of the two veils the second was by far the more important in the rituals of the tabernacle; and it achieved undying fame when its counterpart in Herod's temple was torn from top to bottom at the time of Christ's death at Calvary (Mt. 27:51). For this reason the second veil is often referred to simply as '*the* veil'.

THE TABERNACLE

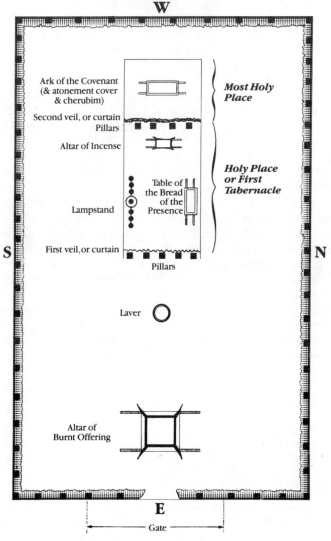

W

Ark of the Covenant (& atonement cover & cherubim)

Most Holy Place

Second veil, or curtain
Pillars

Altar of Incense

Holy Place or First Tabernacle

Lampstand

Table of the Bread of the Presence

First veil, or curtain

Pillars

S

N

Laver

Altar of Burnt Offering

E

Gate

So much for the structure of the tabernacle. The author also lists the major items of its sacred furniture, starting from the contents of the Holy Place and proceeding inwards.[1] It is a short list, though the writer implies that he could have spoken in detail about the significance of each piece of sacred furniture if he had had the time (9:5). But when he comes to the last piece of furniture, his brief description unerringly picks out the most majestic and wonderful thing about the tabernacle: 'Above the ark', he says, 'were the cherubim of the Glory' (9:5). By 'the Glory', of course, he means the actual and immediate presence of God.

Now we do not know where his readers lived, in Jerusalem, Alexandria, Rome or elsewhere. So we do not know whether they had visited the temple at Jerusalem practically every week of their lives, or only once or twice on occasional pilgrimages, or not even once. But we can be sure of this: in the minds of many of his readers the temple at Jerusalem, based as it was in its essential features on the Mosaic tabernacle, would be associated with the most sacred, exalted, and glorious experiences and privileges that they could possibly imagine. It would seem sacrilege to them to suggest that as Christians they must now abandon the temple and its system of worship. Yet that is precisely what the writer is going to require of them (see 13:11–14). Of course, within a very few years God was in any case going to allow the Romans to destroy the temple completely just as our Lord had prophesied they would (Lk. 21:5–6). The old covenant's system of worship was indeed 'obsolete and ageing'; soon it would disappear altogether (8:13). But how will the writer persuade his readers to abandon it forthwith, and after its destruction

---

[1] In v. 4, when he says that the Most Holy Place 'had' the golden altar of incense, he does not mean that the golden altar stood inside the Most Holy Place. This altar 'belonged to' the innermost sanctuary (see 1 Ki. 6:22, NIV) because in function it was closely tied to the ark. When a priest prayed at the golden altar he faced and addressed the God who sat enthroned between the cherubim above the ark. There had to be a veil between the priest and God; but the two vessels were functionally tied together. It was in that sense that the Most Holy Place 'had' an altar of incense, even though that altar stood *outside* the Most Holy Place. So we can say of a modern office complex, 'The managing director's private office *has* a waiting-room', without meaning to imply that the waiting-room is actually inside his private office.

to refrain from trying to reproduce it in their meeting-places for Christian worship?

The inadequacies of the earthly sanctuary

He will do it first by pointing to the way the very structure of the tabernacle proclaims its own inadequacy. 'Yes,' he says in effect (9:1–5) 'the old covenant's system of worship, provided for by the tabernacle, was exceedingly glorious, *but . . .*'. Notice that 'But' at the beginning of verse 7. So many translations either omit it altogether, or begin the sentence with a word like 'Now' and so fail to indicate to the reader that verse 7 begins to put the opposite side of the case: the tabernacle was glorious, *but* it had a glaring limitation. It was so arranged that only for a few brief moments on one day a year was the high priest and representative of the people ever allowed to enter the immediate presence of God! And as for the ordinary priests, they were never allowed to enter that presence at all, but had to content themselves with ministering in the first tabernacle, that is, the Holy Place (9:6–7).

This, of course, was not due to some oversight or mistake in the design of the tabernacle. Nor is it a carping criticism thought up by the Christians to throw at the Jews. The Holy Spirit himself was responsible for the design – on that both orthodox Jews and Christians would agree. And he deliberately designed the tabernacle with its two completely distinct compartments to be a parable, to convey a message, indeed a number of messages, loud, clear and unmistakable (9:8–9).

The first message is so clear as to be immediately obvious – at least, it would be if the translators had only allowed our author to be consistent in his use of technical terms. The significance of the Holy Spirit's design for the tabernacle is that 'the way into the Most Holy Place has not yet been made openly manifest while the first tabernacle still has (*i.e.* retains) standing' (9:8). That is a literal translation. What does it mean?

Look back at the diagram on p. 181. 'The first tabernacle', in the author's terminology, is the first division of the building, the Holy Place. The thing that gives this first tabernacle its separate status, separate, that is, from the second tabernacle, the Most Holy Place, is of course *the* veil, the second veil as our author calls it. Stretched right across the building from floor to ceiling and from wall to wall, it divides the building into two separate compartments, and at the same time blocks the way from the first tabernacle into the Most Holy Place.

The lesson conveyed is so simple, a child could see it: so long as the veil gives the first tabernacle its separate status,[2] the way into the Most Holy Place is automatically barred, closed, cut off, not made manifest. On the other hand, rend, cut down, or remove the veil, and two things automatically happen. First, the way into the Most Holy Place is immediately made manifest. Secondly, the first tabernacle no longer has separate status or standing from the Most Holy Place.

Why, then, did the Holy Spirit's design for the tabernacle so effectively block the way into the Most Holy Place? After all, if we may speak naively but reverently, what was the point of God's coming down from his heaven and of dwelling in the tabernacle, if even the people's high priest could still

DIAGRAM OF THE TABERNACLE WITH THE SECOND VEIL REMOVED

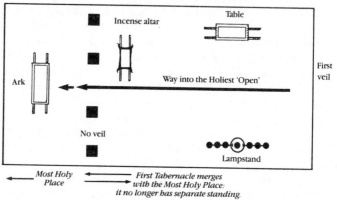

2 For examples of Greek *stasis* meaning 'position' or 'place', see *A Greek-English Lexicon of the New Testament and Other Early Christian Literature*, edited by W. Bauer, adapted and translated by W. F. Arndt and F. W. Gingrich, second edition revised and augmented by F. W. Gingrich and F. W. Danker (University of Chicago Press, 1979).

not enter his presence for more than a few brief moments each year? Why must there be a veil to shut him in, and everybody else, out?

The answer is given us in verses 9–10, which, literally translated, say that the ancient Israelites' sacrifices, ritual washings and gifts, were unable to 'make the worshipper perfect in regard to the conscience'. No Jew, therefore, would have felt fit to enter the immediate presence of God, and none would have been welcome there anyway.

But here we must be careful not to misunderstand our author. He is not denying that the Israelites were forgiven when in repentance and faith they brought their sacrifices. The Old Testament explicitly says they were (see, *e.g.*, Lv. 4:20, 26). True, it was not the animal sacrifices they brought which secured their forgiveness. Those sacrifices were only token payment; the real price of their sins was to be paid by Christ at Calvary. But when in repentance and faith they brought their animal sacrifices as God commanded them, they were forgiven. God says they were; and our author certainly had no intention of contradicting God.

But the forgiveness they received, though real and good, was limited. They brought their sacrifice, confessed their sin, and were forgiven. But that did not mean that they were then permanently in the clear with God. If they had been, they would never have had to offer another sacrifice (see 10:1–2). As it was, if the very next minute they did another (or the same) sin, the whole process of sacrifice had to be repeated. At the very best, all they could claim was that they were forgiven up to the present moment; but what the position between them and God would be next morning, next week, next year, or at life's end, remained, and had to remain, an open uncertain question. Their conscience was never 'made perfect'.

Of course, there are many professing Christians who still feel the same way about forgiveness. They regularly confess their sins, but the most they feel entitled to say is that they are forgiven up to the moment. They hope that at life's end they will be fit enough to enter God's immediate presence, but they have no assurance that they will. And as for being fit here and now to enter God's immediate presence, they would regard the idea as wholly out of the question. Anyone

185

who claimed it would in their eyes be fanatically presumptuous.

Their conscience has obviously not been made perfect. They are not yet fully or truly Christian. Their attitude is no different from that of the Jews who lived when the first tabernacle still retained its separate status, when even the godliest people in Israel (except the high priest) would never have felt fit to draw aside the veil and step into the immediate presence of God on earth – let alone in heaven.

It could be that someone reading this book feels like that. If so, do allow the Holy Spirit now to show you what full-blown Christianity is and what it teaches on this matter of forgiveness and entry in to God's presence, and how immeasurably superior it is to Judaism – and to the kind of forgiveness you yourself believe in at the moment.

Differences between Christianity and Judaism

The first difference concerns the sanctuary in which our high priest ministers. Unlike the old covenant's earthly sanctuary, his tabernacle is not man-made; it is not a part of this creation (9:11). Moses' man-made sanctuary was at best only a copy of the true one (9:24). Christ has entered into heaven itself (9:24). He ministers in the greater and more perfect tabernacle (9:11), the real thing. Compared with this greater and more perfect tabernacle, all the gold and silver and jewels of Moses' tabernacle were but the toys and tinsel of a child.

> No temple made with hands
>   His place of service is;
> In heaven itself he stands,
>   A royal priesthood his.
> In him the shadows of the law
> Are all fulfilled and now withdraw.
>
> (Thomas Kelly)

The second difference concerns the nature of his entry into that heavenly sanctuary. Israel's high priest entered the earthly Most Holy Place on the day of atonement, and came out again the same day – the same hour in fact. The next year he entered again – and came out again. He never stayed in

186

the divine presence. Even on the day of atonement he made at least two entries and two exits; for he could not perform all he had to perform the first time he entered, but had to come out to make another sacrifice (Lv. 16:12, 15).

How different Christ's entry! He entered the Most Holy Place in heaven once and for all (9:12). He did not have to keep entering and coming out and re-entering. His great sufficient sacrifice obtained for us eternal redemption and was already complete when he entered heaven. So having entered, he has remained there in the immediate presence of God as our representative these two thousand years.

Which brings us to the third contrast. Israel's sacrifices, in so far as they did any good at all, provided priests and worshippers with ceremonial cleansing for their bodies. For people still in their spiritual infancy such ceremonial cleansing was not without its value. It began at a lowly level to teach Israel concepts of defilement and cleansing that later on could be applied at a much higher level. One ceremony in particular (referred to here as 'the ashes of a heifer', which, 'sprinkled on those who are ceremonially unclean sanctify them so that they are outwardly clean'; 9:13) had to be applied to anyone who had touched a dead bone or body (see Nu. 19). It made the Israelites feel that physical death is abhorrent to the living God, and defiling to man. (We can only imagine the abhorrence and distress felt by our Lord as he stood at the open grave in which lay his friend Lazarus' stinking corpse; Jn. 11:34–39.)

But if physical death is bad, spiritual death and corruption are worse. And that is our real problem. To worship and serve the living God acceptably nowadays, we must approach not some earthly shrine made of wood, and granite with stained glass windows, either in Jerusalem or in any other place – we must come direct to the living God in heaven. God is spirit, and, as our Lord taught us (Jn. 4:21–24), he must be worshipped in spirit and according to truth. But the unregenerate person is dead – not physically, but spiritually – dead in his transgressions and sins (Eph. 2:1). Obviously he cannot serve and worship God acceptably in that state. He needs cleansing. Not ceremonial cleansing of his body, effected by holy water mixed with ashes, but spiritual cleansing of his conscience and spirit. This Christ provides.

'How much more . . . will the blood of Christ, who through the eternal Spirit offered himself unblemished to God, cleanse our conscience from dead works, that we may serve the living God!' (9:14) (AV/KJV, RV).

And sometimes we who have been genuinely born again, and possess eternal life, find our minds and consciences defiled by some wrong deed or thought by the influence of the world's corruption around us. We then feel unfit to approach God and to worship and serve him. What must we do? If the sin we have done is against a fellow-Christian (or a non-Christian for that matter), we must first go to the one against whom we have sinned and put the matter right (Mt. 5:23–24). But suppose it is a matter between us and God alone. We must confess our sin, and then allow the Holy Spirit by his living Word to apply to our mind and conscience the value of the blood and sacrifice of Christ offered for us at Calvary. Listen again to what the Holy Spirit says: 'How *much more* . . . will the blood of Christ . . . cleanse our conscience from dead works, *so that we may serve* the living God!' We need not be kept back by false consciences. In the full value of Christ's sacrifice we may ever come freely and enjoy access into God's immediate presence.

But what about our relatives who died before the new covenant was made?

Once more we must use our imaginations and try to understand what the readers of the letter felt like when they read it and began to realize the vast superiority of the new covenant over the old. Some of them would sooner or later start to wonder about their grandparents and relatives who had died. 'What about all our ancestors?', they would ask. 'They lived in days when this new covenant was not in existence. Have they all perished? It was not their fault, it was not Moses' fault or Joshua's, that they knew nothing of the new covenant. They did as they were told and brought their animal sacrifices. Now you are telling us that those animal sacrifices never actually put away sin, and never made the conscience perfect. Are they all lost then?'

Thank God, the answer is No; and it is spelled out with the

utmost clarity and certainty in verse 15. The animal sacrifices certainly did not pay the price of the sins that were committed by people living under the old covenant. But the sacrifice of Christ has. Because he offered his sacrifice in the power of the eternal Spirit, the benefit of his sacrifice applies equally to the past and to the future as it does to the present. It avails as much for Moses' sins and Joshua's as it availed for Paul and Peter and avails for you and me, and will avail for people in the future. All who at any time have been, or are, or will be forgiven and saved, have been, are, and will be forgiven and saved in virtue of the sacrifice and blood of the Lord Jesus.

That does not mean that every Israelite in Old Testament times who offered an animal sacrifice for his sins is covered by the sacrifice of Christ. There were unfortunately many ancient Israelites who looked on the offering of a sacrifice as if it were simply the paying of a fine. They had no intention of repenting. Having paid one fine, they would happily go out and repeat the same sin, with the idea that if they were caught, they could afford to pay another fine. Their sacrifices were, in their eyes, simply a licence to sin. God never accepted even their token animal sacrifices. They did not repent, they were not true believers. They are certainly not covered by the sacrifice of Christ. Nor are their counterparts today.

Covenant and will

But now the writer begins to talk about covenants and wills. He points out that with wills the testator, that is the one who makes the will and testament, must die before the will comes into force. Now some readers will be aware that there are certain difficulties in this passage because the Greek word rendered 'will' in verses 16–17 is rendered 'covenant' everywhere else in the chapter. In our modern legal terminology a covenant is not normally the same thing as a will. But in Greek the word in question can be applied both to a covenant and to a will. And what is more, the nature of the new covenant made by Christ is such that it can be properly regarded both as a covenant and as a will. Let us try to think the matter through.

A covenant is made normally by two parties, a will by one. In a covenant, in ancient days, you brought your covenant sacrifice; the two parties agreed to the covenant; the covenant sacrifice died, the blood was shed, and thus the covenant was ratified. But in a matter of a last will and testament, you had no covenant sacrifice. The will was drawn up, but it remained inoperative until the testator, the one who made the will, passed away. And that is still the fact now; if you make your will, it will remain inoperative until you die. But, you see, whereas with the old covenant there were two parties and a covenant sacrifice, what the Lord Jesus has put into operation by his death is a one-party covenant, a testament, a will. And we are not a party to that testament in the sense that we have conditions to fulfil in order to earn its benefits; we have no conditions to fulfil except to repent, believe and accept the benefits.

But do you remember how when Moses came down to the people from Mount Sinai, he put to them the proposition that God had put forward, namely that God was prepared to go with them so long as they fulfilled all that was written in the book of the old covenant, all the law that had been announced on Mount Sinai, all the ceremonial rites that God required of them? These were the conditions which the people had to fulfil. They were weighty and burdensome. It was a system that could not possibly be worked. It was far too heavy a yoke for any human to bear (as Acts 15:10 openly says). And yet the people in their eagerness, as they listened to the terms, replied to God: 'We will do everything the Lord has said; we will obey' (Ex. 24:7). Poor people, they scarcely knew what they said. They stood as parties to the old covenant; the covenant sacrifice was killed, the blood was shed, the blood was sprinkled on the people, and it was ratified. They gave their word solemnly, over the death of the sacrifice, that they would keep the covenant. They had scarcely given their word when they broke the covenant violently and forfeited all their blessings.

It was only the mercy of God that he continued to dwell with them after that as long as he did. The people were constantly sinning, often knowingly but even more often in ignorance. Their very presence around the tabernacle defiled the dwelling-place of God. How then could God consent to continue dwelling among them without compromising his holiness and without allowing the people to think that their sin and uncleanness did not matter?

The answer is that once a year the tabernacle had to be cleansed. It was only a copy of the true heavenly tabernacle (9:23). Nonetheless once a year on the day of atonement Israel's high priest had to go through a most elaborate ceremony so that, as God put it, 'In this way he will make atonement for the Most Holy Place because of the uncleanness and rebellion of the Israelites, whatever their sins have been. He is to do the same for the Tent of Meeting, which is among them in the midst of their uncleanness' (Lv. 16:16). By this means, then, God made his point to ancient Israel. They were alerted to the fact that they were sinful and that only by the shedding of blood could the tabernacle be cleansed and God be enabled to remain dwelling among them.

Contrasts and similarities

But, like the tabernacle itself, the elaborate ceremonies of the day of atonement were only tokens and symbols. They were in themselves no answer to mankind's real need. Our problem is not: On what terms can God put up with us living and working round or near the outside of some consecrated building in the centre of town? But how can we sinners ever enter the immediate presence of God in heaven and be accepted – and know ourselves accepted – there, and form for God a spiritual tabernacle made not of wood or stone but of redeemed human personalities?

Token, animal sacrifices were adequate for cleansing a physical tabernacle that at best contained only 'copies of the heavenly things': they will not do for cleansing 'the heavenly things themselves' (9:23). But what they could not do, Christ has done. So the first thing we notice now is once more the sheer contrast and difference between Judaism's animal sacrifices and the sacrifice of Christ; between Israel's earthly, man-made sanctuary, and heaven itself where Christ now ministers for us (9:23–24). But keep these basic and all-important differences firmly in our minds – the author will certainly not let us forget them – and another very interesting thing will emerge. Because the ancient tabernacle was built

191

(as 8:5 has already reminded us) as a copy and shadow of heavenly things, and because its ceremonies were designed by God, we can use them as a God-given parable (as 9:9 points out). They can serve us as a model to think with as we try to understand what Christ did for us at Calvary, what he is doing for us now, and what he will yet do for us at his second coming.

At the heart of the ceremonies of the day of atonement in ancient Israel were three 'appearances' of the high priest.

1. He first 'appeared' at the altar of sacrifice in the court of the tabernacle in full view of the people, and killed a goat as a sin-offering to put away sin (Lv. 16:7–10, 15).

2. He then took the blood of the sacrifice in a basin and entered the tabernacle. He passed through the first veil as he did every day. But then he did what he did only on this day in the whole of the year: he drew aside the second veil, entered the Most Holy Place and appeared in the immediate presence of God on behalf of the people who continued waiting outside. These were tense moments both for him and for the people. They were self-confessed sinners deserving God's judgment. He was their representative. In the ark that formed God's throne were the tables of the law. He and the people had broken that law. They deserved to suffer its penalty. In acknowledgment of this, he reverently sprinkled the blood of the sacrifice in front and on top of the golden cover of the ark, called 'the atonement cover' in the NIV (in the older translations, 'the mercy seat'), right under the eyes of the symbolic cherubim, the executives of God's throne and judgment. If God accepted the sacrifice, then both he and the people he represented were accepted. If God rejected his sacrifice, both he and the people would perish (Lv. 16:15–17).

3. He then left the Most Holy Place, came out of the tabernacle and appeared a second time before the people waiting outside. Then he took another goat, confessed the nation's sins over its head, and had the goat driven out into the wilderness as a symbolical expression that the people's sins had been forgiven and their guilt removed (Lv. 16:18–28).

What an instructive parable it is! How vividly it helps our minds and imaginations to understand and grasp the significance of our Lord's three great appearings.

First, says our writer, 'he appeared . . . at the end of the

ages to do away with sin by the sacrifice of himself' (9:26).
That great sacrifice was not made in secret. The Son of God,
as pictured by the symbols and shadows of Israel's
ceremonies, and foretold by Israel's prophets, came out of
heaven, appeared on our planet, and, in full view of human
beings and demons, angels and God, offered himself as the
one great and only sacrifice for sins. But notice that unlike
Israel's high priests he appeared once only: 'he has appeared
once for all at the end of the ages' (9:26). They had to appear
at the altar on the day of atonement every year. Why? Because
the token sacrifices they offered could only cover the nation's
sins – and that in symbol only – for one year at a time. If
our Lord's sacrifice had been like theirs, says our writer
(9:25–26), he would have had to come from heaven to Calvary
once every year from the creation of the world to the end of
time. No, thank God, his sacrifice is not like theirs. Do grasp
the difference. He offered it once for all time and for all
eternity.

But some people find this difficult to take in. They can
understand the idea that you sin, offer a sacrifice and are
forgiven; then do another sin, offer another sacrifice and are
forgiven, and so on to the end of life. But they cannot take
it in that the one sacrifice of Christ at Calvary has already
paid the penalty of the believer's sins, all of them, past,
present, and future. So let us notice carefully what is said at
this point.

'Man is destined to die once,' says 9:27, 'and *after that* to
face judgment.' In other words, God does not summon us
into his court, and try our case, and give judgment on us
every day, or every year, of our lives. There is only one final
judgment, and it comes *after* a person has died. It deals with
the whole of his life and all his sins at one and the same court
session. The marvellous news is that in view of that one
judgment covering the whole of a person's life, Christ's one
sacrifice offered once and for all, has for the believer already
paid the penalty of each and every sin that could possibly be
raised at that judgment. (It's well that it has; for Christ is
never going to die again. If some of a believer's sins were not
covered by Christ's death at Calvary, they would remain
unatoned for ever.)

Indeed, the actual situation is even better than we have just described it. Since the penalty of a believer's sins has already been paid, the Judge himself has already declared that the believer 'does not come into judgment' (Jn. 5:24, RSV). The case has already been settled out of court. And the Holy Spirit is about to reassure us that God will never again raise the question of the guilt and penalty of a believer's sins (10:17).

You say, perhaps, 'But how can we be sure of that?'

The answer is to be found in what Christ is doing for us now. He has entered not some specially sacred room in some earthly sanctuary. He has entered heaven itself. And what he is now doing is appearing in the immediate presence of God 'for us' (9:24). Mark those two words 'for us'. It is not surprising that when the Lord Jesus ascended and entered into the immediate presence of God, he was personally accepted for his own sake. But the point is that he did not enter merely for his own sake. He entered as our high priest and representative; and he now appears in the presence of God for us, just as Israel's high priest on the day of atonement appeared in the presence of God as the representative of the people who waited outside. In their case, if their representative high priest was accepted, it meant that the people he represented were accepted. If he was rejected, they were rejected.

And so it is in our case too! If our representative has been accepted, so have we. The question I find myself asking is, 'Does God fully realize that as the Lord Jesus appears now in his presence, he appears not simply for his own sake, but as my personal representative?' The answer is, Yes, of course.

'But does God know all the sins I have done and will yet do?' The answer is, Yes, of course.

'Well, then – and here comes the crucial question – knowing the Lord Jesus has entered and is now appearing for me as the one who died for me at Calvary and now lives as my representative, has God accepted *him*?' The answer once more is, Yes, of course. God has completely accepted him, knowing him to be representing me. Not once in all these 2,000 years has he ever been told that his sacrifice at Calvary is not enough to cover quite all the sins I shall yet do, and that he must leave heaven, come to earth again, and like Israel's high priest, supplement his original sacrifice with another. No, as my representative he sits at the very right hand of God, and not once in 2,000 years has he been asked to move back an inch. It means that all believers can know at this very moment that they are already accepted, and will ever remain so, at the highest level of God's heaven.

And that is not all. Just as Israel's high priest eventually left the Most Holy Place and appeared a second time before the waiting people in and around the court of the tabernacle, so Christ will one day appear a second time at what we call his second coming (9:28). When Israel's high priest appeared before the people the second time, he had to offer another sin-offering. Christ will not have to do that at his second coming. He will come to save those who wait for him (see 1 Thes. 1:10). That is he will complete their salvation by saving their very bodies. The dead will be raised incorruptible; the living will be changed and made immortal. Every believer will be given a body like the risen and glorified body of the Saviour (1 Thes. 4; 1 Cor. 16; Phil. 3:21). And he will take all his ransomed people to his Father's house: not to an earthly tabernacle, or to the temple in Jerusalem which he once called 'my Father's house' (Jn. 2:16), but to the eternal tabernacle of God (Rev. 21:3).

Questions

1 In what way was the ancient tabernacle, built by Moses, unique?

2 What lesson was the Holy Spirit's design of its structure intended to convey (9:8)?

3 What is the counterpart in Christianity of Israel's tabernacle?

4 How does it help our understanding of the terms of our salvation to think of the new covenant as a will (9:16–17)?

5 Were true believers who lived before the death of Christ really forgiven? If so, on what basis? Is our enjoyment of forgiveness better than theirs? If so, in what respects?

6 How many contrasts and similarities can you see in this chapter between what Israel's high priest did for his people on the day of atonement and what Christ has done, is doing, and will yet do for us?

11

THE SUPERIOR SACRIFICE
Hebrews 10

In our last chapter we were thinking about the Lord's appearing for the second time 'to bring salvation to those who are waiting for him'. And very exhilarating it was, for we learned that then our very bodies will be redeemed (Rom. 8:23). At the present time we ourselves are forgiven and have the first fruits of the Spirit; but our bodies are not yet redeemed. True, God, in his creatorial goodness, from time to time heals them when they grow sick – normally through natural means; sometimes, though rarely, miraculously. But we cannot *claim* healing. Our bodies, Scripture insists (1 Cor. 15:53–54), will remain corruptible and mortal, that is, subject to disease and death, until the Lord comes. They could not as they are at present enter God's immediate presence. Flesh and blood cannot inherit the kingdom of God (1 Cor. 15:50). We must wait for that: 'We eagerly await a Saviour, the Lord Jesus Christ, who . . . will transform our lowly bodies so that they will be like his glorious body' (Phil. 3:20–21). The prospect is superbly glorious.

Yet as we wait, there is something else which in its way is more wonderful still. Even now, while we cannot possibly have bodily access into God's presence, we can have spiritual access there. 'Therefore, brothers,' our writer now exhorts us, 'since we have confidence to enter the Most Holy Place by the blood of Jesus, by a new and living way opened for us through the veil, that is, his body, and since we have a great high priest over the house of God, let us draw near to God with a sincere heart in full assurance of faith, having our hearts sprinkled to cleanse us from a guilty conscience and having our bodies washed with pure water' (10:19–22).

The new way

The whole idea, like the way itself, is startlingly new. It did not exist before (9:8). Christ has opened it up. Let's make sure we grasp what is so new and revolutionary about it. The verse is not simply saying that we can pray to God with confidence. God's people all down the centuries have always felt free to pray to him. Nor is it saying that Christ has opened the gates of heaven and so made it possible for us to enter God's presence when we die. It is saying that Christ has made a way for us to enter here and now into the immediate presence of God. We can now do every day of the week what Israel's high priest could only do once a year: enter the Most Holy Place. And there is no doubt which Holy Place that is: it is the one you get at 'through the veil' that is the counterpart of the second veil in the tabernacle. We can now do what Israel's high priest could never do. He could enter only the Most Holy Place in the tabernacle on earth; every day of our lives we can enter the immediate presence of God in heaven.

To the average Jew, the idea would at first seem strange and incredible. Perhaps it did to the first readers of this letter. It might even do so to some of us. For the ancient Jew it was in part his religious background and traditions that made it difficult for him to take advantage of this new and living way into the Most Holy Place. Centuries of indoctrination had trained him to think that no lay persons, only the priests, were allowed to enter the first compartment of the earthly sanctuary, the Holy Place, while the Most Holy Place was forbidden to any but the high priest. The Old Testament told what happened to a king, called Uzziah, who entered the Holy Place and tried to offer incense on the golden altar. God struck him with leprosy and the priests bustled him out of the temple (2 Ch. 26:16–20). How then could a lay person enter the Most Holy Place in heaven?

For some of us the difficulty might be to understand what it means to enter the Most Holy Place in heaven while we are still on earth. We say to ourselves, 'God is in heaven and we are on earth,' and that's that. He can hear us when we pray because he is God. But how can we enter heaven to talk to him? What we should remember is that we are now thinking in spiritual terms, not physical. At this level distance is not to be measured in miles nor light-years. Two people can be sitting in the same room on the same sofa and yet in heart be very distant from each other. Two people can have a conversation, and afterwards one of them will say of the other, 'Yes, we chatted together, but he seemed very distant.' The tax-collector in our Lord's parable (Lk. 18:10–14) went up into the temple to pray. But 'he stood at a distance. He would not even look up to heaven.' God, of course, heard his cry for mercy and he went to his home justified before God, whereas the Pharisee who trusted in his own good works was not justified. But the point is that now we are justified, we need no longer 'stand at a distance'. In spirit we can come right to God's presence and stand before his very throne, because we know that we are completely accepted by him already and he will never cast us out. 'But now in Christ Jesus you who were once far away have been brought near through the blood of Jesus . . . For through him we both have access to the Father by one Spirit' (Eph. 2:13, 18).

Why then could not the ancient Jews enjoy this nearness of access to God? The trouble lay with their sin-offerings. Though they were ordained by God they were only a shadow of the coming great sacrifice of Christ. They were not the reality itself (10:1). They were merely symbols or tokens of it. They could not therefore make perfect those who approached God on that basis. That we can see from the very fact that they kept endlessly repeating the offering of sacrifices year after year in order to get further forgiveness of sins. At no point did they feel that the price of sin had finally been paid completely. If they had, they would not have offered another sacrifice ever. After all, you don't keep on paying monthly instalments when the mortgage on your house has been completely paid off.

The 'remembrance' of sins

The result was, therefore, that Israel's sin-offerings could not remove the sense of distance between them and God. Quite the reverse: they maintained it. In those sacrifices, says our writer, there was a remembrance (NIV, 'reminder') of sins every year (10:3). That, you should notice, means far more than that once a year God suddenly remembered that the Israelites were sinners and that the Israelites likewise suddenly realized the same thing. Nor, incidentally, does God's promise to us that he will not remember our sins any more, mean that somehow he will forget or banish from his memory the fact that we were once sinners. When throughout eternity we look at the nailprints in the Saviour's hands, we shall surely not find ourselves saying, 'I can't remember now why he has those wound marks. What was it that caused them?' Neither will God!

The terms 'remember', 'remembrance', 'remembrancer', are semitechnical terms. Ancient kings had a court official known as the 'remembrancer' or 'recorder' (2 Sa. 20:24). It was his duty to keep the royal records of all significant happenings. And when the king called for it, the recorder had to bring him the books so that the king could examine the record of any particular citizen he was interested in; and if that citizen's record was found to be bad, the king gave sentence and the citizen was executed. That is what is meant by 'remembering' someone's sins (see Rev. 16:19).

And that is what the Israelites believed happened on the day of atonement each year. God, so to speak, called for the books and examined his people's sins for that year. Their guilt was assessed, the penalty demanded. Only by the offering of sacrifices was the wrath of God averted. And then only for the time being. No sooner was one day of atonement over than next year's loomed on the horizon with the prospect of further investigation of guilt, further condemnation, further demand for the penalty to be paid, further danger of the wrath of God and the further urgent need for fresh sacrifices to be offered to gain further forgiveness. The Israelites could never feel that they were fully and finally accepted by God. However much they had been forgiven in the past, the results of next year's investigation always remained an open question. What if God decided next year that the sin-offerings presented by Israel were not enough to cover the nation's guilt, and responded with his rejection and wrath?

No wonder, then, that the average Israelite was never allowed, and never felt free, to enter the immediate presence of God, but stood at a distance, and kept repeatedly offering sacrifices which he hoped would gain him further forgiveness and, one day perhaps, eternal life and entry into God's heaven. The question for our writer was, therefore, how would he get his readers to stop offering these sacrifices?

Cease offering?

Two things stood in the way. First was the fact that these sacrifices had been commanded by God himself in the divinely inspired books of the Pentateuch. To suggest abandoning them would at first seem to a Jew of that time a direct, outright disobedience to Holy Scripture. The second thing was the common experience that when people have guilt on their consciences, they tend to feel better if they can pay something or do something that they think might make amends for their sins. And so they can be very unwilling to be told that their constant offering of sacrifices actually does no good anyway.

Notice then that to deal with the first difficulty the writer does not attempt to say, 'You must abandon your offering of animal sacrifices because the Christian apostles, or other New Testament writers, say you must.' What weight would Christian apostles carry with Jews if they appeared to contradict the Old Testament Scriptures? No, to make his point he quotes the Old Testament Scriptures themselves. Only instead of quoting the Pentateuch, he quotes from the Psalms. Leviticus was God's Word, but so were the Psalms. And, what is more, the Psalms were given to Israel long after the Pentateuch. So they give God's latest word on the subject; and, of course, last orders stand.

Here then in Psalm 40:6–8 a voice is speaking that the readers of our letter would recognize as the voice of the coming Messiah. He has read the heart of God. He realizes that though all down the centuries sacrifices were offered at the command of God and served their God-intended purpose, God's heart was never satisfied with them. How could it be? It is impossible for the blood of bulls and goats to take away sins. What do animals know about sin? They are never haunted by that characteristically human thing – a guilty conscience. Law and morality mean nothing to them. Maintaining true moral and spiritual values is not something they worry about. When they were offered to God to make atonement for sin and came stalling and kicking at the smell of the blood at the altar, they never knew what the sin was that had been done, or how God felt about it or why he must judge it, or why they had to suffer. How then could the sacrifice of animals ever satisfy God?

The superior sacrifice

So now through the psalmist the voice of Messiah is heard as he enters the world, announcing an altogether different kind of sacrifice:

> Sacrifice and offering you did not desire,
>   but a body you prepared for me;[1]
> with burnt offerings and sin offerings
>   you were not pleased.
> Then I said, 'Here I am – it is written
>   about me in the scroll –
> I have come to do your will, O God.

The first thing to notice about these verses (10:5–9), says the writer, is the order of their statements. First comes the statement that the animal sacrifices commanded by the law did not satisfy God. This is at once followed by Messiah's statement that he has come to do God's will. This second statement therefore is meant to be the answer to the problem mentioned in the first statement. The animal sacrifices are to be done away with because of their inability to satisfy God. In their place is to be put Messiah's doing of the will of God. The first is taken away, the second put in its place.

Here then is the first reason why his sacrifice is infinitely superior to the sacrifice of animals. He did know about sin. He was utterly sinless himself. His conscience was never once blurred or blunted by so much as one wrongdoing or compromise. He saw the evil and horror of human sin as no other man has ever seen it. And being God incarnate in a

---

[1] The Hebrew of this verse says, ' . . . but my ears have you pierced'. To bring out the meaning of this metaphor, the Septuagint renders it dynamically, 'but a body you have prepared for me'. The Holy Spirit has chosen to use this rendering as being easier for New Testament readers to understand.

human body he understood how God in his holiness felt about sin as no other human being could possibly understand it, and understood perfectly what God willed him to do about it. It was God's will that he should sanctify us by the offering of his sinless body. He did the will of God. He offered his body. We were sanctified. And his one act of offering has so completely satisfied God that he has never needed, nor will ever need, to offer his body again. God has what he always wanted; animal sacrifices are obsolete and irrelevant.

Here then is the answer to the first difficulty. But what about the second? How will the writer help his readers overcome the urge to keep on making further offerings because offering sacrifices somehow makes them feel better in their consciences?

First he points to the contrast between the posture of Israel's priests in the earthly sanctuary and Christ's posture in the heavenly sanctuary. Israel's priests, every single one of them, stood: Christ sits (10:14). There was no seat among the items of symbolic furniture in the earthly tabernacle, no seat or throne for even the high priest to sit on. Deliberately and significantly so. The ritual of offering sacrifices was never finished. It was not that they had so many different sacrifices to offer. The sacrifices were the same few sacrifices. But the act of offering had to be repeated time and again. Ceremonially, therefore, they were never allowed to sit down.

But when Christ entered the Most Holy Place in heaven, ceremonially speaking, he sat down, says the writer.

'How does he know that?' we ask.

Because Psalm 110:1 says so. It is God who is speaking and he tells the ascended Messiah to sit at his right hand. Why sit? Because by his one act of offering he has perfected for ever those who are being made holy. His work of offering is done. It is not simply that he does not need to offer further and different sacrifices. He does not need to keep on offering his own one sacrifice. He does not sit in heaven eternally offering his sacrifice to God. He is finished with the process of offering. He sits there simply waiting, as Psalm 110:1 puts it, for his enemies to be made his footstool (10:13).

And then to show that he has interpreted Psalm 110 correctly, the author next appeals to the terms of the new covenant once more. Notice, he says, how carefully the Holy

203

Spirit has arranged the order of those terms. First, 'I will put my laws in their hearts, and I will write them on their minds.'

That great operation on our hearts and minds by the Holy Spirit begins at our conversion to Christ and continues throughout the rest of our earthly days as we learn more and more to live holy lives. Forgiveness is not a licence to live in sin. What happens then if, in the course of learning to be holy, we fall and sin? Is it not then necessary and helpful for us to offer a sacrifice to secure forgiveness for these sins and to get peace of conscience?

No!

Why not?

Look at the last set of terms in the new covenant. Precisely in this context of our ongoing, and sometimes failing, life of progressive holiness, God has guaranteed that he will not remember our sins and lawless acts any more. That is, he will not raise the question of the penalty they deserve and will never demand that it be paid. Why not? Because it has been paid already!

Now where you already have forgiveness like that, says our writer, there is no more offering for sin (10:18). And it will be worth while making sure we understand exactly what he is saying. The Greek word *prosphora*, here translated 'offering', can mean two somewhat different things. It can mean 'something offered', 'a sacrifice'. Or it can mean 'the process of offering something', 'the act of sacrificing'. In the present context it is the second of these two meanings that the author intends. He is not saying that we do not need another sacrifice besides the sacrifice of Christ – true though that is. He is saying that the whole activity of offering sacrifices for sin can now cease. As believers we are to offer sacrifices of praise, and of good works (13:15–16). But not in order to get forgiveness of sins. We need not, and we must not, go on offering any sacrifice for sin, not even the sacrifice of Christ itself. How delightfully and forcefully the Holy Spirit puts it. He might have said, 'Christ's offering is so perfect that as a result all your sins have been forgiven.' And that would have been true. But he steps it up one degree further and says, 'All your sins have been forgiven; as a result of that no further offering is needed or permitted.'

But surely, someone will say, we Christians are expected

to offer our bodies as living sacrifices, holy and pleasing to God, aren't we?

Certainly we are. Paul says that very thing in Romans 12:1. But we don't do it in order to get forgiveness. We do it in gratitude because we have been forgiven. And we must never confuse our sacrifice with his. His sacrifice atoned for our sins. Ours can never do that; and there's no atoning left for us to do anyway. It has all been done long ago. We must not, therefore, try to join our sacrifice to Christ's and offer both to God.

Entry into the Most Holy Place

With complete and utter confidence, then, and with a sincere heart in full assurance of faith, we are now to draw near and enter the Most Holy Place. How the Holy Spirit does delight to emphasize the confidence which every true believer has to enter the Holiest of All! It goes without saying that such confidence is not presumption. It is based on God's own provision. For ancient Israel's priests God provided a double ceremonial cleansing. There was cleansing by literal blood at the altar, and cleansing by literal water at the laver. We have the double reality of which Israel's cleansings were only symbolic.

First, our hearts have been sprinkled with the blood of Jesus (not literally, of course, but metaphorically), and so cleansed from a guilty conscience. That is justification. We do not have to suppress our guilty consciences, or force them in any way. When our consciences see that the wrath of God against us has been righteously appeased, and the penalty of our sins fully paid, they rightly lose all fear and can approach God with total confidence and in peace.

Secondly, our bodies have been bathed with pure water (not literally, again, but metaphorically). Not *sprinkled* with water (as our consciences have been with blood), or even rinsed with water, but bathed all over with water. The Greek word for 'bathed' is the same as that used in John 13:10 where our Lord says, 'A person who has been bathed all over needs only to rinse his feet; his whole body is clean' (my translation). The language, of course, is metaphorical once more. Our Lord is talking of that initial, complete and once-for-all

205

sanctification which takes place when in true repentance and faith someone trusts the Saviour. He is not talking of baptism (one big baptism to start with and many minor baptisms thereafter!?), or of literal water whether common or holy. When our Lord added, in virtue of this once-and-for-all bathing all over in water, ' "You are clean, though not every one of you." For he knew who was going to betray him, and that was why he said not every one was clean', he obviously did not mean, 'You have all been baptized except Judas.' Judas had doubtless been baptized along with the rest; but he had not been 'bathed all over', he had not been sanctified. But every true believer has. 'You were washed,' Paul says, 'you were sanctified, you were justified in the name of the Lord Jesus Christ and by the Spirit of our God' (1 Cor. 6:11).

And thirdly, we have a great priest, that is a high priest, over the house of god. When the young Israelite priests began their complicated duties in the solemn courts of the temple, it must have been a comfort to them to have a high priest who was an expert and could show them just what to do and how to behave in the divine presence. Thank God, as we come into the awesome dwelling-place of God, we have a high priest to take us by the hand, to present us at court, to prompt and lead our praise and prayer, and to tell us how to behave before the Majesty in the heavens. Israel's high priest wore on his mitre a plate of pure gold engraved with the words 'HOLY TO THE LORD'. He did this, Scripture explains (Ex. 28:36–38), so that he might bear "the guilt involved in the sacred gifts the Israelites consecrate . . . It will be on Aaron's forehead continually so that they will be acceptable to the Lord'. So Christ – only in a far fuller sense – has made himself responsible for the imperfections of our worship and prayers. He has borne the guilt not only of the sins we did as sinners, but also of our sins and imperfections as saints and worshippers. We may therefore enter boldly into the very presence of God through the veil, not because we have merit, or have attained to an advanced stage of sanctification; but in spite of all our imperfections, thanks solely to Jesus Christ, our Lord, Saviour and high priest.

An important technicality

But now I must trouble you with an important technicality
– and if you don't like technicalities, perhaps you ought to
skip this next paragraph or two.

It concerns the phrase in 10:20, 'the way which he dedicated
for us . . . through the veil, that is to say, his flesh' (my
translation).

In 6:19–20 we were told that 'our hope enters into what lies
inside the veil where as precursor (AV/KJV; NASB 'forerunner')
Jesus has entered for us' (my translation). There the author
was using the veil which separated the Most Holy Place from
the Holy Place as a metaphor for that veil whatever it is, that
hides the unseen world of God's presence from the visible
world in which we live. That veil, of course, still hangs in
place.

Some people think that he is using the veil in the same
sense in 10:20. They take him to be saying that our Lord has
opened up a way through the veil, and that way is the way
of his flesh, the way, that is, of his humanity. Since as a real
human being he has passed through the veil which still hides
the invisible world of heaven from our eyes, we too may pass
through that veil, in spirit now, later on in body as well. It
is certainly possible to understand the Greek of our verse in
this way.

More likely, however, our author is using the veil in 10:20
in a different way from that in 6:19–20. He is now saying
that the veil in the tabernacle can be taken as a picture of our
Lord's human body. 'Impossible!' say many. 'Our Lord never
acted as a veil to hide God from anybody: he always *revealed*
God to people.'

But that is to fail to notice the full function of the veil in
the ancient tabernacle. It certainly hid the presence of God
in the Most Holy Place from the priests who ministered in
the Holy Place. On the other hand, that veil was a merciful
provision. If it had not been there, the Most Holy Place and
the Holy Place would have all been one, and the priests would
not have been able to enter even the Holy Place. As it was,
with the veil in place, they could come into the Holy Place
right up to the veil; and the outer face of the veil, with its
vivid colours and symbolic cherubim, could begin to give

them some idea of the God who dwelt just on the other side of it.

In that sense our Lord's body acted as a veil when he was here on earth. In him dwelt all the fullness of God (Col. 1:19). Yet sinful men and women, who could not possibly have entered the immediate presence of God, could come near to Christ and touch his very body even though God dwelt within him. How near God must have seemed to people then.

But we can come even closer to God now; for Christ no longer acts as a veil. At Calvary he offered his spotless body to God, and was accepted: now risen from the dead, that body has gone into heaven, and we in spirit are invited to follow him right into the presence of God. In that sense there is no longer any veil for us.

'What about the veil in the temple being torn when Christ died?' you ask. 'What significance did that have?'

A double significance. First, it announced the end of Judaism's system of worship. That system, as we have seen, could not operate without the veil hanging there and permitting the priests to enter the Holy Place. Remove the veil, and, for Jews who would not accept the sacrifice of Jesus, their whole system of worship was unworkable. It was as though God had written 'Cancelled' over the whole thing.

Secondly, for those who had eyes to see it, it proclaimed that the way into the Most Holy Place in heaven itself had been opened up. The earthly tabernacle, that had functioned for centuries as such a fine copy of heavenly things, was no longer necessary. It was now obsolete. Soon it would vanish away.

The Lord's return

We are, then, to draw near in spirit into the Most Holy Place where Christ is now. But we are also constantly to remember that Christ is coming again. As the end of chapter 9 told us, he will appear the second time. He will come bodily and visibly (Acts 1:11). And he will come soon. The Day is approaching (10:25). 'In just a little while, "He who is coming will come and will not delay" ' (10:37).

Only true believers will be ready for him. Only true believers will rise to meet him and be taken to the Father's

house to be for ever with the Lord (Jn. 14:1–3;
1 Thes. 4:14–18). If we are true believers, we must show we
are, and act as true believers. We must *live* by faith, as all
God's righteous ones do (10:38).

What will that involve? It will mean sticking to our guns
and holding unswervingly to the hope we profess. Christ
promised to come again. He is faithful. He will assuredly
keep his promise. We must not allow liberalism to empty that
promise of its meaning. It is not a myth. Our Lord's promise
means literally what it says. We must give equal weight to
the prophetic side of our faith, and to the doctrine of the
second coming as we do to our other Christian doctrines. It
is not irrelevant to practical Christian living. The thought of
his coming is in fact a very necessary spur to holiness and
loyal, diligent service (10:24).

And the nearer we can see the Day approaching, the more
we need to meet together with our fellow-believers to
encourage one another. We need to get and give all the help
we can. To imagine we don't is an ominous sign.

What will it mean if someone who once professed to believe
in Jesus as the Messiah, as the One who died, rose, ascended
and is coming again, now deliberately repudiates that
profession and goes back to Judaism? The author tells us in
10:26–31. We considered this passage in detail in our very
first chapter. We need only summarize now what we found
then and make sure that we have understood what sin it is
that the author is describing here when he says: 'If we sin
wilfully after we have received the knowledge of the truth,
there remains no longer any sacrifice for sins.'

The NIV of this verse says: 'If we deliberately keep on
sinning after we have received the knowledge of the truth, no
sacrifice for sins is left'. If we follow this translation, we must
be careful not to misread it and so form a wrong impression
in our minds. The author is not saying that if true believers
persist in sinning deliberately, there will come a point where
the value of the sacrifice of Christ runs out, so to speak; or
that Christ will say, 'I have paid for your sins up to this
point, but I am not prepared to pay for them any further.'
That would be crude thinking indeed, and wrong on two
counts.

First, the apostle John tells us that true believers do not

constantly make a practice of sinning (1 Jn. 3:6–10). Any one who does is of the devil and not a true believer at all. He never was 'born of God'. True believers certainly sin from time to time (1 Jn. 1:6 – 2:2); but they do not persist in sinning deliberately and in making a practice of it. They confess their sins and ask God's help to forsake them. For them the blood of Christ 'shall never lose its power, till all the ransomed church of God be saved, to sin no more'.

Secondly the author proceeds to describe for us in detail in verse 29 what this wilful, deliberate sin is which he has in mind. It involves deliberately denying the deity of the Lord Jesus and therefore holding that his blood is common and worth no more than anyone else's blood. Further, it involves, by inescapable logic, holding that the new covenant established by that blood is totally invalid and worthless. And it means insulting the Spirit of grace, and deliberately opting to stand upon one's own merits.

To commit that sin and persist in it in ignorance as Saul of Tarsus did for a while is serious enough. But ignorance makes mercy possible. Persist in that sin, no longer in ignorance, but in full knowledge of the facts; deliberately reject the sacrifice of Christ with eyes open and illumined by the Holy Spirit – then there is no longer any sacrifice available. Judaism's sacrifices were never more than symbols; but, such as they were, for many centuries God accepted them and pronounced forgiveness over those who brought them with a true heart. But they are now obsolete. God no longer accepts them, and certainly not at the hands of anyone who has deliberately rejected the sacrifice of Christ. For such a person there remains nothing but the consuming fire of God's judgment and vengeance.

No retreat

Retreat to Judaism and its sacrifices is for ever cut off, then, for a true believer. Our writer is not hard-hearted. He knows the persecution and pressures his readers have endured since they professed faith in Jesus as the Messiah. He knows how the apparent delay in the Lord's return tries their faith and brings on them the arguments of their unconverted friends that Jesus is never going to return, for the simple reason that he was an impostor. And he knows how strong the temptation would sometimes be for them to think that Judaism was still a valid system into which they might retreat, so avoiding the continued pressure and yet retaining spiritual respectability.

But it cannot be done, not at least if they are true believers. Of course if they have all the while been Judases, they will eventually desert the Lord Jesus, go back, join those who crucified him, and incur God's eternal displeasure. But our writer has greater confidence in them than to think that. He is convinced that in spite of their present inconsistencies they are true believers. Joining them with himself he boldly asserts: 'We are not of them who shrink back unto perdition; but of them that believe to the saving of the soul' (10:39, AV/KJV). Their early conviction, produced in them by the Spirit of God, was true: they had in heaven a better and lasting possession, far outweighing their temporary loss and suffering. They would respond now to his call for endurance. Like Peter they would recover from their temporary wavering. They would show themselves to be true believers. They would live and witness boldly for the Saviour. They would loyally wait for his Second Coming, assured by God himself that in the light of what was involved the period of waiting, of trial, suffering and persecution was only for a little while. And then the great and eternal reward would be theirs.

Questions

1 In what sense is the way into the Most Holy Place, which the Lord Jesus has opened up for us, new? And what does it mean to describe it as a living way?

2 When we are urged to 'draw near' (10:22), does that mean (a) that we are to live now in such a way that when we die, or when the Lord comes, we may eventually enter heaven? Or,
(b) that we can in some way enter the presence of God in heaven now? If (b), in what way?

3 What does the new covenant mean when it says that God will not *remember* our sins any more?

4 Why, in spite of their repeated offering of sacrifices, could ordinary Israelites not feel free to enter the Most Holy Place?

5 What is wrong nowadays in offering anything in order to obtain forgiveness of sins or eternal life?

6 What would be involved in a professing Christian returning to Judaism?

7 What part does faith in the second coming of Christ play in your life?

12

FAITH'S DOCTRINES AND PILGRIMAGE
Hebrews 11:1–16

To understand the part this chapter plays in the letter, we should first notice that the virtue it speaks of is *faith*. That may seem to be a very elementary observation to make, but it is crucial. The great need of the Hebrews to whom the letter was written was faith. The thing that had been called into doubt by their behaviour was not their godliness, or their zeal in religion, but their faith.

Do we not remember how the writer early on pointed out that their ancestors failed to enter the promised land for lack of just this quality, for lack of faith, for unbelief? Then at the end of chapter 10 this is how he summed up what the situation was for his readers: It is a question of either going on, waiting patiently for the Lord to come and living by faith (for God has said, 'The just shall *live* by faith'); or, on the other hand, of drawing back, which means to abandon any profession of faith and to be lost eternally.

What is faith?

So now he begins to describe and illustrate what faith really is and does. What does it mean to be a believer? What does it mean to *live* by faith?

We have often observed that the faith spoken of throughout this letter is the faith without which no-one can please God, without which we are not believers at all. The ancient Israelites in the desert failed to believe the gospel. They were not believers in any true sense of the word. They may have believed 'for a while', as the Lord phrased it (Luke 8:13); but they certainly had no root in themselves. That kind of faith is no good. When the test came, they were found never to have truly believed the gospel. Now once more at 11:6 the writer explicitly says that by 'faith' he means that true and genuine faith by which we truly come to God and truly please him; without which it is in fact impossible to please him; without which we are not true believers at all.

On the other hand, we are about to be shown in this chapter that you cannot divide faith into nice, tidy, separate compartments and categories. We start our life with God by faith. It is not a different kind of faith that thereafter carries us on, but that same faith still. And the faith by which we start, though small at the beginning, has within it all the potential for growth, action and endurance that is about to be illustrated for us in chapter 11 of Hebrews.

The faith we exercise when first we receive salvation is such that it will inevitably show itself in life. It cannot be completely hidden. It cannot completely fail to mould our lives. True faith is a living thing. It will result in an altered life, it will be courageous for God, it will act, it will persist and endure.

Sometimes I feel a little uneasy when I hear people say that to be saved you do not have to do anything at all. I know what some preachers mean when they say that. In the sense they mean, it is true. Of course, you cannot earn salvation by good works; of course faith is rest, a resting on the work of Christ; of course, faith is a receiving and not a giving.

But true faith is always active right from the very beginning. The prostitute of Luke 7 believed the Saviour's message, and because she believed, she came to him and wept over his feet. A belief that had stayed put and not come, would not have been true faith at all. In Luke 8, the woman with the haemorrhage believed the Saviour, and because she believed, she elbowed her way through the crowd and touched the hem of his garment. A faith that claimed to believe but did not come, would not be faith at all. It is so even in the act of conversion: true faith is ever active and comes to the Saviour, and deliberately puts out the hand and takes what the Saviour promises.

A description of faith

Faith, then, is the assurance of things hoped for, the conviction about things not seen (11:1, AV/KJV). Or, as the NIV puts it, faith is being sure of what we hope for and certain of what we do not see. Faith makes you sure that the future things you hope for – and therefore by definition do not yet possess (see Rom. 8:24–25) – are really yours, so that you learn to count on them as if you already had them. Some things are invisible, either because that is their nature, or because they are as yet hidden in the future. Faith brings us conviction that they are real so that we count them as certainties and base our choices and decisions on them and guide our lives by them.

That's how the godly men and women of a past age lived. That's how we must live too. You are so used to exercising faith that you would be startled if you were to sit down and think how many things you reckon with as realities, solely by faith. You believe implicitly, don't you, that Christ is coming again? He isn't here yet! You believe he is in heaven, but you have never seen him there! You believe that he prays for you every day, but you have never heard him. You stake everything on his sacrifice, but you were not there to see it. And how do you know he is risen again? Yes, you have become so used to exercising faith that these things have become an integral part of your daily life. Having believed them, you have found that they are real and stand the test of experience. Faith is the assurance of things hoped for, conviction about things unseen.

Faith's basic doctrines

1. Creation

The first major area in which we will show ourselves to be true believers is in holding the basic doctrines of the faith, in standing for them vigorously and in acting upon them.

First, the doctrine of *creation*. 'By faith we understand that the universe was formed by the spoken word of God so that what is seen was not made of what was visible' (my translation).

215

Things are not what they seem. Here we stand on very solid *terra firma*. We are surrounded by things which, because we can touch and smell and taste and see and hear them, seem real to us. And sometimes we are afraid to let them go for the spiritual and unseen. But think a minute. Where did all this solid matter come from, this earth and all its products? Did it always exist? No! All that we can see has come out of things we cannot see. We are standing on something that once upon a time could not be seen, or touched, or tasted, or smelt, or heard. So the whole universe in which we live is one gigantic object lesson for faith. If we could have stood at God's side a moment or two before creation sprang into being, we would have had to have tremendous faith to believe that anything could happen at all, because it all came out of nothing! We should never let this material world seem more real to us than the spiritual. It isn't. The spiritual realm is, if anything, far more real.

Now it is by faith that we understand that the universe was formed by the word of God. That does not mean that the basis of our understanding is somehow inferior to the conclusions of science which can be logically proved. Some things can never in that sense be proved by mere logic; they must be discerned, accepted and enjoyed by faith. Take the beauty of a flower or the motive of an action. An action can be observed, and its results measured. But the love that lay behind the action cannot be measured or finally 'proved'. If we are going to believe that genuine love was the motive that lay behind the action, we shall do so because having surveyed the evidence, we are then prepared to take a reasonable step of faith and believe the claim of the person who did the action, that he or she acted in love.

It is certainly not unreasonable to believe that the universe was formed by the spoken word of God. Everywhere in living nature we find not just matter, but matter programmed with 'information' and able to impart that information to other matter. The original matter perishes; the information persists. Where did the information come from?

Current scientific theory suggests that the universe began with the 'big bang'. Scientists do not seem to regard it as part of their province to ask or decide where whatever it was that went bang came from. They have no answer, therefore (and rightly do not pretend to have one), to the question: What is the purpose behind and the goal in front of human life? As scientists, therefore, they are ultimately purpose-less and hope-less.

We know the answer to this fundamental and all-important question by faith. The Creator has spoken through the prophets and finally in his Son. We believe him; and we have purpose and meaning and hope. If we are true believers, we shall stand firmly and vigorously at every level for the doctrine of creation. Everything else rests on it.

2. Sacrifice

Second, the doctrine of sacrifice and approach to God. This is a fallen world, and the next major question after creation is: how may we approach God acceptably?

Cain made a fundamental mistake. His works, John tells us, were evil (1 Jn. 3:12). He thought he could carry on sinning and yet keep himself right with God by formally bringing an offering to keep God happy while he himself unrepentantly persisted in his sinful way of life. Impossible! Sacrifice is not a bribe, nor a cover-up, nor a licence to sin. God rejected Cain's offering and eventually Cain himself.

Abel offered a better sacrifice than Cain, and God accepted it. That showed, says the writer, that Abel was righteous. Not sinless, of course, but right with God, and living a life pleasing to God. But notice what the verse does not say. It does not say that by faith Abel did righteous works and on that ground his sacrifice was accepted. It says, 'By faith Abel offered God a better sacrifice.' To do something by faith, you must do it in response to, and according to, a word from God. And what Abel is said to have done by faith was to offer his sacrifice. It was by faith because he brought it in response to God's word, whether in response to the example God set his parents in Eden (3:21), or in response to some other word of God which Genesis does not record. It was not that Abel simply 'had great faith in his sacrifice', or felt that his works were so good that he could be sure that God would accept his sacrifice. Many people conceive strong convictions like that in their hearts; but it is not faith: it is presumption, because their conviction is simply their own subjective idea, not based on anything God has said.

Nowadays, if we are true believers, we will show it first by shunning any and every attitude tainted by Cain's mistake, and then by making sure that the sacrifice by which we approach God is the sacrifice described in his Word – and nowhere more fully than in our epistle. To persist in offering sacrifices for sin, now that God has said that all such sacrifice is finished, would raise a query whether we were true believers at all.

3. Final salvation

Thirdly, the doctrine of our final salvation. By faith Enoch was translated, that is removed from our world, so that he should not experience death (11:5–6). We have no need to try to water down this statement. The writer obviously means to imply that Enoch was *bodily* removed from our world, for he adds, '*he was not found* because God had removed him' (my translation). We are reminded of how the sons of the prophets went looking for Elijah after he was similarly removed without experiencing death – and did not find him either (2 Ki. 2:16–17).

Enoch's removal to heaven without dying naturally reminds us of the final stage of our salvation, when the Lord comes. Millions of believers from all over the world will similarly be removed to heaven without dying. 'We will not all sleep, but we will all be changed – in a flash, in the twinkling of an eye, at the last trumpet. For the trumpet will sound, the dead will be raised imperishable, and we will be changed' (1 Cor. 15:51–52).

So we may take a lesson from Enoch. 'By faith Enoch was taken from this life, so that he did not experience death.' How 'by faith'? And how does our author know it was by faith? Because, he points out, before Enoch was removed, it was said of him[1] that he pleased God. And since (so the author argues) it is impossible to please God without faith – indeed, you cannot truly come to God at all without believing – Enoch must have been a true believer. And it was because he was a true believer that he was taken to heaven without dying.

[1] In Scripture: Gn. 5:24. The Hebrew has, 'Enoch walked with God.' The Greek rendering is a dynamic translation.

The lesson is clear. The Lord's coming draws ever nearer. If we are alive when he comes, and we wish to be caught up to meet him in the air (1 Thes. 4:17), we too must be true believers. How, then, shall we show we are? By daily walking with God, by living constantly to please him. The apostle John makes the same point. When the Lord appears, he says, we shall be like him, for we shall see him as he is (1 Jn. 3:2). The hope is glorious. But then he adds, 'Everyone who has this hope in him purifies himself, just as he is pure' (verse 3). Notice that this is a statement of fact, not an exhortation. It is the fact that everyone that has the hope purifies himself. Anyone who consistently neglects to purify himself shows that he does not possess the hope. He is not a true believer.

4. The wrath to come

Fourthly, the doctrine of the coming wrath. Noah is commended because, when God warned him of the coming judgment, he believed it. And not simply as a theory or as a doctrine that fitted neatly into his scheme of systematic theology. He believed it as a practical reality – even though humanly speaking it seemed a most unlikely thing – and he showed his faith by doing something about it. He had a family that needed to be saved. How could he really believe that the flood was coming without doing something about the salvation of his family? True faith acts. Noah built an ark to save them.

Our Lord warned us that his second coming will be like Noah's flood. It will deluge this world with judgment (Lk. 17:26–37). The world at large does not believe this. People have consigned Noah and his ark to the category of fairy story, and they imagine that no-one believes in the literal second coming of Christ except a few deranged fanatics. They will, as our Lord pointed out, thus be totally unprepared for his coming and will suffer its catastrophic judgments.

But how can we claim really to believe in the coming judgment unless, like Noah, we are doing something about the salvation of others? And if we don't really believe in the coming judgment in spite of all that Christ said about it, we cannot claim, like Noah, to be heirs of the righteousness that comes by faith. Justification by faith is based on the premiss that the wrath of God is constantly 'revealed from heaven

219

against all the godlessness and wickedness of men' (Rom. 1:18), and that it will be universally executed on the day when God will judge the world with justice by the man he has appointed (Acts 17:31). Justification has as its prime objective that all who believe shall be saved from the wrath of God through Christ (Rom. 5:9). Fail or refuse to take seriously the fact of the coming wrath, and justification by faith is emptied of its meaning and purpose.

Then there is another thing. By building an ark to save his family, so the writer points out, Noah condemned the world. He couldn't help doing so. He couldn't do the one thing without automatically doing the other. He couldn't believe and preach that people needed to get inside the ark to be saved from the flood without implying that people outside the ark would be lost. Neither can we. We must beware of the illogical sentimentality that says, 'Yes, I believe in Christ and I am waiting for him to come from heaven as my rescuer from the coming wrath (1 Thes. 1:10),' but then adds, 'Of course, I wouldn't like to say that those who reject Christ are in any danger or that they will come to much harm.'

Next let us notice what it was that Noah condemned by building his ark: 'he condemned the world'. That is, he did not merely imply that violence and immorality were wrong and that those who were found guilty of these things would eventually have to be taken out and punished. He believed and preached that the whole world system was wrong, its religion, politics, economics – all were vitiated by sin to the point where God was going to destroy them all, and start again.

As Christians we are called upon to believe and preach the same thing. The second coming of Christ will destroy the world's false political system (Rev. 11:15–18; 13; 17; 19:19–21), its false religious system (Rev. 17; 19:1–4), and its false economic and social systems (Rev. 18).

If Noah-like we believe that the whole world-system stands thus under the judgment of God, which will be executed at the return of Christ, the practical effect it will have upon us will be to make us follow the example of the next hero of the faith, Abraham.

The pilgrimage of faith

Abraham now dominates the lessons which the author teaches us from verse 8 to verse 16. The city in which Abraham was born and brought up, together with the surrounding cities, was a brilliant example of the civilization and culture to which the ancient world attained from time to time. But Abraham left it all and became a pilgrim. The negative reason he left it is plain to see from the goal he set for his pilgrimage: 'he was looking forward to the city with foundations, whose architect and builder is God' (11:10). The clear implication is that in his judgment the cities, cultures and societies of his native land were built on inadequate and unsatisfactory foundations. The positive reason he left it is told us by Stephen (Acts 7:2): 'The God of Glory appeared' to him. After that nothing could content him until he reached the city of the living God (Heb. 12:22).

1. Faith's first step (11:8)

'By faith Abraham, when called, obeyed and went out to a place which he would later receive as an inheritance. He went out even though he did not know where he was going' (11:8).

So the first step in Abraham's pilgrimage of faith was one of blind obedience. He had God's promise and that was enough. When the call came, he obeyed it. He did not demand to have everything explained to him first so that he could then make up his mind whether he would follow God's call or not. Knowing it was God's call, he obeyed it simply because it was God's call. That's what it means to follow *God*. If it had been the call of a mere human being, he would have been wise to demand to know and understand all the details before he decided whether to follow it. But he couldn't treat God that way. If he was the God of glory, the one, true and only God, and if Abraham really believed it, then he must be prepared to do what God said, just because it was God that said it – whether he knew and understood the whys and the wherefores and the hows or not.

And so it is with us and the Lord Jesus. He will not ask us blindly to believe that he is the Son of God. He will give us plenty of evidence on which to base our faith (Jn. 20:30–31). But suppose we come to believe that he is the

221

Son of God. That will do us no good whatsoever unless we then become his genuine disciples. And the very first step he will demand of us as his disciples is that we accept his lordship over everything and everybody, ourselves, our thoughts, decisions and possessions, before we go any further. And we must accept it unreservedly (Lk. 14:25–27, 33). We cannot be his disciples on the understanding that he will first explain to us in detail what he would like us to do, and why, and then leave us free to decide on each occasion whether we like his demands or not and whether or not we consent to them. That would be to treat Christ not as Lord but merely as a professional adviser or as one business person treats another. If we really believe that he is the supreme Lord, we shall do what he says, just because he says it, whether we understand it or not, and whether we like it or not. What does our profession of faith amount to, if we call him 'Lord, Lord', and then do not do what he says? (Lk. 6:46). Unreserved obedience is the first step on the path of discipleship.

2. Faith's ultimate goal (11:9–10)

But if it is important that we start our pilgrimage on the right foot, so to speak, it is also important that we get our ultimate goal clearly in our sights from the very beginning. Abraham did, and so did the other patriarchs. They arrived in the promised land and were informed by God that this was the land which was to be theirs and their descendants'. But they made no attempt to build a city there and to settle down. They continued to live in tents like strangers in a foreign country. It was not that they were ungrateful or that they despised the great earthly possessions that God was giving them or the brilliant career that God had in mind for their descendants in that land. All that was good. They would enjoy it in its day. But nothing on this temporary earth could be their main goal. In their hearts they had already left it all. Only the eternal city could be their goal. So Abraham continued to live as a pilgrim and foreigner. It doubtless took a lot of faith to do so. His secret was that he kept his sights on the eternal city. That nourished his faith in its reality; and faith in its reality kept him from treating anything in this world as though it were his main objective.

His secret may be ours. We are meant to enjoy our God-given present and future earthly blessings and careers; but we must not let them loom so large in our thinking that they virtually become life's chief goal. If we do, the danger is that we shall settle down in this world as if it were our home, cease to live like pilgrims and foreigners, and belie our professed faith that we are looking for the eternal city. Our goals and way of life will then be no different from those of people of the world.

3. Faith's fruitfulness (11:11–12)

Verse 11 has suffered some textual disturbance over the centuries. Perhaps the best reading would be the one that yields the translation: 'By faith he [*i.e.* Abraham], along with Sarah, received strength to beget a child when he was past age, since he counted him faithful who had promised.'[2] Certainly Abraham's persistence in living as a foreigner and pilgrim on earth was no negative, barren, unproductive running away from life. Quite the opposite. Perhaps no-one else recorded in Scripture, except of course our Lord, and perhaps also Paul (the great expounder of Abraham's life), has had such an immense influence on his fellows. His life and Sarah's have been astonishingly – in sober fact, miraculously – fruitful.

We think of the great and distinguished nation, influential out of all proportion to its size, which has sprung physically from him. Its birth was a miracle directly attributable to his faith and Sarah's. More impressive still are the multi-millions of his spiritual progeny from every nation (see Rom. 4:16–17). How many myriads of those who shall inhabit the eternal city, will, under God, owe their initial justification by faith and their persistence in a life of faith to the guidance and encouragement of Abraham's example.

If we would live fruitful and not barren lives (2 Pet. 1:8) and influence others for God, we must discover his secret. How did his faith manage to be so strong that it could bring life out of veritable death? 'He counted him faithful who had promised.' His faith was the result of his considered moral assessment of the character of God. God, so Abraham decided, was faithful. He could never be anything less. There-

[2] On the question of the translation of this verse see the full and very helpful discussion in F. F. Bruce, *The Epistle to the Hebrews* (Marshall, Morgan and Scott, 1965).

fore, if he made a promise, he would keep it. So Abraham believed the promise, and kept on believing it in spite of the all-too-real difficulties and the long delay in the fulfilment. Abraham could not give up believing the promise. To have done so would have been to imply unfaithfulness and moral defect in God.

That is faith, then. It is not some high feeling, mood or emotion, worked up by psychological or religious techniques. It is the result of calm, deliberate moral assessment of the character of God. The apostle John remarks that if you don't believe God's word, you make him out to be a liar (1 Jn. 5:10). In that case true faith is not long in deciding what to do.

4. Faith's consistency and compensation (11:13–16)

It is the mark of true faith in the patriarchs that they not only started their pilgrimage in faith, they finished it in faith as well. And throughout their long lives their behaviour was consistent with their profession of faith. As far as Abraham's spoken testimony was concerned, he made his position unambiguously clear. He explained to the Hittites – and doubtless to many others as well – 'I am an alien and a stranger among you' (Gn. 23:4). Peter uses the very same terms in his letter to remind us what our position in the world is (1 Pet. 1:1; 2:11–12). We live among people that are pagans. Our behaviour should mark us out as aliens and strangers.

The point about Abraham and the patriarchs is that they not only had a clear spoken testimony: their behaviour was consistent with their testimony. They never went back to Ur of Chaldees. They could have done, if they had wished. They had not been thrown out of Ur, or driven out by persecution. Abraham left voluntarily on his own initiative. Had Abraham stayed, or returned, he might well have occupied a very honourable place in the city. But he had no intention of doing so. When he told the Hittites he was an alien and a stranger among them, he did not mean that his fatherland was Ur of Chaldees. Since his conversion, Ur had become as much a foreign country to him as Canaan. He meant that his fatherland was heaven. Paul says the same thing about us. As distinct from those whose 'mind is on earthly things . . . our citizenship is in heaven' (Phil. 3:19–20).

Abraham and the patriarchs, then, were life-long and consistent pilgrims. But they will be adequately rewarded. God is not ashamed to be called after people like that: the God of Abraham, the God of Isaac, the God of Jacob. He admits to being the God who caused Abraham to wander from his father's house and home (Gn. 20:13), and he is aware of the cost and sacrifice involved for Abraham. But he is confident that the city which his almighty power and infinite love have prepared for Abraham will meet and far exceed all Abraham's expectations. No-one will ever be able to say that, having encouraged Abraham to live as a pilgrim, God in the end let him down by providing a city that was an inadequate compensation for his sacrifice, and unworthy of his hopes. Abraham will not be disappointed in God, and God will not be ashamed to be called Abraham's God, for God has prepared for him, and for all the redeemed, a city.

Questions

1 What is the relevance of chapter 11 of Hebrews to the argument of the letter?
2 (a) What is faith?
  (b) Is the faith by which we are saved different from the faith by which we live as Christians?
  (c) Are there degrees of faith? Consider Mark 9:24; Matthew 14:31; Luke 7:9
  (d) Is faith ever a meritorious deed? See Rom. 4:4–5.
  (e) Is faith active or passive?
3 How important is our 'faith' in the sense of the doctrines which we believe? Can you be a true believer if your fundamental doctrines are wrong?
4 In the light of Hebrews 11:11 and 1 John 5:10, consider the proposition that true faith rests on an assessment of God's character.
5 In what sense are believers 'strangers and aliens' in this world? How far would you apply the metaphor? How would you balance it with our duty to act as salt and light in the world? (see Mt. 5:13–16.)

13

FAITH'S TESTING AND WARFARE
Hebrews 11:17 – 12:2

In this chapter we continue our study of what faith is, and of how it behaves; in a word, what it means to be a believer.

The testing and refining of faith
a. Faith justified by works (11:17–19)

True faith must and will be tested. It is not enough to say, 'I believe.' Sooner or later we shall be called upon to justify our profession of faith by our works. Abraham was; and we have already considered what the issues at stake were, and what it was that had to be demonstrated, and to whom it had to be demonstrated, when Abraham was asked to offer up Isaac to God (see pp. 153–155).

What interests us here is to discover how his faith found the strength to go through this extreme test so triumphantly. It found it in logic. I don't suppose for one moment that Abraham ran up the mountain singing and shouting 'Hallelujah!' It was not exuberant spirits or waves of emotion that sustained him in his grim task. It was logic. Abraham reasoned the matter out. God had not only promised that he would have many descendants. God had specified that it was through Isaac that these descendants would come. Isaac as yet had no children. He was not even married. If God was now asking that Isaac be slain, that could not mean that God was going back on his promise. There was only one way out. God would have to raise him from the dead. He could; and he would. So presently Abraham told his servants to stay put: he and Isaac were going to the mountain-top to worship and both of them would come back again (Gn. 22:5).

The logic was simple but breathtaking. It was also sound; and God was delighted to honour it, and to make the giving back of Isaac from virtual death a prototype of our Lord's death and resurrection (11:19).

Faith's logic does not reason that if God loves us he must save us from difficulty, disease, sacrifice and death. It argues rather, 'I am persuaded that neither life nor death can separate us from the love of God or from the fulfilment of his promises.'

b. Faith redirected (11:20)

It may seem to us rather generous to attribute Isaac's blessing of his sons to faith; for when we read the actual story in Genesis 27, his faith seems in many respects to be misdirected. God is generous, of course. He will detect true faith where we might find it difficult to see it. On the other hand the writer is not exaggerating or flattering Isaac when he says that he blessed his sons by faith. Isaac's blessing of his sons shows clearly that he did believe the great promises in regard to the future given to Abraham and to his seed; and it was in a real faith-response to those promises that he blessed Isaac and Esau even concerning things to come.

His mistake was to confuse God's blessing with the emotions and sensations that sometimes accompany or result from that blessing. He had (or at least his wife had; and surely she had told him?) a word from God that of the two nations which would spring from his sons, the elder would serve the younger (Gn. 25:23). That was of course contrary to natural feeling. But instead of putting natural feeling aside and acting on the basis of faith in God's word, Isaac determined to give the official patriarchal blessing to Esau and not to Jacob. Perhaps he had simply forgotten God's word (though Rebekah had not); or perhaps he disregarded it. Rebekah, with scarcely more faith in God than Isaac had, decided to deceive him into blessing Jacob and not Esau. It was easily done.

Isaac had sent Esau off to hunt, kill and prepare some venison for him to eat, so that in that feeling of well-being and contentment which steals over one after a good meal, he might feel assured of God's blessing and pass it on to Esau.

But while Esau was gone, Rebekah dressed Jacob up in goat-skins and sent him in to Isaac with a dish of roast goat which she had faked to taste like venison. Now Isaac was nearly blind, so he could not see who it was; but when Jacob spoke, he immediately recognized the voice. Unfortunately – or fortunately, depending on how you look at it – he did not trust his hearing but allowed himself to be deceived into thinking it was Esau's voice. He tasted the meat and felt sure it was venison. But it wasn't; his taste had deceived him. He touched Jacob's arms and felt sure it was hairy Esau. But it wasn't: his sense of touch had deceived him. He smelt Jacob's clothes and was convinced they were Esau's, carrying the scent of a field which the Lord had blessed (Gn. 27:27). But they weren't: the sense of smell had deceived him.

What a sorry scene it was, with Isaac neglecting God's word and trusting his natural preferences, feelings and sensations, and with Rebekah deliberately playing on his feelings in order to by-pass his intellect and moral judgment in the decision he was making, and all in the cause of promoting the blessing of God! We may be sure that God approved neither of the one nor of the other.

Mercifully God overruled it. He recognized that beneath it all there was a core of genuine faith, and he honoured that faith, though it took him years to discipline out of Jacob's life the effects of that day's deception.

We too need the lesson. It is a common error to mistake the emotions, feelings and sensations that sometimes accompany or result from God's blessing with the blessing itself. Some new Christians so enjoy the feelings of relief and elation that accompany their initial forgiveness, that before they realize what they are doing they rest their assurance of salvation on these feelings instead of pinning it to faith in God's Word. The result is that when the feelings subside, their assurance evaporates.

Some religious leaders, instead of producing conviction and faith by preaching God's Word and allowing emotion and feeling to follow, start the other way round. They try to work up emotion and feeling as if they were in themselves the blessing of God. Some do worse. They try to get 'decisions for Christ' by bypassing people's intellects and moral judgments and moving them by their emotions and feelings.

And all of us, I suggest, from time to time go chasing spiritual 'highs' rather than learning to live by faith in God's Word. We mistake feeling good for becoming holy.

And God is merciful and patient with us too. He recognizes the genuine faith that lies underneath and gives us credit for it. But just as patiently and firmly he will redirect it to its proper object.

c. Faith refined (11:21)

As with Isaac, so with Jacob. The act of faith that is singled out for mention is taken from the end of his life. Of course he had believed in God's promised blessing right from the beginning of his career. But in his early years and for many years thereafter there was a great deal of dross mixed in with the pure gold of his faith. He had very small ideas of the blessing which God designed to give him and very crude ideas as to how that blessing was to be obtained. He thought it was clever, and good business, to take advantage of Esau's moral weakness and offer him an abominably low price for the birthright, and later on to steal the blessing from him by downright lies and deceit (Gn. 25:28–34). He ruined his relationship with his father-in-law and the rest of the family by using Laban's capital selfishly to feather his own nest. Worse still, he thought the result was the blessing of God on him (Gn. 31).

But God had to disabuse him of these ideas. He made him give Esau 220 goats, 220 sheep, 30 female camels with their young, 40 cows, 10 bulls, 20 female donkeys and 10 male donkeys (Gn. 32:13–15). That at least made it clear that God's blessing of Jacob did not depend on cheating Esau.

Rachel, Jacob's favourite wife, who stole her father's gods and deliberately deceived him (Gn. 31:30–37), died prematurely (Gn. 35:16–20). Joseph, his favourite son, Rachel's first child, went missing, presumably killed. Simeon was imprisoned way down in Egypt. In his distress Jacob vowed he would never let Benjamin, Rachel's only other child, out of his sight. But eventually he was forced to do so. A third of his family plus his favourite wife were now gone, and famine stared him in the face. So this is what all his scheming, cheating, and ruthless business deals had accomplished!

What about God's blessing now? That remained what God

had always intended it should be. And when Jacob had been taught that all his scheming contributed nothing to the obtaining of the blessing, God let him discover what that blessing was. He found that Joseph was still alive, and, as head of the whole Egyptian economy, was second only to the Pharaoh. Joseph, his son, had become the economic saviour not only of Egypt but of all the smaller nations dependent on her. God's original promise, 'All peoples on earth will be blessed through you and your offspring' (Gn. 28:14), had found its first major fulfilment. As Joseph's father, Jacob blessed the Pharaoh (Gn. 47:7).

It was with a much purified faith that Jacob, when he was dying, blessed Joseph's two sons. He had been rigorously chastened by God's discipline no longer to trust to his own selfish schemings; yet now he was overwhelmed by the grace of God whose blessing had already proved to be far more than he had ever asked or thought; and he leant on his staff, like the true believing pilgrim he was, and worshipped God. He could bless his grandsons in faith: their future was secure in the promise of God.

d. Faith undimmed (11:22)

Perhaps the greatest test of faith is not sacrifice but success, worldly success. If so, Joseph's faith was supremely triumphant. We may be sure that throughout his long and eventually brilliant career, he had maintained his personal faith in God and his daily spiritual exercises. But it is not his personal piety that the Holy Spirit calls attention to. Many believers in similarly eminent positions in the world have, behind the scenes, maintained an equally strong personal piety. And that is splendid. But the remarkable thing about Joseph is that being in the position he was in, he still retained his boyhood faith that God had a prophetic programme for this world and that that programme was centred in, and would be carried by, Israel and not Egypt.

At the time such a faith must have seemed to the hard-headed politicians, economists and businessmen of the world rather eccentric, not to say bizarre. Egypt in those days was the dominant world power. Israel was a tiny tribe, scarcely more than an extended family. For a member of that family to emigrate to Egypt and eventually to become the Vice-

President of the country was not all that remarkable. Such things have often happened in the history of super-powers. They still do in some quarters. But for such a Vice-President, while still in office, to believe and announce that hope for the world's future lies not with super-powers, but with tiny Israel and with her God-given prophetic role in history – that is quite another thing. It takes a lot of faith to believe that nowadays. It must have taken a lot more in Joseph's day.

Yet that is what he had learnt from Abraham, Isaac and Jacob, and he continued to believe it. He lived in a day when there was an interlude in God's programme for Israel, and Israel was out of the promised land and living among the Gentiles. During that interlude Joseph was happy to serve in Egypt's administration. But he believed the promise given to Abraham (Gn. 15:13–16). The interlude would one day end, Israel would return to the land. God's prophetic programme would be on the march again.

When that happened, Joseph wanted to be identified with it. His bones were not to be left in Egypt to await the general resurrection at the Last Day. Even in death he wanted to be remembered not as a famous prime minister of Egypt, but as one link in the long chain of the fulfilment of God's purpose through Israel. In this, Scripture says, he acted in faith. That is, his action was based on the explicit word of God recorded in Genesis, interpreted literally, and believed whole-heartedly.

God give us the faith of Joseph to believe that before this planet comes to its end, there will be a time of unparalleled blessing for our world. The present interlude in Israel's history, marked by her unbelief in the Messiah and her scattering among the Gentile nations, will one day end. Her Messiah shall return. Israel shall be reconciled and restored. For the world at large it shall be veritable life from the dead (Rom. 11:12–15, 25–27).

Faith and the redemption of mankind

The time eventually came for God's purposes for the redemption of Israel to swing into action. That gave believers in Israel spectacular opportunities to show that their faith was living and real, by co-operating with God and playing their part in his work. Moses was the prime example.

a. Faith's ambitions, choices and motivations (11:23–26)

Moses' career as the evangelist to his people began with the faith of his parents. Their faith saw in him as a baby a potential deliverer of his nation. Risking their lives they hid him from the king's murdering soldiers, trusting God to find some way of preserving him when he could no longer be hidden. That's only natural, you say, for parents to want to protect their child and to have grand ambitions for him. Perhaps it is. But still today the career of evangelist or missionary is the greatest and most noble career known to man. Not every child can grow up to be a Moses; but God give us more men and women of faith whose prime ambition for their children is that they shall grow to be effective co-workers with God in the salvation of their fellow-men and women.

As the adopted son of Pharaoh's daughter Moses grew up surrounded with every possible luxury and privilege. Almost any office in the state, short of being the Pharaoh himself, would doubtless have been open to him. But he gave it all up, even renouncing his right to be known as the son of Pharaoh's daughter. What made him do it?

According to the writer it was not hot-headed enthusiasm. It was the result of a considered weighing of the comparative value of things and a calm deliberate decision to go for the most valuable.

On the one side there were pleasures, the considerable pleasures of life at court with all the dignity and honours of royal society. On the other was positive ill-treatment if he threw in his lot with oppressed Israel. He chose the ill-treatment. Not because ill-treatment is a good thing in itself, or that pleasure is a bad thing in itself. But the pleasures of Egyptian court-life were sinful and temporary: a very poor deal at best. The ill-treatment was unattractive enough, but it was merely a temporary consequence of association with the people of God.

For Moses the expression 'people of God' was no empty religious phraseology. He really believed that Israel stood in a special relationship with the living God, with a unique role to play in the process of God's self-revelation and in his

233

purposes for the redemption of the world. In Moses' opinion it made it the most noble and most exciting society it was possible to be associated with. The fact that most individual Israelites at the time were unpolished, unsophisticated, ill-treated slaves did nothing to detract from the dignity of being *God's* people. Compared with that, life in the Egyptian court was a poor-quality, ignoble thing.

Again, on one side lay treasures of wealth, and art and culture and advanced technology. No other nation at the time had such tremendous treasures. And they were, of course, genuine treasures of real value. On the other side lay reproach, the reproach of Christ. And it was real reproach too. A messianic movement is rarely popular or even respectable in the eyes of the establishment. Belief in the coming of a world Saviour? Denunciation of the present established order as at heart anti-God? Demands for radical repentance? Warnings of plagues if those demands were not met? The encouragement of a mass exodus of the populace out of ordered civilized society into the desert? Moses challenged all Pharaoh's fundamental values. It is no wonder that Pharaoh responded with a mixture of dismay, incredulity, disgust, hatred and vitriolic abuse.

But for Moses this reproach was a wound suffered in the cause of the Christ. Such wounds were in themselves more honourable and valuable than all Egypt's treasures, not to speak of the reward they would bring in the day of Messiah's triumph.

b. Faith's spiritual warfare (11:27–37)

Moses, of course, did not redeem Israel. God did that. But God used Moses to preach redemption to the people, to teach them how they could be redeemed and to lead them once they had been. And that required of Moses a very clear understanding of the principles of redemption, and faith strong enough to apply them and put them into action.

First there was the realism of tactics in face of the foe. The enemy was no man of straw. At the beginning, perhaps rashly, Moses had tried to settle an injustice by secretly killing an Egyptian who was ill-treating some Israelites. It became known, however, and Moses was afraid and fled from Pharaoh's presence to the land of Midian (Ex. 2: 11–15). The writer explains that it was not fear of Pharaoh that made him flee. It was presumably a question of tactics. Had Moses stayed in Egypt at that point, he would have been obliged there and then to bring on a show-down between himself and Pharaoh. It would have been premature. The Israelites were not yet ready for that; witness their rejection of Moses (Ex. 2:14) and their later failure of nerve and hope (Ex. 5:19–21).

So Moses made a tactical withdrawal. But he persisted with his determination to deliver Israel. The opposition was all too powerful and very visible. But Moses' faith could see the One who is invisible – and he was Almighty.

Then Moses had the faith to believe that it was possible to be saved from the wrath of God and from the destroying angel. He believed he knew how. He not only encouraged the Israelites to shelter behind the blood of the passover lamb: he instituted the annual celebration of the passover as a yearly reminder to Israel of the principle of redemption.

He had to be right, for if he wasn't, there would have been a lot of firstborn dead in Israel.

One might ask, 'How is there anything remarkable about that? God had told Moses exactly and in detail how Israel would be saved from his wrath. Anybody would have believed it and acted on it.'

Really? God has told us also how we can be saved from his wrath and know we are (Rom. 5:9). But many preachers appear not to believe it. At least, they seldom preach it. On the one hand they seem not to be sure that there is such a thing as the wrath of God. They talk only in terms of his love. On the other, if there is such a thing as the wrath of God, they feel that no-one can be sure that he will be saved from it. Obviously they do not have Moses' faith. Somewhere along the line they have lost the courage to believe and preach what the Bible plainly teaches.

And then Moses had the faith to believe that if Israel would walk along the recently created channel of dry land through the Red Sea, the water would not flow back again until they got safely to the other side. With tremendous courage he persuaded Israel to take that step and commit themselves to the crossing. 'They were all baptised to Moses in the cloud and in the sea,' says Paul (1 Cor. 10:2).

235

You say, 'But where was his courage, if God had commanded it? Was it not easy for Moses to obey and get the people to obey?' Well, the New Testament commands believers nowadays to be baptized and clearly explains its significance. It has proved notoriously difficult for some to believe it and obey it, and still more difficult to preach it and require it.

The forces of evil were barricaded in Jericho. Joshua had the faith to believe that their defences could be breached. And they were. The tactics God told him to adopt seemed strange indeed. Perhaps the biggest act of faith was to believe that such tactics would work. But they did. We struggle against strongholds of a different kind (2 Cor. 10:3–6), not against enemies of flesh and blood, but against demonic forces (Eph. 6:10–20). But let us not lose our nerve or our faith in the gospel. Though foolishness to the world (1 Cor. 1:18), it is still the power of God to salvation. The enemy's walls can still be breached (2 Cor. 10:4).

When Jericho fell, Rahab was saved. But consider what faith in the true God and in the gospel involved for Rahab. It meant receiving the Israelite spies and transferring her loyalties from her native people to the invading Israelites whom she had come to believe were God's people. The people of Jericho would have regarded her as a traitor. But it is not treachery to leave the world's side and to stand with God and his people. 'Save yourselves from this corrupt generation,' said Peter to his fellow-Jews on the day of Pentecost (Acts 2:40). We must have the faith to take up the challenge and re-echo it in our modern evangelism.

c. Faith's victories and apparent defeats (11:32 – 12:2)

And now the author summarizes in a very impressive and moving list the exploits of numerous men and women of faith. Some were obviously victorious by faith even in their life-times. Others, equally men and women of faith, suffered apparent defeat. They died without being vindicated. Faith is not always seen to be triumphant in this life. And it takes greater faith to suffer apparent disaster, unvindicated, and to go on believing still.

Now all in the list of those who faced disaster through faith are nameless, except One. Of him we read in chapter 12. For when all the vast army of witnesses has gone past, there comes One at last who takes our attention away from all else and fastens it on himself. We look off to the author and perfector of our faith. And what do we observe? A great success in this life, with people thronging round to praise him that his way has worked and has been vindicated and proved right? No. We follow the Man of faith to Golgotha's hill and see him trust God's leading and guidance till it brings him to the cross. We watch the nails driven in, and we say, 'Surely God will vindicate his faith now and work a miracle to bring him down.' The crowds pass by and say, 'He saved others, but he can't save himself. Let this Christ, this King of Israel, come down' (Mk. 15:32).

But he doesn't. The hours pass, and he dies. The world says, 'There you are. He was an impostor.'

What is there to prove otherwise? Why, the One who went to the cross is risen now, seated on the right hand of the throne of God. And he who once seemed such a victim of circumstances, sits on the right hand of the very throne that controls the universe. Courage! If you dare to believe this Christ and follow him, come what may, you too shall sit down on his throne, as he also overcame and sat down on his Father's throne. This is Christ's explicit promise (Rev. 3:21; 2 Tim. 2:12). Let us dare to believe it.

But to follow his faith we shall need to share his sense of values. He despised the shame and endured the cross for the sake of the joy set before him – not only the joy of his own exultation and glory, but the joy of having us there to see it and enjoy it with him eternally (Jn. 17:24). May God give us a true sense of values and help us to choose the best.

Questions

1 Would you distinguish between the testing of faith and the refining of faith?

2 What is meant by talking of the logic of Abraham's faith (11:19)?

3 How reliable are our emotions and feelings as an indication (a) that we are saved, and (b) that we are enjoying God's blessing?

4 In what way does Joseph's request (11:22) demonstrate his faith?

5 Is it fair to say that our attitude to evangelism shows whether we are true believers or not? Consider Philippians 1:3–7.

6 How and in what sense did Moses, who lived centuries before the birth of Jesus, bear reproach for the sake of Christ (11:26)?

7 Analyse Moses' sense of values (11:24–26). If we shared his values, in what practical ways would they affect our lives and careers?

8 In the light of 11:35–38, would it be true to say that faith and obedience always lead to success and prosperity?

9 What will it mean to reign with Christ (2 Tim. 2:12)?

14

THE LONG RACE
Hebrews 12 – 13

Arguments, painful disputes, accusations, contradictions, bitter words, hurt feelings, broken friendships – all are very wearisome and wearing. No wonder if the readers of our letter were discouraged, and sometimes felt like giving up altogether. Since they had been converted there had doubtless been many such arguments. Friends of years had become virtual enemies, relatives had been alienated. The rabbis had been ferocious in their opposition, and on top of all that there had been the physical persecution, damage and loss. It is not surprising if they felt spiritually and mentally drained.

But there is relief for mind and heart. 'Consider him', says the writer, 'who endured such opposition from sinful men, so that you will not grow weary and lose heart' (11:3). The mind finds healing and encouragement in its distress, sometimes, by forgetting itself and thinking of the greater distress of someone else. And there was never distress like that which the Lord suffered.

The Greek word the writer uses for 'opposition' or 'contradiction' is the same as Jude uses to describe the 'gainsaying' (AV) or 'rebellion' (NIV) of Korah (Jude 11). The Lord Jesus and his disciples were not the first or the only ones to be bitterly opposed from within Israel. Moses himself and Aaron had been similarly treated (Nu. 16). Korah, who was a Levite and should have known better, got together with certain prominent leaders from other tribes and forcefully disputed the claim of Moses to be their apostle and the claim of Aaron to be their high priest. God showed his disapproval: the earth opened and swallowed them up. Even so the whole congregation then turned on Moses and Aaron and accused them of having killed the people of the Lord! (Nu. 16:41). Thereupon the glory of the Lord appeared and a plague broke out. Thousands died. And so would thousands more, had not Moses mercifully instructed Aaron to intervene as high priest on behalf of these their very critics.

Israel were running true to type, then, when they disputed the claims of their Messiah, mocked and crucified him. But he endured it without retaliation and without giving up. 'When they hurled their insults at him, he did not retaliate . . . Instead . . . he bore our sins in his body on the tree, so that we might die to sins and live for righteousness' (1 Pet. 2:23–24). If he had refused to endure it, all sinners everywhere would have perished along with their sins.

Shall we not show similar endurance? We too are involved in a fight against sin; in our own lives as we endeavour to progress in holiness; and in other people's lives as we preach the gospel, teach God's Word and pastor people in difficulties. The fight is real and costly. We must expect opposition. We must expect to get hurt. But cheer up, says the writer, you're not dead yet! (12:4). It's not that bad – yet. You have not resisted to the point of shedding your blood in your struggle against sin. But one day we might have to, who knows? The battle is as serious as that. Anyone who thinks that the struggle against sin is a pastime or hobby probably hasn't joined in the war yet.

The Father's discipline

And then, the writer explains, there's another reason for enduring opposition. Persecution may seem unfair and outrageous to us, but behind it all stands God. He could stop it instantly if he chose, and would do so if it would be for our good. But he does not choose to stop it. He means to use it. For a quite different purpose from what the enemy intends, of course: he means to use it to discipline us and perfect our Christian character. A ship's captain that gets his ship to port in spite of the tempest is a conqueror. A ship's captain that uses the tempest's winds to get his ship home in spite of the tempest is more than a conqueror. The enemy opposes believers in order to destroy their faith; God takes the opposition and uses it to strengthen their faith and to bring out the character of the divine life within them.

There are two attitudes, therefore, which we should avoid. 'My son, do not make light of [or despise] the Lord's discipline, and do not lose heart when he rebukes you.' It is possible on the one hand to despise discipline, to grow hard and cynical, and to let it pass without profiting from it. It is possible on the other hand to faint under it and to give in; instead of standing up to it courageously, to go under, until the Lord is obliged to ease the pressure lest he ruin us; and thus we miss a lesson we might have learned.

Let us avoid these two extreme attitudes, not despising, nor yet fainting under the discipline of the Lord. For those whom the Lord loves he disciplines. And if the way is hard, and if we think that overmuch discipline is coming our way, then we must begin to develop the habit of thinking that the Lord must love us very much. The very fact that he does not relieve the pressure for a while is evidence of his persistent intention to do us good. He will let the persecution or the difficulty or whatever it is do us the utmost good before he removes it. For 'the Lord disciplines those he loves and he punishes [or scourges] everyone he accepts as a son.' So much is this true, that if we receive no discipline at all, then we might have grave doubts about the reality of our profession. 'If you are not disciplined . . . then you are illegitimate children and not true sons' (12:8).

Now the word translated 'discipline' means, of course, correction; but it includes the wider thought of general spiritual education, all that is involved in bringing up a child. Thousands of people are for ever grateful to human parents who were careful with their upbringing and education. How much more ought we to be grateful to God that he is prepared to use all means, even the difficulties caused by sin, to educate us as his children.

God's purposes in discipline

'We have all had human fathers who disciplined us', says the writer, 'and we respected them for it. How much more should we submit to the Father of our spirits and live!' No right-minded father would discipline a child to kill it. No right-minded father puts a child through exercises at school, or through a training in business, in order to make life unpleasant for the child. A father, as he trains his child, is thinking to develop the child's abilities so that the child will be able, not only to cope with life better, but to enjoy life better: to do more things, more enjoyable things and bigger things. And when we grow up, we learn to respect fathers who did this for us. 'And what do you think God is doing?' asks the writer; 'do you think he is out to ruin you? Of course he is not. He is out to lead you into a fuller life. Shall we not rather submit to the Father of our spirits and *live*?'

Let us see what it is that God is doing in our trials. Things went so smoothly for us at first, perhaps, and we were enjoying spiritual life so much – and then days of difficulty came. We look back with a sigh to the earlier days and wish we were there still. We enjoyed spiritual life then, but not now; it is all so difficult. Why can't we go back? To reason like this is to reason like a child in the nursery. She has been enjoying life so far. There have been gifts from the parents, and endless play, and the child has enjoyed it. But now comes the day when the parents take the child off to school, and the child does not care for it. Why can't she go back and play as she used to instead of having to be made to face lessons in school that are tedious and uninteresting? But see that child in ten years' time, and she will not want to go back to the nursery. She has now been trained so that she sees greater possibilities in life.

And though God gives us times of great enjoyment in spiritual life, yet sooner or later he allows things to become difficult, so that he might develop us, and so that we get more out of spiritual life. And that not only here; God thinks not only about the few years of our preparation in this life, but has in mind a whole eternity. We have to learn to share in his holiness, to behave as he behaves. It is the way the divine persons behave that makes heaven heaven. How short life is to prepare us for eternity! Shall we not rather, then, submit to him? Shall we not trust his wisdom? Shall we not agree that he sees and foresees far better than we do? And shall we not co-operate with him and live? Why of course! By his grace we will.

Now at the time discipline seems painful and not at all pleasant. Afterwards, however, it produces a harvest of righteousness and peace for those who have been trained by it.

There will be an afterward; as surely as there is a trial, there will be an afterward. Of course, the trial itself is not meant to be enjoyable. All discipline is for the time being painful. If we enjoyed the trial, it would not be a trial, would it? Often, when a trial begins to hurt, we quickly run to the Lord and ask him to take away all the pain and all the difficulty. But if he did, it would not be a trial. We must expect to feel the trial. For all discipline for the time being is painful; but there is an afterward with its rich harvest.

I suppose trial trains us all to some extent; but just as it is possible to waste money on some people's education, it is possible for us to despise God's discipline and not value it; and thus much of his care goes unrewarded. We need to let ourselves be trained by the discipline. Look on to the afterward and lift up those hands that hang down, strengthen those paralysed knees, and though you feel fit to drop, your knees sag in the middle, and your hands hang down, press on! For there is an afterward.

Our Father knows. While we think, at times, that things are well, our Father can see a hidden weakness within us, and allows a trial to come that exposes that very weakness in a way that is unpleasant. We ask God for the trial to be taken away so that the weakness will not be exposed so much. But God probes it all the more. Just as a physician will come to an ailing body and put his finger right on the mark, and of course it hurts – you would rather he put his finger anywhere else than there – so God, with unerring skill, very often allows a trial to come that exposes the very weakness that up till now we have sheltered and tried to forget. He is not fault-finding, delighting to criticize and to humiliate us. He is out to heal our weaknesses. Let us only understand this, and then in time of trial we shall find grace to pray not so much that the trial be stopped, but that the weakness be dealt with and we come through refined.

Yet what do we know of trial? As once more we remember the plight of those to whom this letter was written, we must admit that we scarcely know anything. Many of them stood with broken homes, with everything lost, family connections severed. Their knees were sagging, their hands were hanging down. In spite of it, many of them, with their eyes on the mark, valiantly ran to the end and gained the winning-post somehow. The Lord help us in our easier circumstances to run with perseverance, putting off everything that hinders and the sin that so easily entangles us, running with endurance till we sit down beside the Lord at the winning-post above.

The stark alternatives

But there is nothing like persecution for the sake of Christ to bring into sharp focus the stark alternatives that everyone must face. As the Lord himself put it, either we confess him before our fellow-human beings and he will confess us before the angels of God, or we deny him, and he will deny us (Lk. 12:8–9). Of course we can fall into grave, temporary inconsistency. Once more remember Peter. But there is no permanent third way involving neither denying nor confessing Christ that we can deliberately take and still be saved.

Without holiness no-one shall see the Lord (12:14). Salvation offers us that holiness, both initial sanctification and progressive sanctification. It is open to all to receive the initial sanctification as a gift, and with it the power step by step to perfect holiness in the fear of God. It is also open to all to reject it. But there is no third option that allows people to receive salvation without the obligation to seek holiness. The grace of God 'teaches us to say "No" to ungodliness . . . and to live self-controlled, upright and godly lives in this present age, while we wait for the blessed hope – the glorious appearing of our great God and Saviour, Jesus Christ' (Tit. 2:12–13). Anyone who thinks that salvation by grace means permission to live an unholy life, has not yet understood God's grace. He hasn't yet come anywhere near it. He has come short of it, he has missed it altogether (12:15).

When Moses was expounding the terms of the old covenant to the assembled people, he warned them of the possibility that there might be among them what he called 'a root that bears gall and wormwood' (NIV, 'a root that produces such bitter poison') (Dt. 29:18–21). He meant that kind of person who, even while listening to God's solemn warnings, invokes a blessing on himself and thinks, 'I will be safe even though I persist in going my own way.' He hears God's call to faith, loyalty, righteousness and holiness, and the solemn curses on those who reject the call. He has no intention of obeying the call. Far from it: he is intent on following other gods. But he persuades himself that everything will be all right nonetheless. God's curses, he thinks, do not really mean what they say. There is somehow a third way in which rejection of God's word, outright idolatry, disobedience and sin are perfectly compatible with salvation and blessing.

The writer repeats the warning (12:15), not so much for the sake of the person himself – he is an obvious unbeliever and will perish – but for the sake of the effect such a person can have on the genuine believers while he mixes among them under the pretence of being a believer himself. They can become defiled, and encouraged to lax living and compromise. Carried away by the error of lawless people, as Peter puts it, they can fall, not from their salvation, but from their steadfastness (2 Pet. 3:17).

So let there be no Esau among you, says the author. Esau was a decent enough man, as men go, but he was utterly profane (NIV, 'godless'). By God's gracious providence he was Isaac's eldest son and so held the birthright. If there was anything at all in the promises of God to Abraham and Isaac, then the firstborn son's inheritance-rights were an exceedingly valuable thing. But to Esau they meant virtually nothing.

Jacob was cooking some stew one day when Esau came in from the open country rather hungry. 'Quick,' he said to Jacob, 'let me have some of that red stew! I'm famished.'

'Sell me your birthright,' said Jacob, 'then I will.'

'Look, I'm about to die,' Esau said. 'What good is the birthright to me?' So he sold his birthright to Jacob for a bowl of stew.

Now some young men are given to violent exaggeration; so when Esau said, 'I am about to die,' we may take it, I suppose, that he was quite hungry, perhaps painfully so. But to barter his God-given birthright for a bowl of stew to pacify his momentary hunger-pangs – God brands it as profanity. 'He *despised* his birthright,' says God, and all things sacred with it. God's promise to Abraham and to his descendants, wonderful though they were, necessarily related to the future. Esau was saying, in effect: 'As for all those promises for the future, you can have the lot, Jacob, if you like. As far as I'm concerned, one bowl of stew now is worth more than all those promises for the future. I'm not prepared to put up with the pangs of hunger for the sake of a few promises, even God-given promises. I intend to have a full stomach here and now. If holding on to the promises means hunger and pain, you can have them. Give me relief from pain, present satisfaction and enjoyment.'

The relevance of the lesson to the readers of this letter is obvious. For them as for us there were but two alternatives. One was to follow Christ, which means taking up the cross and sharing the rejection he suffered at the hands of the world that gave him that cross. It can lead – and for our readers it had literally led – to a very empty feeling in the stomach. On the other hand they could refuse Christ and his cross and say with Esau, 'I care nothing for God's promises in Jesus Christ. I care nothing for living by faith. Hunger-pangs, persecution, social ostracism are more than I can, or will, put up with. I demand to have a good time and a full stomach now. You can live on empty promises if you like. I will not put up with rejection by my family, social group and nation, not even for Christ's sake.'

Two alternatives then, and only two. Where shall we find strength to make the right choice?

The solemn warning

Life's ultimate choice cannot be other than solemn. It means either accepting God and his Word, or refusing him (12:25). In making up our minds which to choose, it is of the utmost importance that we have a true and realistic fear of God.

Some fear is bad. Neurotic fears that stem from a wounded and disturbed personality are obviously bad and unhealthy. So is fear that springs from a concept of God as a cruel tyrant. Discover the reality of the love of God, and it will drive out that fear (1 Jn. 4:17–18). But not all fear is bad. Fear-mechanisms within us enable us instinctively to anticipate real danger and avoid it; and give us the extra strength successfully to run away when disaster threatens. These mechanisms are healthy. They are common to bird, animal and man. They are the gift of a wise and loving Creator.

And there are things which it is healthy to fear: damaging

a child, for instance, or breaking a loved one's heart. Supreme among these things is the possibility of incurring the displeasure and wrath of God.

When the Lord Jesus prepared his disciples to face hostility and persecution, he spoke to them not only of the love of God but of the fear of God. 'Do not be afraid of those who kill the body and after that can do no more. But I will show you whom you should fear: Fear him who, after the killing of the body, has power to throw you into hell. Yes, I tell you, fear him' (Lk. 12:4–5). The greater fear will overcome the lesser.

The writer now adopts the same approach. 'Do consider the situation well and realistically,' he says. 'You have not come to Mount Sinai with its thunder, fearful as that was; you have come to something far more august, far more awesome. Not to a mountain that can be touched, a tangible thing. You have come to the spiritual realm. You have come to Mount Zion; here is your glorious and eternal goal.

'Here you have to do with God, not now as the Father of all, but as the Judge of all. To be sure, Jesus is there as Mediator of the covenant, and his blood speaks pardon. But we are now dealing with the solemn realities of the august majesty of heaven. Those who refused him who spoke from Mount Sinai perished. How much more shall those who refuse him who speaks from heaven perish!'

In previous chapters the writer has comforted these Jewish believers with the thought that Christ is superior to Aaron and to Moses and to Joshua, and that his sacrifice is superior to their animal sacrifices. He has pointed out that the two things cannot go together. They cannot have the new covenant and the old together. They cannot have Christ and the animal sacrifices together. They must have one or the other. They cannot combine them. But now he warns them that if they choose to stay where once they were, if they cling to the seen, if they cling to their Judaism, they must beware, for God is not to be trifled with. God does not give people an alternative choice.

God will win us by love if he can; he will hold out the better thing, and woo us to himself, if he can, by all the glories and wonders of the salvation that Christ offers; and Christ is supremely wonderful. He is so wonderful that it is worth going through persecution for his sake. Let's grit our teeth and go through it. But, if we do not go through with it, and if we do not follow him, and if we do not love him, and if we do not believe him, then what? Well, there is no second best, no moderately acceptable alternative. Without Christ there is nothing but the ultimate disaster from which his salvation was designed to save us.

God once shook the earth, but he has promised that in a soon-coming day he will shake not only the earth but the heaven as well. And when he says he will shake it, he means that the whole of creation as we know it will utterly disappear; for there is to be a new heaven and a new earth. How pathetic it is that men and women grasp so tightly the material and the seen! Presently it will flee away and they will be left with nothing. Can you not see, the writer is saying to his reader, that the vestments and the animal sacrifices and the glorious temple and the gorgeous pageantry and the Aaronic priesthood – can you not see that the whole lot of it put together, though it attracts you so much now, is destined to pass away? It is a nothing really, it will soon be gone and forgotten. If you cling to that, you will find yourself in eternity without anything. The only real thing is Christ and the salvation that God provides through him.

We do well to keep this in our minds as we present the gospel. Let us see to it that we put first and foremost the love of God in all its wonderful extent. Let us see that we speak well of the Saviour and of his salvation, that people's hearts might be opened by the warmth of God's love. But let us see to it that we are fair to them, and tell them that through much tribulation they must enter the kingdom; that if they come, drawn by this Saviour's love, yet at the same time they must take up the cross and endure persecution for him. If they should hesitate, let us not fail to point out that there are only two alternatives: to believe God is to be saved; to refuse his voice is to be lost for ever.

And the choice has to be made now. When God brought the Israelites out of Egypt, he did not wait until they were on the brink of entering the promised land before he put before them what the real goal of redemption was. He himself came to meet them in the desert. Stationing himself in all his majesty on Mount Sinai, he explained to Israel that he had carried them on eagles' wings and brought them *to himself* (Ex. 19:4). He himself was the goal. There and then he offered them the awesome glory of entering a covenant relationship with him. There and then they had to decide their response. God was speaking to them. They had to reply. Decision could not be deferred.

So it is with us. 'You *have* come to Mount Zion . . . to Jesus the mediator of a new covenant.' Not 'One day you *will* come to Mount Zion, to the border between time and eternity, and then the Judge will take the decision whether or not you are to be admitted into his heaven.' In Jesus eternity has already invaded time. He is our Creator, he is the Redeemer. He is the true goal of life. He is the Judge (Jn. 5:22–27). Here in this life he confronts us *now*. He is speaking to us *now*. This is not some preliminary exam: this is Finals. Our eternity depends on our response to him; and we must respond now. 'Now is the day of salvation' (2 Cor. 6:2). '*Today*, if you hear his voice, do not harden your hearts' (3:7).

But once more the writer's confidence in the genuine faith of his readers comes to the surface. 'Since we', he says, 'are receiving a kingdom that cannot be shaken, let us be thankful and so worship God acceptably with reverence and awe.'

Final exhortations

With these solemn thoughts in mind, we may conclude by reading the last chapter. It is noteworthy that a letter of this sort, which has lifted us to the very heavens with the glorious things it has spoken about the Saviour, ends with a chapter full of exhortations and practical instruction. These glorious things are real; necessarily they must affect the ordinary, everyday details of life.

In fact, we shall show how much we have enjoyed our study of this letter by the way it works out in the detail of our living. It is not too much to say that our enjoyment is worthless, if it does not lead us by God's grace to seek to fulfil these things. Let us not think, then, that these practical exhortations are incidental and mean little. They come to us with the whole weight of all the preceding chapters behind them. They need little comment. When it comes to practical exhortation, it is not more understanding we need, but the heart and intention to carry it out.

13:1–3

We remember what persecution the readers were going through. If persecution came to our country, we should see more point in this exhortation; and many of our trifling points of disagreement would disappear. We would learn to love and value our brothers and sisters in Christ more than perhaps we do now. Still to this day in many countries many believers live in fear of imprisonment or are actually in prison. How we would pray if we were in prison! Then let us remember those in prison as if we were in prison with them. For in a sense we are! They are in prison because of their stand for the gospel on which our salvation depends, out of loyalty to the Saviour whom we too must never deny. We cannot afford to forget the battle they fight. We are in the same war!

And let love be pure and the Christian community kept free from the sexual immorality, easy divorce and perversions that plague contemporary society.

13:5–6

These verses are excellent psychology. They tell us how we may live confidently as genuine Christians in a fiercely competitive and unprincipled world. We have to have money; we have to live ordinary lives; we have to have homes; and most will want to get married and raise a family. How then can our minds be free from the *love* of money?

We start with what God has said. He himself has said, 'Never will I leave you; never will I forsake you.' The promise is a composite one made up of promises given to Jacob when he left home and went off to find himself a job and a wife and enough money to set up a home of his own (Gn. 28:15); repeated to Israel when Moses was about to leave them (Dt. 31:6,8); and repeated again to Joshua as he stood at the beginning of his mighty enterprise (Jos. 1:5); and now repeated to us.

Since God has spoken and committed himself, we may speak and say with confidence, 'The Lord is my helper.' That

is a fact. It bears repetition. Aloud! And then we can make
an assertion of our own: 'I will not be afraid.' We can make
it with confidence and with a determination that has looked
all possibilities in the face and dares to ask, 'What can man
do to me?' Why, the very worst he can do will but translate
us from this world into the Lord's presence. Our wages and
our bread and butter are ultimately in the Lord's hand. We
need not fear; only we must be content with what he gives.

13:7–8

'Remember your leaders, who spoke the word of God to
you. Consider the outcome of their way of life and imitate
their faith.' Remember them, but don't idolize them or pine
after them. Doubtless some of them were spiritual giants, but
they would have freely admitted that they got their everything
from Jesus Christ. They have died, but Jesus Christ is the
same, yesterday, and today and for ever.

In Old Testament days, God was the God of Abraham,
and the God of Isaac, and the God of Jacob, making himself
known to each generation, as each generation required. The
same is true of our Lord Jesus. What he was to Paul, and
what he was to Luther, and what he was to Spurgeon, that
he can be to us. We do not ask God to send back again
the worthies of the past. We watch their lives, we see their
triumphant end, and we thank God that we still have the
source of all power with us today, unchanged: Jesus Christ
the same yesterday, and today, and for ever.

13:9–18

If we leave Judaism behind, how shall we order our ways?
Well, beware of strange doctrines! Beware particularly of
doctrines about ceremonial foods, which are of no value to
those who eat them. It is God's grace that strengthens us.
Doctrines about meats and drinks and holy days and things
like that are useless. Take Judaism itself, says the writer: it
was a religion that was full of observances of food and meats
and drinks and washings and ceremonies and holy days, a
religion given of God. And yet, at its very heart, it had a
ceremony that showed the emptiness of it all. The bodies of

the offerings, the blood of which was brought inside into the Holy Place, were taken and burned outside the camp, so that the priests who ministered at the altar were given no part of those sacrifices to eat. They offered the offering, they brought its blood in, but instead of eating it as they did the other sacrifices, they had to take the body out and it was burned outside the camp (see Lv. 4:13–21).

Look, says the writer, I will show you the fulfilment of that. In order to sanctify the people with his blood, Jesus suffered outside the gate and outside the camp. He did not offer his sacrifice as a ceremony within Judaism. He left the whole thing. True enough, Judaism with its sacrifices was a picture; but when it came to making the sacrifice that put our sin away, Christ was taken outside the gate, outside the camp, outside Judaism and all its rituals. Those who still cling to Judaism have no benefit from his sacrifice, any more than the priests who ministered at the altar could eat the sacrifice that was burned outside the gate. God has had enough of animal sacrifices, enough of holy days, vestments, incense, foods, and ceremonial washings. His Son has died outside the camp. Let us come out to him and bear his reproach.

And then the writer adds something that must have driven a sharp pang through the hearts of his readers. 'For here we do not have an enduring city, but we are looking for the city that is to come.' What? Must they give up Jerusalem city as well as the temple? Yes, they must. That sacred city was about to be overrun and trodden down by Gentiles for centuries. And God would put no other sacred city in its place. The day of the sacral state, in which religion and politics were but the two sides of one and the same thing, were over as far as God was concerned; and it would have been a happy thing for Europe and the world if Christians had never tried to go back to that old order and to marry Christianity with politics, to set up cities on earth, whether Rome or Byzantium or Geneva, as their religio-political head-quarters. Think of the misery and the persecution of minority groups, the repression of conscience, and the sheer empire-building and worldliness in the church that would have been avoided!

On the other hand, may the Lord help us to pursue the true thing. Let us not be content with being negative. Let us worship the Lord in the beauty of holiness. Let us make the teaching about God our Saviour attractive by the way we live and worship. True worship is 'the fruit of lips' in constant praise, confessing and giving thanks to the name of God's Son who has 'called us by his own glory and goodness' (2 Pet. 1:3). And true worship also consists of practical doing good, sacrificial living, godly and glad submission to responsible, spiritual leadership, and prayer for evangelists and teachers. Life in the church, for all its joys – and pains! – is serious business. Our spiritual leaders watch over us as people who must one day account for us to the Lord and Head of the church. Shepherds are responsible for the sheep committed to their care. It is a demanding task. But above the lesser shepherds, stands the great Shepherd.

13:20–21

So now the writer reminds us once more what God's unbreakable commitment to our sanctification has done in order to achieve it. If we were ever to be made holy, we should need a Supreme Shepherd to guide our feet in the paths of righteousness. That being so, God who had covenanted to make us holy, raised from the dead our Lord Jesus, that great Shepherd of the sheep. We may rest assured that through him God will fulfil every term of the covenant to which he has committed himself by the blood of his Son. The glory and the credit for it will eternally be his.

13:22–25

The letter is finished; but as the writer adds his personal greetings, we get a brief glimpse through his eyes of the community he has been writing to.

'I want you to know that our brother Timothy has been released. If he arrives soon, I will come with him to see you.'

Our minds go to that able and sensitive young man from Lystra who joined Paul on his missionary journeys. In the course of the years he helped to plant churches in different cities and countries, and carried the onerous task of shepherding the large, multi-racial church at Ephesus. Apparently he had been imprisoned and then more recently released;

and the writer wants his readers to hear the news. He had become to them, as well as to the writer, 'our brother Timothy'. Doubtless they had been interested in his work, and had prayed for him during his imprisonment. His release would be a victory for their prayers and a boost to their faith. A visit from him would be an occasion of great joy.

We pause to think. How true faith in Christ enlarges our horizons! It lifts us out of our narrow personal and selfish or even national concerns, and gives us a common international interest in Christ's work and workers throughout the world, making us feel an integral part of his great enterprise.

'Greet *all* your leaders and *all* God's people. Those from Italy send you their greetings. Grace be with you all.'

We think again. What a marvellous reality is the family of God into which faith in Christ has brought us! And, in spite of our family squabbles, how real is the affection, born of God's Spirit, which unites us in Christ across the world and across the ages.

Marvellous people, these ancient Hebrew Christians. We have read and thought much about them. We have been stimulated by their courage. We have profited from their mistakes. We have learned to love them in the Lord. For they were real people, and even now they live with Christ. One day we shall meet them and be able to tell them how immensely we enjoyed reading the letter that was originally addressed to them.

Questions

1 How does 'considering Christ' help us not to grow weary and lose heart?

2 What is meant by the phrase 'struggle against sin'?

3 What reasons does the writer give us for submitting to God's discipline? Does God discipline us always and only when we have done something wrong?

4 For buying Jacob's red stew at the cost of his birthright, Esau got the nickname Edom (Gn. 25:30), which he passed on to his descendants, the Edomites. The Herods of the New Testament were Idumaeans, that is, Edomites. Do you see in their behaviour anything resembling Esau's?

5 In what sense have we already come to Mount Zion? Are

you confident that your name is already written there as one of its citizens (*cf.* Lk. 10:20; Phil. 3:20; 4:3)?

6 What is the true Christian attitude to the question of making a living?

7 'Let us, then, go to him outside the camp . . . for here we do not have an enduring city.' What were the practical implications of this exhortation for the readers of our letter? What are they for us?